Strategic Marketing
Planning and Control

Second edition

Graeme Drummond

Napier University Business School

John Ensor

Napier University Business School

Ruth Ashford

Manchester Metropolitan University

ELSEVIER
BUTTERWORTH
HEINEMANN

AMSTERDAM • BOSTON • HEIDELBERG • LONDON • NEW YORK • OXFORD
PARIS • SAN DIEGO • SAN FRANCISCO • SINGAPORE • SYDNEY • TOKYO

Elsevier Butterworth-Heinemann
Linacre House, Jordan Hill, Oxford OX2 8DP
30 Corporate Drive, Burlington, MA 01803

First published 1999
Second edition 2001
Reprinted 2002, 2003 (twice), 2004, 2005

British Library Cataloguing in Publication Data
Drummond, Graeme
  Strategic marketing: planning and control. – 2nd ed.
  1. Marketing – Management
  I. Title II. Ensor, John   III. Chartered Institute of Marketing
  658.8′4

Library of Congress Cataloguing in Publication Data
A catalogue record for this book is available from the Library of Congress

ISBN 0 7506 5236 5

Composition by Genesis Typesetting, Rochester, Kent
Printed and bound in Great Britain

Strategic Marketing
Planning and Control

The Chartered Institute of Marketing/Butterworth-Heinemann Marketing Series is the most comprehensive, widely used and important collection of books in marketing and sales currently available worldwide.

As the CIM's official publisher, Butterworth-Heinemann develops, produces and publishes the complete series in association with the CIM. We aim to provide definitive marketing books for students and practitioners that promote excellence in marketing education and practice.

The series titles are written by CIM senior examiners and leading marketing educators for professionals, students and those studying the CIM's Certificate, Advanced Certificate and Postgraduate Diploma courses. Now firmly established, these titles provide practical study support to CIM and other marketing students and to practitioners at all levels.

The Chartered Institute of Marketing

Formed in 1911, The Chartered Institute of Marketing is now the largest professional marketing management body in the world with over 60,000 members located worldwide. Its primary objectives are focused on the development of awareness and understanding of marketing throughout UK industry and commerce and in the raising of standards of professionalism in the education, training and practice of this key business discipline.

Books in the series

Below-the-line Promotion, John Wilmshurst
CIM Handbook of Export Marketing, Chris Noonan
CIM Handbook of Selling and Sales Strategy, David Jobber
CIM Handbook of Strategic Marketing, Colin Egan and
    Michael J. Thomas
CIM Marketing Dictionary, Norman A. Hart
Copywriting, Moi Ali
Creating Powerful Brands, Leslie de Chernatony and
    Malcolm McDonald
Creative Marketer, Simon Majaro
Customer Service Planner, Martin Christopher
Cybermarketing, Pauline Bickerton, Matthew Bickerton and
    Upkar Pardesi
Effective Advertiser, Tom Brannan
From Brand Vision to Brand Evaluation, Leslie de Chernatony
Integrated Marketing Communications, Ian Linton and Kevin Morley
Key Customers: How to manage them profitably, Malcolm McDonald,
    Beth Rogers and Diana Woodburn
Market-led Strategic Change, Nigel Piercy
Marketing Book, Michael J. Baker
Marketing Logistics, Martin Christopher
Marketing Research for Managers, Sunny Crouch and
    Matthew Housden
Marketing Manual, Michael J. Baker
Marketing Planner, Malcolm McDonald
Marketing Planning for Services, Malcolm McDonald and Adrian Payne
Marketing Plans, Malcolm McDonald
Marketing Strategy, Paul Fifield
Practice of Advertising, Norman A. Hart
Practice of Public Relations, Sam Black
Profitable Product Management, Richard Collier
Relationship Marketing, Martin Christopher, Adrian Payne and
    David Ballantyne
Relationship Marketing for Competitive Advantage, Adrian Payne,
    Martin Christopher, Moira Clark and Helen Peck
Retail Marketing Plans, Malcolm McDonald and Christopher Tideman
Royal Mail Guide to Direct Mail for Small Businesses, Brian Thomas
Sales Management, Chris Noonan
Trade Marketing Strategies, Geoffrey Randall

Contents

Preface

The aim of this text is to enable the reader to develop a sound theoretical and practical understanding of marketing planning and control. Although primarily written for those studying for the Chartered Institute of Marketing Advanced Certificate Stage 2 and Diploma Stage 3 professional marketing qualifications, this text is equally useful for industry practitioners. This is not an introductory text to the subject of marketing planning, but builds on the existing knowledge that students and practitioners already hold about the principles of the subject. The aim has been to provide a clear, concise guide to the tools, techniques and concepts necessary to undertake strategic marketing decisions.

The text also covers contemporary issues by exploring current developments in marketing theory and practice including:

- The concept of a market-led orientation
- A resource/asset-based approach to internal analysis and planning

Innovation is a theme throughout the text, reflecting the growing importance of this issue, both in terms of its academic profile and current business practice. There is also an emphasis on developing a view of the future through various forecasting techniques.

This new edition also includes a new chapter on competitive intelligence. Chapter 9 has been revised with new material on strategic brand management. There is also a new chapter at the end of the text which consists of four mini case studies. Throughout the new edition new illustrative examples have been included to reinforce the material covered in each chapter.

An instructor's manual is available to academic staff adopting this text. This contains expanded versions of selected illustrative examples featured in the main text, new cases and a pack of lecture material.

Information for students studying for the CIM Qualifications

The Chartered Institute of Marketing has relaunched their suite of professional marketing qualifications. The new CIM Advanced Certificate Stage 2 qualification, was launched in September 2003. There are now new modules which comprise this CIM Stage 2 qualification, which are: Marketing Research and Information; Marketing Planning; Marketing Communications; Marketing Management in Practice.

The CIM intends to launch their Stage 3 qualification in September 2004, which will replace the CIM Diploma. Again, the modules are different at this stage which are (at time of going to press): Analysis and Evaluation; Competitive Strategy; Performance Management; Strategy in Practice.

The text therefore has been designed to cover the new Marketing Planning syllabus (CIM Advanced Certificate Stage 2 professional marketing qualification), the old CIM Diploma for the Planning and Control syllabus (for the year 2003/4), and will underpin the new Stage 3 professional marketing qualifications syllabus (from 2004 onwards).

The new Marketing Planning syllabus (CIM new Advanced Certificate Stage 2) is divided into four major areas:

- The marketing plan in its organizational and wider marketing context
- Marketing planning & budgeting
- The extended marketing mix and related tools
- Marketing in different contexts

The CIM has designed their new syllabus around the statements of marketing practice, which were developed by the Standard Setting Body for marketing under the direction of the Chartered Institute of Marketing. These statements identify the practical tasks that marketers undertake within their marketing career. These standards are available on the CIM website (www.cim.co.uk).

This text still includes important strategic theory, some of which is not specifically included within the Marketing Planning syllabus, however, this does add further understanding for the student and thus goes beyond this syllabus. Also it is not the intention of this text to cover the theory relating to the marketing mix elements, as this is available in most fundamental marketing texts. However, the Marketing Planning syllabus requires candidates to be able to discuss the operationalization of their marketing planning decisions using the marketing mix and so students should ensure that they have this knowledge also.

Links with other papers

The Marketing Planning syllabus was developed to provide the key skills and knowledge required by an operational marketing manager. This module replaced the 'Marketing Operations' module in the old CIM Advanced Certificate. It aims to prepare marketers for practice at management level and does consider operational issues as well as strategic marketing decisions. The general basis of this module is the marketing planning function and the implications for the operational decisions. However, as many organizations today are small or medium sized businesses, the marketing planning process is undertaken at a lower level of management than in larger multi-national organizations as cited in many other text books.

Therefore, the Marketing Planning module acts as a central base for the other CIM modules to build upon at the Advanced Certificate Stage 2 level and also is very much required for Diploma Stage 3 as underpinning theory for this higher level of study.

This text will provide students with an understanding of the nature of strategic marketing decisions and the marketing decision process. This text covers key elements of the syllabus (such as forecasting, control mechanisms and budgeting) which are not covered well in other textbooks on the market and so is of major benefit to all students studying for this examination. Indeed, these are the areas of the syllabus which tend not to be taught well and consequently students do not perform well in response to questions in this area. Therefore, this text offers a useful and directed aid to this section of the Marketing Planning syllabus both for lecturers, students and practitioners.

The Marketing Research and Information module, which is another new CIM module within the new CIM Advanced Certificate Stage 2, includes the management of information and this is important to understand in relation to inform the marketing planning. This unit offers knowledge to operationalize the concepts discussed in this text (such as offering information for the external analysis and competitive intelligence audits Chapters 2 and 3)

The new CIM Marketing Communications module within the new Advanced Certificate at Stage 2 offers understanding of customer dynamics, which again offers information to make marketing planning decisions discussed in this text.

The final new CIM Advanced Certificate Stage 2 module, Marketing Management in Practice, requires students to operationalize and illustrate their skills and their knowledge of marketing planning processes as discussed in this text. Therefore, this text can add value to the reading for this syllabus also.

The CIM have now introduced two assessment routes for the new Advanced Certificate Stage 2 syllabus, which are by examination or assignment. Any CIM centre at which students are studying will be able to inform them of the assessment route, which will be offered at that centre.

The CIM examination route

The Chartered Institute of Marketing has slightly redesigned their examinations for the new Advanced Certificate Stage 2 and Diploma Stage 3. The examination paper for the Marketing Planning module (from September 2003) will now be in two parts. Part A is a mini case study with three or four compulsory questions and this is worth 50 per cent of the examination (this was previously 40 per cent of the paper). Each element of the syllabus will be tested in some way in Part A. Part B of the paper is made up of four questions, of which candidates are required to answer two and each question is worth 25 per cent of the paper. There used to be a choice of three questions out of six – therefore, there is some reduction in the choice of questions and candidates should be aware of this.

Part A is normally a mini case study (similar to the ones found in Chapter 15 of this text) but it could also be an abstract of an article. Normally it will be up to one or one and a half sides of A4. Students will be asked to analyse the material, make comments upon it and propose further actions. Therefore, it will be expected that candidates can illustrate their knowledge and understanding of appropriate theory and apply their knowledge to the case study. Normally the answers will be required in report format.

Part B will contain four questions from across the syllabus, and there will normally be two or three parts to one question. Students should be aware that in some questions two areas of the syllabus will be tested. These will require students to understand marketing theories and concepts and show that they can apply them to a given situation. Students will also need to demonstrate that they have an ability to critically appraise appropriate models and concepts. Again, answers will be required in report format.

In the examination the CIM examiners are looking for candidates to demonstrate interpretative skills, insight and originality in answering the questions. At the same time, it is expected that candidates will show a critical awareness and understanding of the relevant theoretical framework surrounding the issues being discussed.

To perform well on this paper the following characteristics should be observed and adhered to:

- Candidates need to concentrate on the specifics of the question which may be strategic or operational in nature.
- Candidates have to demonstrate that they have the knowledge and skills required to critically appraise and apply models and concepts, not merely describe them.
- Candidates have to illustrate their answers, wherever possible, with relevant examples and provide the examiner with evidence that they have undertaken wider reading about the subject.
- Candidates need to ensure that they concentrate on the specifics of the question set, rather than answering in a generalized way, and that they answer all elements of the question (which have now been increased due to the new syllabus requirements).
- Candidates should ensure that they answer the question in the format requested. If the question asks for a report format they need to ensure that this is provided. Generally candidates should try to give well-presented answers. Where possible candidates should use diagrams as this helps them to use their time more efficiently.

In order for candidates to do well on this paper they need to be fully prepared. The best preparation would include:

- Practice on selected questions from either past examinations or the CIM specimen papers.
- Reading the examiners' reports and specimen answers that are available for each past paper.
- Reading as widely as possible, not only textbooks but also the marketing and business press on a regular basis. *Note:* suggestions for further reading will be found at the end of each chapter in this text.

The CIM assignment route

The CIM have introduced an assignment route for all modules within the new Advanced Certificate Stage 2 qualification. Therefore, certain CIM study centres may now offer the assignment route as an alternative to the examination route (launched in September 2003).

The assignment route requires candidates to complete coursework instead of sitting an examination for the Marketing Planning module. The Chartered Institute of Marketing devises the coursework and assessment criteria and these are then delivered at the Study Centres which have been given CIM approval to run this type of assessment rather than the examination.

This route comprises:

- **Core section** – this attracts a 40 per cent weighting and is often about the creation of an effective marketing plan. The word count for this would be 3,000 words.
- **Elective Section** – this is worth 25 per cent weighting and requires two pieces of work (where the candidate can choose 2 out of 4 areas). Examples of such areas are: the role of environmental analysis; a report on the potential for a new Internet-based service; a report on the extended marketing mix in not for profit organizations; an external analysis of an organization of choice. Each assignment would be 1,500 words.
- **Final Reflective Statement** –10 per cent weighting. This would include specific aspects of module, application of learning to work based environment and points for future development. The word count would be 750 words for this piece of work.

This is a new assessment strategy and CIM has to approve a study centre before this route can be offered to students. Therefore, CIM has written guidelines for study centres offering this route.

Whatever assessment route candidates undertake, they should always ensure that:

- They focus upon the application of models in a variety of markets and industry sectors, e.g. the service sector, small business sector or business to business sector.
- Wherever possible, they make use of their own business experience and other illustrative sources to provide relevant examples. Regular reading of the business press is useful in order to identify illustrative examples.
- They make themselves aware of the broader implications of marketing planning decisions. In particular, as well as understanding the benefits of planning and control techniques, they should be aware of the drawbacks, in terms of costs, and other resource implications.

Acknowledgements

The authors and publisher wish to thank the following for permission to use copyright material:

The Free Press, a division of Simon & Schuster, Inc., for Figures 8.2 and 8.8 adapted from Michael E. Porter, *Competitive Strategy: Techniques for Analysing Industries and Competitors*, Figure 1.3, p. 12, Figure 2.2, p. 37. Copyright © 1980 by Michael E. Porter.

Harvard Business Review for Figure 13.1 adapted from Thomas V. Bonoma, 'Making Your Marketing Strategy Work', *Harvard Business Review*, **62** (2), March/April 1984, p. 72. Copyright © 1984 by the President and Fellows of Harvard College.

The Controller of Her Majesty's Stationery Office for Figure 4.9 data from 'New Earnings Survey', Office for National Statistics. Crown copyright © 1991.

Pearson Education for Figures 8.9 and 8.10 from Kotler, Armstrong, Saunders and Wong, *Principles of Marketing*, 2nd European edition, Prentice Hall (1999), Figure 12.6, p. 531 and Figure 12.5, p. 527; and for Figures 1.2, 5.2, 7.1 and 7.2 from Johnson, G. and Scholes, K., *Exploring Corporate Strategy*, 5th edition, Prentice Hall (1999).

Penguin Books Ltd for adapted material from Hugh Davidson, *Even More Offensive Marketing*, Penguin Books (1997), Table 120, p. 285. Copyright © Hugh Davidson, 1997.

John Wiley & Sons Ltd for Figure 5.9 adapted from J. R. Montnari and J. S. Bracker, article in *Strategic Management Journal*, **7** (3), 1986. Copyright © 1986 John Wiley & Sons Ltd.

John Wiley, Inc. for Figure 14.7 from Watson, *Strategic Benchmarking* (1993) p. 4.

Whilst every effort has been made to contact copyright holders, the publisher would like to hear from anyone whose copyright has unwittingly been infringed.

The Authors would also like to thank Paul Newman of TBWA\ and Julie Tinson of Southampton Business School for their contribution of the National Westminster Bank plc case study.

Chapter 1

The strategic perspective

About this chapter

Increasingly competitive market conditions require strategic responses. Strategic decisions define core competencies and integrate activities. Strategic management recognizes the importance of implementation and managing change. Essentially, strategic marketing management, and subsequent marketing strategies, contribute to overall business goals via a three-stage process: analysis, formulation and implementation.

Introduction

The concept of marketing is inherently simple – business success via a process of understanding and meeting customer needs. Few would argue with this basic principle, and even the most inexperienced of business managers would intuitively see the sense in this. Given this basic simplicity, why do we need something as complicated, and time-consuming, as a marketing strategy?

While basic business principles may be simple common sense, achievement involves many complex, interdependent or even conflicting tasks. Increasingly, such tasks are undertaken against a backdrop of constant change, intense competition and limited resources. To further enhance the challenge, managers are often at the mercy of incomplete data and unexpected events, often being left to 'second guess' customer and competitor reactions. It is to this end that marketing strategy has become a vital component of success. A well-considered, effectively implemented, marketing strategy should go some way to alleviating such problems and reduce the complexity of business tasks. Strategy should restore simplicity to the art of management. In essence, it is a series of tools and techniques that guide (hopefully) the organization to the marketing panacea – success via a process of understanding and meeting customer needs.

The modern business world now recognizes the importance of strategic issues and the contribution of strategic management to business success. While this has many benefits it also brings many problems. It could be argued that 'strategy' (or 'strategic') is the most overused/misused phrase in business today. Everybody seems to have a 'strategy' for everything. By attaching the term 'strategy' to an activity, it somehow becomes more important – more grand – but in reality very little actually gets done! To illustrate this, the authors recall the recent experience of sitting through a seemingly endless meeting, listening to people talk on and on about their 'strategy' or the need for a strategic view. Finally, someone said something sensible: '. . . *there's too much strategy and not enough people doing things!*' This blunt comment is memorable for two reasons. Firstly, it ended a tedious meeting. Secondly, and more importantly, it illustrated a key point: strategy must lead to action, not be a substitute for it. Ultimately, all organizations need '. . . people doing things'. The goal of strategy is to ensure they are doing the right things. These actions need to be co-ordinated, efficiently executed and focused on meeting customer need.

Essentially, strategy is a three-stage process involving analysis, formulation and implementation. During the analysis phase management needs to look both internally and externally. Understanding the wider business environment is fundamental. It is then necessary to formulate plans appropriate to current and future circumstances. Finally, implementation is needed to make sure our plans are put into practice. Managers must ensure that due care and attention is paid to each of these stages. In this way, strategy avoids being little more than rhetoric and starts to become a practical reality of business life.

What is strategy?

Over the years, many definitions of 'strategy' have been developed and close examination of such definitions tends to converge on the following – strategy is concerned with making major decisions affecting the long-term direction of the business. Major business decisions are by their very nature strategic, and tend to focus on:

- **Business definition**. A strategic fundamental is defining the business we are in. organizations need to anticipate and adapt to change by keeping in touch with the **external competitive environment**. Business leaders need to define the **scope** (or range) of the organization's activities and determine the markets in which the organization will compete. We are defining the boundaries of activity and ensuring management face up to the challenges of change.

- **Core competencies**. The organization must be competitive now and in the future. Therefore, strategic decisions need to define the basis of **sustainable competitive advantage(s)**. What skills and resources are needed in order to prosper within our defined markets and how can they be used to optimum advantage? It is essential that this is considered over the long term and aims to **match** organizational capability with desired goals and the external environment This process often has **major resource implications**, both in terms of investment and rationalization.

- **An integrative approach**. Strategy has a wide-ranging impact and therefore affects all functional areas within the organization. Effective strategy is able to **co-ordinate** the different functions/activities within the organization in order to achieve common goals. By taking a 'whole-organization' view of the corporation, managers should be better able to target resources, eliminate waste and generate synergy. **Synergy** occurs when the combined effect of functions/activities is greater than their individual contribution. It is vital that business leaders articulate a common **vision** and sense of purpose, in order to achieve an integrative approach.

- **Consistency of approach**. Strategy should provide a consistency of approach, and offer a focus to the organization. Tactical activities may change and be adapted readily in response to market conditions, but strategic direction should remain constant. Additionally, strategic management can provide common tools and analytical techniques, enabling the assessment and control of complex issues, situations and functional areas.

The process aims to specify corporate objectives and establish ways of achieving such objectives. The intent is to react to, and of course influence, the competitive environment to the advantage of the organization. Any such advantage must be sustained over the long term, but be flexible enough to adapt and develop as required.

Note that strategy and a **corporate/strategic plan** are not one and the same. Strategy defines the general concepts of future competitive advantage and reflects intent, whereas a strategic plan specifies the selection, sequence, resources, timing and specific objectives required to achieve the strategy.

Figure 1.1 summarizes the above issues. Issues of strategy, tactics and corporate planning are further developed in Chapter 12.

Figure 1.1 The basics of strategy

Towards strategic management

Over a period of some thirty years, we have seen the concept of strategy evolve. Aaker (1995) provides a historical perspective showing how this evolution has progressed and acknowledges that strategic activity has been described over the years as:

- **Budgeting**. Early strategic activity was concerned with budgetary and control mechanisms. Structured methods of allocating, monitoring and investigating variances from budget provided a means of managing complex processes. The process was often based on past trends and assumed incremental development.
- **Long-range planning**. Here greater emphasis was placed on forecasting. Planning systems and processes tended to extrapolate current trends (with varying degrees of sophistication) and predict factors such as sales, profits and cost. Management could use such forecasts as a basis for decision making.
- **Strategic planning**. The 1970s and 1980s were the era of strategic planning, with emphasis placed on: (i) specifying the overall direction, and (ii) centralized control of planning activities. While still based

around forecasting and extrapolation of past trends, far greater attention was paid to understanding the business environment. Managers hoped to be able to anticipate events via a detailed analysis of cause-and-effect relationships. Planning systems aimed to provide data and logic as a means of decision support. While promoting more awareness of strategic issues in terms of the external environment, the process still tended to focus on the preparation of corporate-wide plans. This was often achieved in a highly bureaucratic, centralized fashion.

● **Strategic management**. We are currently in the age of strategic management. Strategic management concerns both the formulation of strategy and how such strategy is put into practice. While still undertaking analysis and forecasting, far greater prominence is placed on implementation. The concern is with managing change and transforming the organization within an increasingly turbulent business environment.

Johnson and Scholes (1999) provide a useful model (see Figure 1.2) summarizing the main elements of strategic management. Strategic problems can be viewed as having three distinct components. Firstly analysis: we need to understand the business environment and the

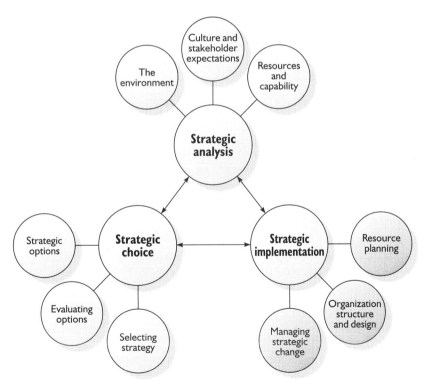

Figure 1.2 Elements of strategic management (*Source:* Johnson and Scholes, 1999)

resource capabilities of the organization. This needs to be considered in the context of the organization's culture and the aspirations and expectations of the stakeholders. ('Stakeholders' are taken to be anyone with a stake in the organization, for example, customers, employees, suppliers.) Secondly, managers need to make strategic choices. This is achieved via a process of identifying, evaluating and selecting options. The organization needs to define: (i) what is the basis of our strategy – so-called 'generic' strategy, (ii) what product/market areas will we operate in, and (iii) the specific strategies to achieve corporate goals. Finally, the issue of implementation must be considered. There is the need to plan actions, allocate resources and, where appropriate, restructure to achieve strategic change.

It is important to remember that strategic management is not the orderly, logical sequence of events/activities that managers wish for. Practical reality means that processes are interlinked and overlapping. For example, strategic analysis does not stop (or at least should not stop) when other stages take place. Analysis is an ongoing activity. Equally, creativity, vision and leadership are required to turn analysis into successful strategy. Given the volatility in today's business world, a contingency approach may be required. This provides flexibility by developing contingencies for a range of future scenarios.

Porter (1998) provides an interesting perspective and views strategy in terms of: (i) developing a unique position by choosing to perform

---

Illustrative Example 1.1: Sainsbury's strategic return to core values

---

Major strategic decisions have to be made if Sainsbury is to regain its former glory. The UK's second biggest food retailer is looking to establish a more upmarket position, in order to reverse the recent downturn in fortunes. A new 'flagship' store in London will feature luxury product ranges. These include a juice bar, an upmarket bakery counter, a premium wine merchant – 'The Cromwell Cellar' – and a seasonal produce counter. The move sees the group attempting to return to its core competencies (see Figure 1.1) of being a top-quality food retailer. Sainsbury's traditional strength is not price but rather quality, with the above developments aiming to position the company upmarket. Sainsbury struggled to compete in a price war with larger groups such as Asda and Tesco. Previous Sainsbury campaigns (e.g. 'Value to shout about' featuring actor John Cleese) promoted price competitiveness – not something traditionally associated with the company. It is now committed to offering the highest quality food at the most competitive prices. This focus gives the group strategy a consistent approach.

---

differently from the opposition; (ii) making 'trade-offs' with other possible competitive positions, in order to protect the organization's competitive advantage; (iii) combining activities to fit into, and reinforce, an overall competitive position; (iv) ensuring operational effectiveness when executing activities.

Change – shaping strategy

Change is an accepted consequence of modern life. Indeed, the phrase *'change is the only certainty'* has become something of a business mantra. All organizations are subject to increasing levels of change. We can view change in terms of cyclical change and evolutionary change. Cyclical change involves variation that is repetitive and often predictable (e.g. seasonal variation in demand or fluctuation in economic circumstances). Evolutionary change involves a more fundamental shift. It may mean sudden innovation or a gradual 'creeping' process. Either way, the result can have drastic consequences for strategic development.

Given that strategic management is concerned with moving the organization to some future desired state, which has been defined in terms of a corporate vision and corporate-wide issues, it is important to see the concept of 'change' as an integral part of strategy. We can examine this in terms of the following questions: (i) What drives change? (ii) How does change impact on our markets/business environment? (iii) What is the result of change on the organization's strategy? Figure 1.3 summarizes these three questions.

● **Drivers of change**
  Consistently, current products and methods of operating are rapidly being displaced by a combination of competitors' actions and shifting customer needs. This discontinuity is being driven by the following factors: **P**olitical, **E**conomic, **S**ocial (e.g. demographics) and **T**echnological. A so-called **'PEST'** analysis (see next chapter) provides a useful analytical framework with which to study the business environment.

Figure 1.3 Strategy and change

- **Impact of change**
  Quite simply, change means that we need to redefine our markets. While fast growth is still possible within certain 'sunrise' industries, many industries have to accept that the days of incremental annual growth are over. Variation in consumer habits and demographic patterns means traditional markets are becoming more challenging. Change is accompanied by intense competition, which the phenomenon of business globalization can only intensify. Increasingly, we see shorter product life cycles and increasing difficulty in predicting the future.
- **Result of change**
  There are two main outcomes. First, change creates opportunity. Organizations that are flexible and in touch with customer needs are likely not just to survive, but to prosper. Second, past actions, strategies and methods offer no guarantee of future success. There is a need to guard against complacency and ensure that the strategic thrust of the organization does not drift from the true needs of the market place (beware of strategic drift).

Balanced scorecard approach

As change pervades all aspects of business strategy, it is important to set appropriate measures of business success. Rather than relying on a few narrow financial measures, a system is needed which provides an overall view of business success. To this end, Kaplan and Norton (1992) advocate using a '**balanced scorecard**' approach. This involves taking both financial and non-financial measures and examining the benefits delivered to all the organization's stakeholders. A balanced scorecard approach involves four sets of measures:

- **Financial measures**. Here we examine how we are perceived by investors and shareholders.
- **Customers**. How do our customers view us?
- **Internal activities**. By examining the key areas of activity which deliver customer satisfaction, we can identify where the organization must outdo its competitors.
- **Innovation and learning**. To survive and prosper, all organizations need to improve and adapt. Any business activity can be viewed as a learning experience with the goal of continuously creating value.

Performance indicators are established within each of these areas. These become an objective basis with which to evaluate and formulate strategy. A winning strategy should address the above and offer a range of initiatives for the future.

The role of marketing within strategy

As noted earlier, all organizations need to make strategic decisions relating to their external environment. Strategy must address issues such as customers, competitors and market trends. It needs to be proactive as opposed to simply reacting to events. In this way, strategy can detect and influence changes in the business environment. By its nature, marketing defines how the organization interacts with its market place. Consequently, all strategic planning, to a greater or lesser degree, requires an element of marketing. Only in this way can organizations become strategically responsive to customer need and commercial pressures. Indeed, it is possible to view marketing as more than a functional activity. It can be adopted as a business philosophy. Here the organization adopts a marketing orientation – *success by a process of understanding and meeting customer need*. Basically, the company's orientation defines its fundamental business philosophy, highlighting what is perceived as the primary route to success. Market orientations are now widely established within the business world (and often seen as the 'holy grail' of marketers) but other business orientations are equally common.

- **Production orientation**. Here business success is attributed to efficient production. The emphasis is on mass production, economy of scale and cost control. Management's key concern is with achieving volume and meeting production schedules. This philosophy has its place, but risks limiting operations to low added-value assembly work.
- **Product orientation**. The belief is that product innovation and design will have buyers beating a path to the door. Management's perception is that their products are so good they will, in effect, sell themselves. Little or no effort is put into establishing what the customer actually wants – a dangerous route! Naturally, product innovation is important but it needs to appeal to the market place, otherwise it risks being innovation for the sake of innovation.
- **Sales orientation**. This views sales volume as the key determinant of success. The focus is on aggressive selling that persuades the customer to buy. Given that the process is driven by sales targets, a short-term perspective dominates, with little regard to building longer-term relationships. Often, this follows on from a production orientation, as management tries to create a demand for unwanted products.
- **Market orientation**. As previously stated, success is derived from understanding and meeting customer needs. This process starts with the customer and uses actual customer demand as a means to focus resources. In simple terms, we provide what the market wants. Additionally, the importance of building long-term relationships with

customers is recognized. We seek to build loyalty and consistently offer superior value. An awareness of competitors' proficiency and strategy is required in order to optimize this process.

It is not our intention to decry production, product innovation or selling – indeed they are vital. However, the truly 'world-class' organization understands how to marshal these factors into a coherent market-led orientation. Creating such focus will facilitate the sustainable competitive advantage required to prosper.

How do we go about achieving a market orientation? The answer to this question can be summarized as follows:

1 **Customer focused**
   Understand your customer base and be responsive to their needs. Treat loyal customers as assets and strive to build ongoing and long-term relationships. Regularly monitor levels of customer satisfaction and retention. To achieve this we must: (i) define our markets; (ii) effectively segment/target customers, and (iii) listen to customers.
2 **Competitor focused**
   In terms of competitors, be watchful and assess their objectives, strategies and capabilities. There is the need to 'benchmark' their products, processes and operations against our own.
3 **Integrate marketing into the business**
   Marketing should not be confined to the marketing department. Every function and person within the organization has a role to play in creating value and achieving the goal of being a market-led organization. This may require fundamental changes in culture and organization structure.
4 **Strategic vision**
   Develop a long-term, market-orientated strategic vision by viewing marketing as more than a series of promotional tools and techniques. It must be on the agenda of senior management, who should develop and implement market-led strategy and define the future in terms of creating long-term value for stakeholders.
5 **Realistic expectations**
   We cannot be all things to all people. Expectations have to be realistic and matched to capabilities, resources and external conditions. We may well need to make 'trade-offs' to ensure we focus on activities that add value.

What is marketing strategy?

In a strategic role, marketing aims to transform corporate objectives and business strategy into a competitive market position. Essentially, the concern is to differentiate our activities/products by meeting customer needs more effectively than competitors. Marketing strategy can by characterized by:

(a) analysing the business environment and defining specific customer needs
(b) matching activities/products to customer segments, and
(c) implementing programmes that achieve a competitive position, superior to competitors.

Therefore, marketing strategy addresses three elements – customers, competitors and internal corporate issues (see Figure 1.4).

Figure 1.4 The basis of marketing strategy

Firstly, we consider customers. How is the market defined, what segments exist and who should we target? Secondly, how can we best establish a competitive position? A precursor to this is a detailed understanding of our competitors within targeted market segments. Finally, we need to match internal corporate capabilities with customer need. The successful achievement of these factors should enable the organization to develop, and maintain, a strong market position.

Essentially, a marketing strategy aims to deliver the following:

1 Segmentation
This process breaks the market down into groups displaying common characteristics, behaviours and attitudes. Fundamentally, this process aims to understand need and forecast reaction and/or demand.

2 Targeting

This involves evaluating and selecting market segments. We aim to look for opportunities which are sustainable, where we can build long-term relationships with customers.

3 Positioning

As previously stated, we establish a distinctive superior position, relative to competitors. The competitive position adopted should be based on matching product attributes to customer need.

It goes without saying that the three key constituents of marketing strategy – customers, competitors and internal corporate factors – are dynamic and constantly changing (summarized in the section on Change – shaping strategy in this chapter, p. 7). Therefore, organizations must develop and deploy processes, procedures and techniques that ensure market strategy is:

(a) relative to the current/future business environment,
(b) sustainable,
(c) generating optimum benefits to both the organization and customers, and
(d) correctly implemented.

This is the process of **strategic marketing management**.

Illustrative Example 1.2: Torex: – marketing strategy and the drivers of change

Rather than trying to cover all possible users, information technology company Torex has two distinct areas of operation – retailing and health care. Having adopted a clear segmentation and targeting strategy, Torex is able to establish a distinct competitive position, setting it apart from more general IT providers. A PEST analysis demonstrates how the organization can benefit from the drivers of change. Consider the following statement in terms of **P**olitical, **E**conomic, **S**ocial and **T**echnological factors.

The UK government's commitment to modernize the health service (*political*) is excellent news for specialist information technology provider Torex. Growing demand for health care (*social*) will generate a need to modernize existing health service systems with specialized health service/care technology. As a provider of computer technology to the medical profession, Torex is well placed to benefit from increased government expenditure (*economic*). The company is also reported to be working on the 'Gpnet' project (*technological*) – an electronic information system which links doctors together.

As a process, strategic marketing (and the subsequent structure of this book) has three distinct phases:

- **Strategic analysis**

  To move forward we must first answer the question: where are we? This stage entails a detailed examination of the business environment, customers and an internal review of the organization itself. Tools such as portfolio analysis and industry structure models help management to assess objectively the organization's current position. Equally, it is important to develop some view regarding future trends. This is achieved via forecasting and defining assumptions about the future market trends.

- **Formulating strategy**

  Having analysed our situation, we then determine a way forward. Formulation involves defining strategic intent – what are our overall goals and objectives? Managers need to formulate a marketing strategy that generates competitive advantage and positions the organization's products effectively. To be successful, this must be based on core competencies. During this stage, product development and innovation are strategic activities, offering the potential to enhance competitive position and further develop products and brands. Additionally, formulation emphasizes the need to form relationships with customers and other businesses. Increasingly, we see organizations recognizing that they cannot do everything themselves and looking to form joint ventures and partnerships.

  The formulation stage culminates with the development of a strategic marketing plan.

- **Implementation**

  Consideration needs to be given to implementing the strategy. Marketing managers will undertake programmes and actions that deliver strategic objectives. Such actions, will often focus on individual elements of the marketing mix. Additionally, a process of monitoring and control needs to be put in place. This ensures compliance and aids decision making.

Figure 1.5 provides an overview of the process of strategic marketing management. It also provides a template for the structure of this text. The three components form a planning cycle (analysis, formulation and implementation) and are interactive in nature, with information being fed back to enable objectives and strategy to be reviewed and amended. Ultimately, the process will establish the organization's marketing mix – products, price, promotion and place, which underpins and conveys our marketing strategy.

Figure 1.5 Strategic marketing

Summary

Today's business world recognizes the importance of strategy and strategic management. Normally, any strategic process has three distinct stages – analysis, formulation of plans and implementation. Increasingly, the importance of implementation is recognized as an integral part of the strategic framework. Strategy aims to define core competencies, understand the external environment and offer an integrative, consistent approach to decision making.

Any strategy is significantly influenced by environmental change. Political, economic, social and technological factors drive change and impact on the organization. This results in a volatile, intensely competitive market place. Organizations need to ensure that they fully embrace the opportunities change brings and guard against complacency and strategic drift. To this end, a 'balanced scorecard' approach is advocated, thus encouraging the organization to address wider strategic issues.

Marketing has a role to play within the strategic process; namely, marketing can be adopted as a business philosophy. This sees commercial success as stemming from a process of understanding and meeting customer needs.

Marketing strategy involves achieving a superior competitive position within a defined market. Essentially, it involves segmentation, targeting and positioning. This must address customers, competitors and internal corporate factors. Strategic marketing management is the process of ensuring our marketing strategy is relevant and sustainable.

References

Aaker, D., *Strategic Market Management*, 4th edition, Wiley, 1995

Johnson, G. and Scholes, K., *Exploring Corporate Strategy*, 5th edition, Prentice Hall, 1999

Kaplan, R. and Norton, D. 'The balanced scorecard: Measures that drive performance', *Harvard Business Review*, Vol. 70, No. 1, 1992

Porter, M., 'What is strategy?', cited in Segal-Horn, S. (ed.), *The Strategy Reader*, Blackwell in association with The Open University, 1998

Part 1

Strategic analysis

- External analysis
- Competitive intelligence
- Segmentation
- Internal analysis
- Developing a future orientation

Undertaking a strategic analysis is the foundation upon which strategic decisions are constructed. In this text strategic analysis is broken down into three constituent elements: external analysis, customer analysis and internal analysis. Undertaking the analysis is not, however, a linear process and there are areas of the analyses that overlap. The aim of the process is to develop a detailed and all-embracing view of the company and its external environment to permit the organization to formulate informed strategic decisions.

Chapter 2 explores the external analysis. This consists of an initial audit of the macro-environment. The organization's micro-environment is then considered and an initial analysis of the company's competitive position is undertaken.

Chapter 3 explores the increasingly critical function of competitive intelligence and examines how organizations can employ such a practice to support and develop successful marketing strategies.

Chapter 4 examines the customer. Consumer behaviour is explored to illustrate what effect changes in the external environment can have on customers. Market segmentation techniques are then discussed.

Chapter 5 describes the process of internal analysis. This looks at the ways of identifying the organization's assets and competencies.

These four chapters illustrate the groundwork that needs to be undertaken by an organization before it can begin to form a view of the future.

Chapter 6 discusses different approaches that organizations can take to form a view of what developments may occur, and affect their activities, in the future. Part 1 also covers the process that is at the heart of strategic choice – matching the organization's resources and competencies to attractive market opportunities (the theme of Part 2 of this text).

Chapter 2

External analysis

About this chapter

The external analysis is the first stage of the auditing process. It creates the information and analysis necessary for an organization to begin to identify the key issues it will need to address in order to develop a successful strategy. The chapter explores the process of PEST analysis, industry analysis, competitor analysis and market analysis. The various approaches used to facilitate this process, in particular the 'five forces' model and strategic groups, are covered.

Introduction

An analysis of the external environment is undertaken in order to discover the opportunities and threats that are evolving and that need to be addressed by the organization. A study by Diffenbach (1983) identified a number of positive consequences that stem from carrying out organized environmental analysis (see Figure 2.1).

An analysis of the external environment can be broken down into three key steps, each becoming more specific to the organization. The first step is an analysis of the macro-environmental influences that the organization faces. This is followed by an examination of the competitive (micro) environment the organization operates within. Finally, a specific competitive analysis is undertaken.

Scanning

The environmental audit is reliant on the monitoring activity that is undertaken by the organization. The process is normally referred to as scanning.

Awareness of environmental changes by management:	Industry and market analysis:
■ Enhanced ability to anticipate problems arising in the longer term ■ Senior management awareness of a range of possible futures and their effect on the organization ■ Greater inclination to act in advance of changes	■ Quality of market and product forecasts improved ■ Identification of changes in buyer behaviour as a result of changes in social trends ■ Ability to identify future needs and anticipate new products
Strategic planning and decision making:	**Diversification and resource allocation:**
■ More flexibility and adaptability in plans as they reflect greater awareness of political events and economic cycles ■ Scope of perspectives broadened ■ Organization has greater ability to allocate resources to opportunities arising due to environmental change	■ Ability to focus resources in business areas that have long-term attractiveness ■ Guides the acquisitions process ■ Move away from products exposed to greater social and political pressure (environmental issues, etc.) towards other areas of the product portfolio
Relationship with government:	**Overseas businesses:**
■ Improved understanding and relationship with government ■ Ability to be proactive on government legislation	■ Improved ability to anticipate changes in overseas markets ■ Improved ability to anticipate how to undertake business in overseas markets

Figure 2.1 A selection of benefits derived from organized environmental analysis. (*Source*: Adapted from Diffenbach, 1983)

There are four forms of scanning according to Aguilar (1967):

- **Undirected viewing**. This activity concerns the viewer exploring information in general without carrying a specific agenda. The viewer is exposed to a large amount of varied information but this is not an active search looking for particular issues, just a broad attempt to be aware of factors or areas that may have changed.
- **Conditional viewing**. Again this is not an organized search but the viewer is sensitive to information that identifies changes in specific areas of activity.
- **Informal search**. This is an organized but limited search for information to support a specific goal.
- **Formal search**. This type of search is actively pursued and specifically designed to seek particular information.

There is, of course, an unlimited amount of information that can be scanned but any organization can only scan a certain amount of this information. A balance has to be struck between the resources allocated to this activity and the potential benefits. More information also does not lead to better decision making. Understanding the dynamics of the environment, not the volume of information reviewed, is the critical aspect to this activity (see the section on Market sensing in Chapter 6, p. 120).

Managers search for information in five broad areas (Aguilar, 1967) (see Figure 2.2):

- market intelligence
- technical intelligence
- acquisition intelligence
- broad issues
- other intelligence

(*Note*: Aguilar uses the word 'tidings' rather than intelligence.)

The study showed that 58 per cent of managers saw market intelligence as the most important area for obtaining external information, three times

Area of external information	Category	General content
Market intelligence	■ Market potential ■ Structural change ■ Competitors and industry ■ Pricing ■ Sales negotiations ■ Customers	➡ Capacity, consumption, imports, exports ➡ Mergers, acquisitions, new entries ➡ Competitor information, industry policy ➡ Effective and proposed prices ➡ Information on specific current or potential sales ➡ Current or potential customers, markets and problems
Technical intelligence	■ New product, processes and technology ■ Product problems ■ Costs ■ Licensing and patents	➡ Technical information relatively new or unknown to enterprise ➡ Involving current products ➡ For processing, operations, etc. for suppliers, customers and competitors ➡ Products and processes
Acquisition intelligence	■ Leads for mergers, joint ventures or acquisitions	➡ Information concerning possibilities for the organization
Intelligence on broad issues	■ General conditions ■ Government actions and policies	➡ General information: political, demographic etc. ➡ Decisions affecting the industry
Other intelligence	■ Suppliers and raw materials ■ Resources available ■ Miscellaneous	➡ Purchasing information ➡ Availability of people, land, other resources ➡ Any other information

Figure 2.2 Critical areas of external information (*Source*: Adapted from Aguilar, 1967)

more important than the next most significant area, technical intelligence at 18 per cent. The importance placed on market intelligence was true across all functional areas. The most significant categories of information within this area were market potential, accounting for 30 per cent alone, and structural change, accounting for 10 per cent. The only other category that reached double figures was for the category of new products, process and technology under technical intelligence.

One crucial aspect of this activity, especially where it underpins futures forecasting, is to detect weak signals. That is, identifying fragments of information that indicate significant changes, but whose potential impact has generally not been perceived. This is obviously difficult, especially as many organizations fail to recognize major signals in the environment.

Macro-environmental analysis

The macro-environment audit examines the broad range of environmental issues that may affect the organization. This will include political/legal issues, economic factors, social/cultural issues and technological developments. This is normally referred to as a PEST (Political, Economic, Social and Technological) analysis, although some writers use the alternative acronym STEP (see Figure 2.3). The aim of

Political/legal issues	**Economic factors**
■ Taxation policy ■ Monopoly controls ■ Environmental protection measures ■ Employment law ■ Environmental legislation ■ Foreign trade agreements ■ Stability of the governmental system	■ Interest rates ■ Inflation rates ■ Money supply ■ Business cycles ■ Unemployment ■ GNP trends
Social/cultural issues	**Technological factors**
■ Age profiles ■ Social mobility ■ Changes in lifestyles ■ Family structures ■ Levels of education ■ Work behaviour ■ Leisure activities ■ Distribution of income ■ Patterns of ownership ■ Attitudes and values	■ Focus of government research ■ Rate of technology transfer ■ Materials ■ Developing technological processes

Figure 2.3 The PEST analysis of influences in the external environment

this analysis is to identify the critical issues in the external environment that may affect the organization before moving on to judge the impact they may have on the organization.

- **Political/legal issues**. There is a range of political organizations that have to be considered when looking at influences in this area of the audit. The structure of a political system defines the centres of political influence. A state with a federal political structure will differ from a unitary political system. In the UK there is a parliament for Scotland and an assembly for Wales. There are, however, a number of decision areas that are still the responsibility of the Westminster parliament. At the same time there is also an increasing range of decisions being taken both politically and legally within the framework of the European Union. Political pressure groups such as Greenpeace can also affect the political agenda. Therefore when considering this area of the environment a much wider view has to be taken than just the domestic national government or the legal process.
- **Economic factors**. Similarly, economic factors have to be viewed from a wider perspective than the organization's domestic economy. In the global economy, domestic economic conditions are heavily influenced by events in other areas of the world. Economics is concerned with the allocation of resources. Therefore issues such as conservation of natural resources, costs of pollution, energy consumption and the whole area of the management of natural resources should be considered under this heading.
- **Social/cultural issues**. Demographic changes are important and can be used as lead indicators in certain areas, such as health care and education. However, other critical areas such as social/cultural values and beliefs that are central to changes in consumer behaviour are harder to predict and can be subject to more dramatic shifts.
- **Technological developments**. There is a great danger in using a particular technology to define an industry. In a situation where technological developments are fast-moving it is critical to understand the fundamental consumer needs which the organization's technology is currently serving. Identifying new technologies that can service those consumer needs more completely or economically is the critical part of this area of the analysis.

The central role of this PEST analysis is to identify the key factors that are likely to drive change in the environment. Then the aim is to establish how these key factors will affect the industry in general and the organization in particular.

Illustrative Example 2.1: WAP and UMTS technology

WAP is the acronym that stands for Wireless Application Protocol and UMTS is the term for Universal Mobile Telecommunications System. WAP is the technology that allows miniaturized internet sites to be accessed through mobile phones. UMTS will support mobile video as well as audio, graphics and text. These new technologies link two areas of dynamic growth, the mobile phone market and internet usage. Mobile phone networks, telecommunication equipment manufacturers and e-commerce operators are all actively developing WAP phones and associated services. Airlines are developing journey information sites and check-in facilities using WAP services. The BBC, in association with Vodaphone Airtouch, is developing a mobile news service using both WAP and UMTS. Companies in the banking sector are also committed to developing services based on current web delivery but with added features such as text messages being sent to customers who are in danger of becoming overdrawn.

Despite all this activity there is still uncertainty about how this area will develop. It is unclear exactly what the technology is able to deliver and what consumers will demand. This technology is a major development in the external environment faced by companies across a range of industry sectors. Organizations confronting this type of development face a dilemma about whether to embrace the technology early and commit the resources necessary to develop products and services or to stand back until it is clearer exactly what the technology can deliver. Despite some early difficulties it appears many organizations feel they cannot afford to stand back.

Industry analysis

An organization has to understand the nature of the relationships within its industry in order to allow the enterprise to develop strategies to gain advantage of the current relationships.

A useful framework that can be utilized when undertaking this analysis is Porter's 'five forces' model of establishing industry attractiveness for a business (see Figure 2.4). This analysis should be conducted at the level of the individual strategic business unit (SBU) rather than at the level of the organization as a whole, otherwise the range of relationships facing a company with several divisions causes the analysis to lose focus. Porter identified five factors that affect the level of competition and therefore profitability within an industry:

- **Suppliers**. The power of suppliers is liable to be strong where:
  - Control over supplies is concentrated into the hands of a few players.

- Costs of switching to a new source of supply are high.
- The supplier has a strong brand.
- The supplier is in an industry with a large number of smaller disparate customers.
- **Buyers**. The power of buyers is liable to be strong where:
  - A few buyers control a large percentage of a volume market. For example, grocery and electrical goods retailers in the UK dominate the market and are in a very strong position versus their suppliers as a result.
  - There are a large number of small suppliers. In the meat industry in the UK there are a large number of small farmers supplying a retail sector dominated by a small number of large supermarkets.
  - The costs of switching to a new supplier are low.
  - The supplier's product is relatively undifferentiated, effectively lowering barriers to alternative sources of supply.

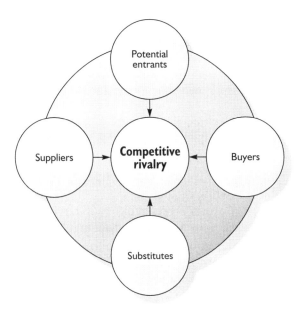

Figure 2.4 The five forces model (*Source*: Adapted from Porter, 1980)

- **Potential entrants**. The threat of potential entrants will be determined by a number of barriers to entry that may exist in any given industry:
  - The capital investment necessary to enter the industry can be very high in areas such as electrical power generation or chemical production.
  - A well-entrenched competitor who moved into the industry early may have established cost advantages irrespective of the size of

their operation. They have had time to establish crucial aspects of their operation such as effective sources of supply, the best locations, and customer franchises.
- Achieving economies of scale in production, distribution or marketing can be a necessity in certain industries.
- Gaining access to appropriate distribution channels can be difficult. Peugeot/Citröen bought Chrysler's entire UK operations in order to gain an effective dealership network in Britain.
- Government legislation and policies such as patent protection, trade relations with other states, and state-owned monopolies can all act to restrict the entry of competitors.
- The prospect of a well-established company's hostile reactions to a new competitor's entry to the market may be enough to act as a deterrent.
- **Substitutes**. Substitution can arise in a number of ways:
  - A new product or service may eradicate the need for a previous process. Insurance services delivered directly by producers over the phone or internet are substitutes for the services of the independent insurance broker.
  - A new product replaces an existing product or service. Cassette tapes replaced vinyl records, only to be replaced in turn by compact discs.
  - All products and services, to some extent, suffer from generic substitution. Consumers may choose to substitute purchasing an expensive holiday instead of buying a car.
- **Competitive rivalry**. The intensity of competition in the industry will be determined by a range of factors:
  - The stage of the industry life cycle will have an effect. Natural growth reaches a plateau once an industry reaches maturity, so the only way an organization can continue to grow in the industry is to take market share from its rivals.
  - The relative size of competitors is an important factor. In an industry where rivals are of similar size, competition is likely to be intense as they each strive for a dominant position. Industries that already have a clear dominant player tend to be less competitive.
  - In industries that suffer from high fixed costs, companies will try to gain as much volume throughput as possible. This may create competition based on price discounting.
  - There may be barriers that prevent companies withdrawing from an industry. This may be plant and machinery that is specialist in nature and therefore cannot be transferred to other uses. The workforce may have non-transferable specialist skills. If the industry is in maturity, moving towards decline, and rivals cannot easily leave the industry then competition will inevitably increase.

The 'five forces' model allows an organization to identify the major forces that are present in the industry sector. This can be related to the critical factors that were identified by the PEST analysis. Several issue then need to be considered:

- What is the likelihood that the nature of the relationships identified by the 'five forces' model will change given the trends in the external environment? Are there ways of benefiting from these potential changes?
- What actions can the organization undertake that will improve its position against the current forces in the industry? Can the company increase its power, relative to suppliers or buyers? Can actions be taken to reduce competitive rivalry, or are there ways of building barriers to dissuade companies from considering entering the industry? Are there ways of making substitute products less attractive?
- The organization will also need to consider its competitors. Given the forces in the industry, what is the relative position of the organization's rivals? Do conditions favour one particular operator? Could conditions change in favour of one particular competitor? Consideration of the relative competitive position of rivals is an important aspect of an audit and needs now to be considered in more detail.

Competitor analysis

The 'five forces' analysis has examined the overall industry and is a starting point in assessing a company's competitive position. This is likely to be a rather broad definition of an industry and contains a number of companies that would not be direct competitors. For instance. Toyota is likely to have a number of natural direct competitors but TVR is not likely to be one of them, although both companies are in the car industry. Toyota's scale is global and it manufactures cars across the full range, TVR is a specialist, low-volume prestige sports car manufacturer. Companies that are direct competitors in terms of products and customer profiles are seen as being in a strategic group. The car industry would be made up of a number of strategic groups.

Strategic groups

Strategic groups are made up of organizations within the same industry that are pursuing equivalent strategies, targeting groups of customers that have similar profiles. TVR's strategic group is likely to contain

Ferrari, Lotus, Lamborghini, Aston Martin etc. All these companies are following similar strategies and facing similar strategic questions. They are also aiming at very similar market segments. In the airline industry there are at least three strategic groups. One group consists of airlines with regional operations who offer scheduled flights and compete on cost. There is a group of major airlines who have global operations and offer scheduled flights with quality environments and service. The third group offer charter services to a range of holiday destinations (see Figure 2.5).

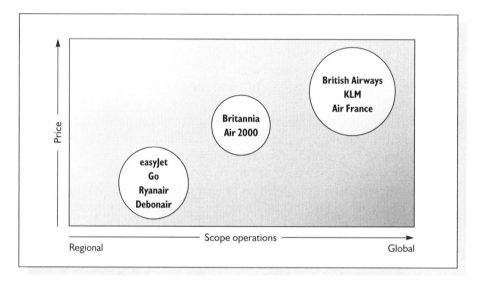

Figure 2.5 Strategic groups in the airline industry

There are a range of attributes that can be used to identify strategic groups. Some examples are:

- size of the company
- assets and skills
- scope of the operation
- breadth of the product range
- choice of distribution channel
- relative product quality
- brand image

For many companies, analysing every competitor in its generic industry would be a difficult task in terms of management time and company resources. Defining an organization's strategic group allows a company to concentrate its analysis on its direct competitors and to examine them in more detail.

Tools which are used to analyse the internal environment, such as the value chain, can of course be used to analyse competitors (see Chapter 8). For each competitor in their strategic group an organization needs, as far as possible, to establish the information discussed in the following subsections.

Competitor's objectives

A competitor's objectives can be identified by analysing three important factors:

- Whether the competitor's current performance is likely to be fulfilling their objectives. If not, the competitor may initiate a change of strategy.
- How likely the competitor is to commit further investment to the business. Financial objectives may indicate this. Investment is more likely from companies that have objectives which are long-term in nature, such as market share and sales growth, rather than organizations under pressure to produce short-term profitability. This also reveals potential trade-offs the competitor may be willing to take. If short-term profitability is the key objective then the rival is likely to be willing to lose market share in the short term in order to achieve its profitability targets.
- The likely future direction of the competitor's strategy. The organization may have non-financial objectives, such as gaining technology leadership.

Competitor's current and past strategies

There are three areas that should be explored in order to establish a competitor's current activities:

- Identification of the current markets, or market segments, within which the competitor currently operates. This will indicate the scope of the business
- Identification of the way the competitor has chosen to compete in those markets. Is it based on quality of service, brand image or on price? This may be an indication of whether a low cost or differentiation strategy is being pursued (see Chapter 8).
- Comparison between the current strategy and past strategies can be instructive. Firstly it can illustrate the direction in which the competitor is moving, in terms of product and market development, over time. It can also highlight strategies that the organization has

tried in the past and which have failed. The competitor is unlikely to attempt these approaches again without considerable reservations.

Competitor's capabilities

An analysis of a competitor's assets and competencies allows a judgement to be made about how well equipped they are to address the market, given the dynamics in the industry and the trends in the external environment. In order to evaluate a competitor's potential challenge to an organization a number of areas need to be examined (Lehman and Weiner, 1991):

- **Management capabilities**. The background and previous approaches of leading managers in a competitor company can give clues as to their likely future strategy. The level of centralization, or decentralization of management decisions will also affect decision making. Recruitment and promotion policies, along with the remuneration and rewards scheme, all give an indication as to the culture and style of the management team.
- **Marketing capabilities**. An analysis of the competitor's actions, with the marketing mix, uncovers the areas where their marketing skills are high and also areas of vulnerability. There are a number of questions that can be asked: How good is the competitor's product line? Do they have a strong brand image? Is their advertising effective? How good are their distribution channels? How strong is their relationship with customers?
- **Innovation capabilities**. Evaluating a competitor's ability to innovate allows an organization to judge how likely the rival is to introduce new products and services or even new technology. Assessing the quality of a competitor's technical staff, its technical facilities and its level of investment in research and development will all help indicate its likely potential in this area.
- **Production capabilities**. The configuration of a competitor's production infrastructure can highlight areas that may place them at an advantage, or conversely point out areas that are problematic to them. Such factors could be geographic spread of plant, level of vertical integration, or level of capacity utilization. Low capacity utilization can increase fixed costs per unit of manufacture. On the other hand, it offers a competitor production capacity for new products. The flexibility of production staff is also an important issue to identify. In the service sector, capacity and staff flexibility are just as important. Factors such as the ability to pull in additional staff on a temporary basis give a service company an important capability.

- **Financial capabilities**. The ability to finance developments is a critical area. Competitors that have strong cash flows, or are a division of a major group, may have the ability to finance investment not available to other competitors.

Competitor's future strategies and reactions

One of the aims of the competitor analysis so far has been to gather information on rivals to establish their likely future strategy. It is equally important to evaluate a competitor's likely reactions to any strategic moves the organization might instigate. The reactions of organizations can be categorized into four types of response (Kotler *et al.*, 1996):

- **Certain retaliation**. The competitor is guaranteed to react in an aggressive manner to any challenge. Market leaders, in particular, are likely to react in this manner against any threat to their dominant position. Companies that have an aggressive culture may also fall into this category.
- **Failure to react**. Competitors can be lulled into a false sense of security in an industry that, over a long period of time, has seen very little change. In this situation companies can be extremely slow to react to a competitive move. The classic example is British motorcycle companies failing to react to the entry of Japanese manufacturers into the lower end of the market.
- **Specific reactions**. Some competitors may react, but only to competitive moves in certain areas. For instance, they may always react to any price reductions, or sales promotions, as they believe these will have an important impact on their business, but they may fail to respond to a competitor's increase in advertising expenditure. The more visible the competitor's move the more likely a competitor is to respond. Actions that are less visible, such as support material for the sales force or dealerships, are less likely to face a response.
- **Inconsistent reactions**. Other companies' reactions are simply not predictable. They react aggressively on occasion but at other times ignore similar competitive challenges.

Problems in identifying competitors

Analysing members of a strategic group provides crucial information on which to base strategic decisions. However, there are risks in the

Illustrative Example 2.2: Sainsbury

On 20 November 2000 Sainsbury's announced that its home delivery service, called 'Sainsbury's to You', was being geographically extended to include Manchester. This move takes Sainsbury's home delivery service's coverage up to 45 per cent of the UK market. The company's aim is to reach 60 per cent coverage by spring 2001 and turnover of £125 million. Tesco already claims to have 90 per cent coverage for its rival service, called Tescodirect, and a turnover of £350 million. Sainsbury, however, is pursuing a different strategy to Tesco who send goods to online customers from stocks at its current retail outlets. Sainsbury is building dedicated warehouses to deliver 15,000 product lines. Each warehouse will have the capacity to make 15,000 deliveries a week to customers within a 40-mile radius. Sainsbury's approach is based on the belief that current retail outlets would struggle to service more than 500 online orders a week as well as carry out the normal retail services.

Sainsbury's research indicates that consumers who buy online also tend to use the retail store outlet for top-up purchases. In total, online customers purchase 25 per cent more than customers who only shop in-store. Online shopping is a growing market and is particularly attractive to dual income families who are affluent but face constraints on their free time due to the pressures of sustaining two careers. Both Sainsbury and Tesco have developed strategies to service changing patterns of consumer behaviour that are emerging due to changes in the technological and social environment. Only time will allow a judgement to be made as to whether either approach has created a strategic competitive advantage in this growing market sector.

process of identifying an organization's competitors and a number of errors should be avoided:

- Overlooking smaller competitors by placing too much emphasis on large, visible competitors.
- Focusing on established competitors and ignoring potential new entrants.
- Concentrating on current domestic competitors and disregarding international competitors who could possibly enter the market.

The competitive analysis has allowed the organization to establish its relative position versus its competitors on a range of important criteria. However, the organization has to judge itself and its competitors against the market it is operating within. At this stage in the external analysis it is useful to establish a range of information about the market. The customer and market segmentation would also be considered in a market analysis and this will be explored in detail in Chapter 4.

The market analysis

A market analysis will be made up of a range of factors relevant to the particular situation under review, but would normally include the following areas:

- **Actual and potential market size**. Estimating the total sales in the market allows the organization to evaluate the realism of particular market share objectives. Identifying the key sub-markets of this market, and potential areas of growth, is crucial to developing a marketing strategy, as is establishing if any areas are in decline.
- **Trends**. Analysing general trends in the market identifies the changes that have actually taken place. This can help to uncover the reasons for these changes and expose the critical drivers underlying a market.
- **Customers**. The analysis needs to identify who the customer is and what criteria they use to judge a product offering. Information on where, when and how customers purchase the product, or service, allows an organization to begin to understand the needs of the customer (Chapter 4 will look at consumer behaviour in more detail). Identifying changing trends in consumer behaviour may begin to signal potential market developments and opportunities (see Chapter 6).
- **Customer segments**. Identifying current market segments and establishing the benefits each group requires allows an organization to detect if it has the capability to serve particular consumers' needs.
- **Distribution channels**. Identifying the changes of importance between channels of distribution, based on growth, cost or effectiveness, permits a company to evaluate its current arrangements. Establishing the key decision makers in a channel of distribution also helps to inform strategic decisions.

Summary

The external auditing process creates the information and analysis necessary for an organization to begin to identify the key issues it will have to address in order to develop a successful strategy. The PEST analysis uncovered the critical areas in the external environment that the organization needed to consider. The industry analysis revealed the structure and strengths of players in the industry that any strategy will be required to address. The competitor analysis disclosed the relative position of the direct competitors in the strategic group. Finally, the market analysis began to explore current trends and areas of growth. More importantly, it began to build a picture of the consumer.

The external analysis is the initial step in the process of establishing the key issues facing an organization. The next stage is to examine the consumer, before establishing methods for segmenting markets.

References

Aguilar, F. J., *Scanning the Business Environment*, Macmillan, 1967

Diffenbach, J., 'Corporate environmental analysis in large U.S. corporations', *Long Range Planning*, Vol. 16, No. 3, pp. 107–116, 1983

Kotler, P., Armstrong, G., Saunders, J. and Wong, V., *Principles of Marketing: The European Edition*, Prentice Hall, 1996

Lehman, D.R. and Weiner, R.S., *Analysis for Marketing Planning*, 2nd edition, Irwin, 1991

Porter, M.E., *Competitive Strategy*, p. 4, Free Press, 1980

Further reading

Aaker, D., *Strategic Market Management*, 4th edition, Chapters 4–7, Wiley, 1995

Davidson, H., *Even More Offensive Marketing*, Chapter 5, Penguin 1997

Mudie, P., *Marketing: An Analytical Perspective*, Chapter 2, Prentice Hall, 1997

Chapter 3

Competitive intelligence

About this chapter

Business success is as much determined by the actions of competitors, as by the actions of the organization itself. For example, the success of Coca-Cola is partly determined by the actions of Pepsi-Cola. This chapter explores the increasingly vital practice of competitive intelligence and examines how organizations can use such a function to support/develop successful marketing strategies. Gathering, analysing and disseminating intelligence relating to competitors' strategies, goals, procedures and products greatly underpins competitiveness.

What is competitive intelligence?

Competitive intelligence has something of an image problem. The term conjures up an image of illicit activities involving private detectives, telephoto lenses and hidden microphones. While such images are not completely unappealing, they are far removed from the truth. Put simply, competitive intelligence is a structured, ethical and legal process designed to gather, analyse and distribute data/information relating to current, and potential, competitors. The key to successful competitive intelligence is the ability to turn basic raw data into actionable intelligence. Actionable intelligence involves providing decision makers with timely, appropriate information which facilitates action. Additionally, competitive intelligence stresses the need to protect business activities against competitors' intelligence-gathering operations.

The need for competitive intelligence (CI) has always been recognized. Indeed, Sun Tzu's *The Art of War*, written in China over 2000 years ago, makes many references to CI.

> *Know the enemy and know yourself, in a hundred battles you will never be defeated.* Sun Tzu, *The Art of War*, 400 BC.

Such reference is equally applicable to today's business world. Given the established business trends of: (a) globalization; (b) rapid technological development, and (c) merger and acquisition, CI is likely to be a strategic priority for most organizations. Currently management information tends to fall into two main categories. Firstly, reporting and control information. This monitors what has happened internally within any given period. Secondly, information relating to key performance indicators providing measures of success/failure relative to pre-set benchmarks (accounting ratios, profit and loss accounts, etc.). Such data is of course necessary, but managers increasingly need to be forward looking. CI serves this purpose.

Illustrative Example 3.1: Nike – the sports footwear market

Reebok established that design and fashion, as opposed to functional performance, were increasingly driving the sports footwear market. Reebok viewed their products as being image-driven as opposed to Nike's performance-driven product development. At first, Nike ignored the Reebok product lines and subsequently lost significant market share. It took layoffs and a management restructuring before Nike acknowledged their competition. Nike paid the price for failing to pay close attention to one of their key competitors.

CI can provide a number of useful functions within any organization. These can be summarized as follows:

- **Anticipating competitors' activities**
  The most obvious advantage of CI is in the provision of systems to consider the likely action of specific competitors. The various strengths and weaknesses of the opposition can be considered and frameworks established to anticipate and pre-empt competitor initiatives. Early warning of competitors' actions enables the organization to judge the seriousness of a threat and develop appropriate responses. The process may also uncover potential competitors who are about to target your existing customer base or industry activities.

- **Analysing industry trends**

  By examining the actions of groups of competitors within specific segments and/or market leaders it is possible proactively to establish growing trends. If management can spot the convergence of technologies and operating procedures, it is possible to 'steal a march' on competitors.

- **Learning and innovation**

  The CI process offers tremendous opportunities to learn. CI forces managers to have an external focus. By constantly reviewing the opposition, we are better able to develop, adapt and innovate our own product offerings. For example, the process of reverse engineering – involving detailed examination of competitors' products – can provide a valuable insight into improving our own products. Scenario planning exercises, which anticipate competitors' actions, can enhance the organization's understanding of the competitive environment.

- **Improved communication**

  Key principles of CI are: (a) the delivery of concise, timely information to decision makers and (b) the ability to share information across functional boundaries and provide wider access to knowledge. These general concepts do much to enhance overall corporate communication and promote teamwork. Correctly applied, the CI concept enables staff to overcome many problems associated with information overload.

The reality is that most organizations have some form of competitive intelligence. For example, they conduct benchmarking exercises, commission market research or monitor competitors' prices. CI offers the opportunity to bring together the various strands of information which already exist into one cohesive, practical system.

The competitive intelligence cycle

Kahaner (1997) develops the concept of the CI cycle (see Figure 3.1). This basic concept is derived from government agency intelligence-gathering operations (e.g. CIA).

I Planning and direction

The cycle begins with establishing intelligence requirements. It is important to prioritize information needs and set appropriate time-

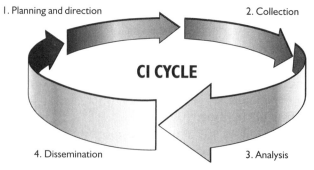

Figure 3.1 Competitive intelligence cycle (*Source:* Adapted from Kahaner, 1997)

scales/reporting periods. This phase requires a detailed understanding of what business decisions are being taken and how information will be used. When prioritizing information it is important to differentiate between 'targeted intelligence' – collected to achieve a specific objective – and 'awareness intelligence' – general information which will be 'filtered' in order to build a general picture of the competitive environment. Targeted intelligence is used to resolve specific problems, while awareness intelligence is designed to monitor the competitive environment on an ongoing basis. The planning process is concerned with obtaining the correct balance between the two.

2 Collection

Based on established intelligence requirements, a collection strategy is now developed. Pollard (1999) advocates translating key intelligence requirements into more specific key intelligence questions and then identifying and monitoring intelligence indicators. These intelligence indicators are identifiable signals that are likely to precede particular competitor actions. Figure 3.2 illustrates this process.

Common sources of competitive information are considered later in this chapter.

Key intelligence question	Intelligence indicators
■ Is the competitor about to initiate a customer loyalty scheme?	■ Actively recruiting customer service staff ■ Buying media advertising space

Figure 3.2 Example of intelligence indicators

3 Analysis

Analysis is concerned with converting raw data into useful information. The process involves classification, evaluation, collation and synthesis. Once information has been processed informed judgements relating to competitors' intent can be established.

The classification stage may involve tagging data as: (i) primary – facts directly from the source (interviews, annual reports, promotional material, etc.), and (ii) secondary – reported by third parties (e.g. newspaper comment, books, and analysts' reports). Data can then be prioritized in terms of importance. When necessary, triangulation can be used to confirm findings. This involves cross-checking an item against a number of sources. The CIA (1999) offers the following guidelines relating to classification of data/information:

- *Fact* – Verified information, something known to exist or to have happened.
- *Information* – The content of reports, research and analytical reflection on an intelligence issue that helps analysts evaluate the likelihood that something is factual and thereby reduces uncertainty.
- *Direct information* – Information which can, as a rule, be considered factual, because of the nature of the sources, the sources' direct access to the information, and readily verifiable content.
- *Indirect information* – Information which may or may not be factual. The doubt reflects some combination of sources' questionable reliability, lack of direct access to information and complex content.
- *Sourcing* – Depicting the manner, or method, in which the information was obtained, in order to assist in evaluating the likely factual content.

History teaches us the importance of evaluation and classification. Most military, political and commercial intelligence failures have not been due to inadequate information collection, but due to poor evaluation of available information.

Many analytical tools and techniques exist to facilitate management decision making and such techniques provide vehicles for forecasting/speculating competitive intent. Common techniques included:

- **SWOT/portfolio analysis**. The classic SWOT or portfolio analysis (e.g. Boston Matrix, Ansoff Matrix – see later chapters) are applied to the competitor(s) in question.
- **Behavioural traits**. While not an absolute indicator of future action, it is true to say that organizational leaders tend to repeat past successful behaviour and avoid previous mistakes. Therefore, to

some degree, future behaviour is likely to be predictable. Understanding the behaviour and reactions of rival corporate leaders to
given sets of circumstances can be highly revealing of future intent.

- **War gaming**. In-house teams take on the simulated role of competitors for a workshop exercise. The team is provided with actual
  data and asked to simulate the strategies/actions they believe the
  competitor is most likely to follow. Their responses are then analysed
  in a debriefing session. Numerous advantages stem from this
  process, such as: identifying competitors' weaknesses, enhancing
  teamwork and identifying information 'gaps' relating to knowledge
  of competitors.
- **Synthesis reports**. Information from numerous sources is collated
  under common key themes. It is possible to scan electronically large
  amounts of text for key words (brand names, patent applications, etc.)
  and selectively extract/flag information. Techniques such as word and
  pattern analysis can identify underlying themes and trends.
- **Mission statement analysis**. The main aim of analysis is to predict
  what a competitor will do. Therefore it is possible to analyse
  competitors' mission statements in order to establish their goals,
  values and generic strategies. Analysing how mission statements have
  changed or been interpreted over time is highly insightful. Rumours of
  likely activity can be checked against a rival's stated mission. Does the
  rumour seem to equate with overall corporate aims?

4 Dissemination

CI has to be tailored to meet user needs. Effective dissemination is
based on clarity, simplicity and appropriateness to need. CI should (if
merited) form the basis of competitive action plans. A useful test is to
consider what the implications are of the intelligence not being passed
on. If there are no real implications, it is questionable whether it is
necessary. Research shows that many CI projects fail during this phase.
Therefore, presentation of CI is critical. Pollard (1999) recommends
developing structured templates for reports: (i) information – bullet
points, graphics, etc.; (ii) analysis – interpretation of information; (iii)
implication – what could happen, and (iv) actions.

Sources of competitive intelligence

As outlined above, data/information can be classified in a number of
ways and the source is important in establishing its reliability.

Competitive information comes from three general areas. Firstly, **public domain** information – information available to anyone. Most industries are heavily regulated and any publicly listed company has legal obligations to make certain information available. Additional promotional materials, product advertising, annual reports and recruitment activities are, by nature, publicly available. Secondly, **internal** information. It is often surprising just how much information organizations already hold on competitors. The problem is one of analysis and dissemination. The sales force and customer service staff are a primary source of CI. They are well positioned to 'pick up' CI from customers, suppliers and industry contacts. Organizations need to establish mechanisms, such as internal networks, to facilitate this process. It is also possible to set up internal systems to monitor competitors (e.g. monitoring competitors' prices on a weekly basis). Finally, **third party** information – specific sources not directly connected to the competitor (e.g. market research agencies, media/journalists, credit rating organizations and consumer groups). Many electronic sources exist, providing powerful search engines enabling detailed enquiries to be made. The internet provides a vast array of free and fee-paying information services. Some commonly used internet sites are listed in Figure 3.3. However, the problem is often how to deal with the sheer volume of information internet searches generate.

Summary

CI provides an increasingly vital function which underpins marketing strategy. The process provides numerous benefits including anticipating competitors' actions, improved teamwork and promoting learning and

Search engines	Financial/business information
www.lycos.co.uk www.yahoo.com www.altavista.com	www.FT.com www.thisismoney.com www.realnames.com
Meta search engines	**Specialist search engines**
www.Askjeeves.com www.MetaCrawler.com	www.DejaNews.com www.Newsbot.com
Note: realnames.com has been established to alleviate the problem of matching company and products names to actual web addresses. Essentially, it operates as a specialist search engine.	

Figure 3.3 Common internet sources

innovation within the organization. Competitive intelligence is based on a four-stage cycle. The cycle starts with planning and direction then moves on to collection, analysis and dissemination. Internal and electronic data sources have greatly widened the availability of data/information.

References

Kahaner, L., *Competitive Intelligence*, Touchstone, 1997

Pollard, A., *Competitor Intelligence*, Financial Times/Pitman Publishing, 1999

Taylor, J., 'Competitive intelligence: A status report on US business practices', *Journal of Marketing Management*, Vol. 8, No. 2, 1993

Further reading

Pollard, A., *Competitor Intelligence*, Financial Times/Pitman Publishing, 1999

Chapter 4

Segmentation

About this chapter

The segmentation process is a crucial aspect of strategic marketing. This chapter explores both consumer and organizational segmentation. Initially both consumer and organizational behaviour is summarized to illustrate the areas from which segmentation criteria have developed. A full analysis of segmentation is then undertaken, to provide the foundation of the targeting and positioning activities that will be addressed in Chapter 9.

Introduction

At a fundamental level an organization's marketing objectives become a decision about which products or services they are going to deliver into which markets. It follows that decisions about the markets to be serviced are a critical step in strategy formulation. The segmentation process is therefore central to strategy and it can be broken into three distinct elements: segmentation, targeting and positioning. This chapter will examine the segmentation aspect of both consumer and organizational markets.

Successful segmentation relies on a clear understanding of the market. Knowledge of consumer behaviour is the crucial foundation on which that market understanding is built. The chapter will briefly summarize both consumer and organizational buyer behaviour as an introduction to market segmentation criteria.

Why segment?

There are a number of reasons why organizations undertake segmentation (Doyle, 1994):

- **To meet consumer needs more precisely**. In a generic market customers' demands will differ. By developing a distinct marketing mix for each consumer segment an organization can offer customers better solutions for their needs.
- **To increase profits**. Different consumer segments react in contrasting ways to prices; some are far less price sensitive than others. Segmentation allows an organization to gain the best price it can in every segment, effectively raising the average price and increasing profitability.
- **To gain segment leadership**. In any particular market the brands that have dominant shares of the market will be highly profitable. Their market leadership gives them economies of scale, while in marketing and production they will also have established access to distribution channels. Small companies or new entrants in a market are unlikely to be able to gain leadership; they can, however, take a dominant share of a particular market segment. This focus can allow them to develop a specialist marketing mix to satisfy the needs of the consumers in that group while at the same time building a competitive cost position relative to other companies in that segment.
- **To retain customers**. Providing products or services aimed at different consumer segments allows an organization to retain customers' loyalty as their needs change. As an individual moves through life their needs in financial services will change. For example, young single individuals may need a minimum of credit and banking facilities and car insurance; younger families, however, will need in addition life insurance policies and mortgages, while in middle age these needs will turn to pension provision. If an organization can provide all these services they may retain a customer who otherwise would transfer to another brand.

    An organization may also be able to use segmentation as a way of moving a customer over time from entry level products or services to products at the premium end of the market.
- **To focus marketing communications**. Segmentation allows an organization to identify media channels that can specifically reach the target groups. For example, young women interested in fashion are likely to read certain fashion magazines. Rather than spend money on mass-market media that reach far wider than the target group, organizations can target their money and effort by using media focused directly on their potential consumer group.

The segmentation process

The segmentation process involves establishing criteria by which groups of consumers with similar needs can be identified. These criteria have to establish consumer groups that have the following characteristics:

- The consumers in the segment respond in the same way to a particular marketing mix.
- The consumers within the segment have to react in a clearly different way from other groups of consumers to the marketing mix on offer.
- The group has to be large enough to provide the return on investment necessary to the organization.
- The criteria used to identify the segment have to be operational. Recently a small company in the magazine market identified a group of customers that had clear needs. Overseas nationals living in the UK wished to buy magazines from their home country. The organization's proposed marketing offer was to import magazines from overseas and mail them out directly to the consumers' homes. This was a potential customer group that all responded in the same way to the proposed marketing mix. They clearly acted differently from other groups in the magazine market. This potential segment was large and potentially profitable; however, this was a difficult group to make operational. You cannot identify overseas nationals easily as no official organization or overseas institute will give you their names and addresses. The only way of pursuing this opportunity was to persuade overseas nationals to identify themselves. This could have been accomplished by attracting consumers to respond to a promotional campaign, allowing the organization to build a customer database. However, for a small organization this was likely to be a costly operation and the idea was dropped in favour of other options.

Given the fact that segments need to demonstrate these four characteristics, the next step is to examine the variables that can be usefully employed to segment a market. Understanding consumer buyer behaviour theory is central to the successful development and application of segmentation criteria.

Consumer buyer behaviour

Consumer buyer behaviour relates to the end customer, the individuals who purchase products and services for personal consumption. This section of the chapter will summarize the main sources of influence on consumer buyer behaviour (see Figure 4.1), in order to illustrate the

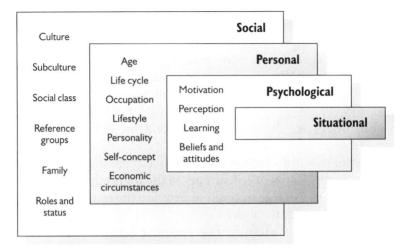

Figure 4.1 Influences on consumer behaviour

influences that affect consumers' purchasing decisions. These influences can be broken down into four major categories: social, personal, psychological and situational.

Social influences

There is a range of social influences on a consumer's purchasing behaviour, in particular culture and social class.

Culture

Behaviour is largely learned so the traditions, values and attitudes of the society an individual is brought up in will influence their behaviour. Cultural norms form the codes that direct behaviour. Therefore in an informal culture such as the USA or the UK the use of first names in a formal business meeting may be acceptable. In other cultures such as mainland China more formal behaviour would be the norm. Within a larger culture there are obviously some subcultures; these may be based on religion, nationality, geographical areas or racial groups.

Social class

An individual's social class has been seen as an important influence on consumer behaviour, with individuals in lower social groups generally being seen to be more culture-bound. Social class groupings are heavily dependent upon a society's cultural background. Some societies are more hierarchical than others – many have a few people in the top and bottom classes with the majority in the middle. However, some societies, such as Scandinavia and Japan, have much flatter structures (see Figure 4.2). Some societies are more open than others, that is, individuals can move from one class to another in an open society; in a closed society this is not possible.

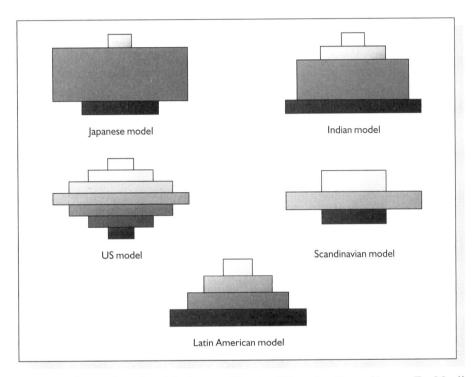

Figure 4.2 Examples of social class profiles in different cultures (*Source*: **De Mooij and Keegan, 1991**)

In Western societies social classification has been criticized as a predictor of purchasing behaviour. In the UK a household in the higher AB category, after paying for a mortgage and private school tuition for their children, may have less disposable income than a lower category C2 or D household. There can also be wide discrepancies in purchasing patterns within social groups. Individuals are also influenced by smaller social groups, such as friends, co-workers and family. These can be categorized into reference groups and family:

- **Reference groups**. Reference groups can be formal (members of a professional association or society) or informal groupings (social, friends, etc.). These reference groups influence an individual's attitude or behaviour. Individuals will tend to exhibit purchasing behaviour that is deemed to be acceptable by their reference group. Group norms and the role an individual plays within a group exert considerable influence on their behaviour. Recent research into the behaviour of first-time mothers illustrated the power of reference groups in shaping their expectations of the quality of service they would experience during their stay in the maternity ward. For individuals from residential areas of lower economic status, doctors, midwives and information from ante-natal classes were less influential than friends with young children – and, more importantly, the individual's sisters and mother. These reference groups influenced their subsequent behaviour in terms of length of stay and treatment (Tinson, 1998). This also underlines the power of one key reference group, the family.

- **Family**. The family is a key group not only because it is a primary reference group but also because it is the group within which individual purchasing behaviour is socialized. Attitudes and beliefs in general and patterns of purchasing behaviour in particular are all learnt initially from the family into which an individual is born and raised (the family of orientation). Once individuals start to have their own children they set up their own family unit (family of procreation). This developing family group also exerts an influence on the behaviour of individuals. There are, moreover, purchasing decisions that are taken by the household as a unit which reinforce the family as a key primary reference group.

Personal influences

An individual's personal attributes will have an influence on their purchasing behaviour. Factors such as the individual's age, occupation and financial situation, their personality, their family life cycle stage and their lifestyle in general will affect the pattern of their consumption decisions. These factors are commonly used as criteria to segment consumer markets and will be explored in greater detail later in this chapter.

Psychological influences

Four key psychological factors – motivation, perception, learning, and beliefs and attitudes – are further influences on consumer behaviour.

Motivation

Individuals have a range of needs, from basic biological needs such as the need to satisfy hunger, thirst and physical distress to psychological needs like the need for social recognition, esteem or belonging. These needs may lie dormant at any particular time but once aroused to a high enough level of intensity they become a motivational force. A motive is a need that has reached a level that drives an individual to search for ways to alleviate its demands. There is a whole body of theory in this area that cannot be explored in this text (see Further reading at the end of this chapter); however, it is worthwhile summarizing two of the most influential theories to illustrate their effect on marketing practice:

- **Freud's theory of motivation**. Freud proposed that individuals are motivated by unconscious psychological factors. Moreover, as an individual grows up they conform to social norms which require them to repress a range of desires and passions (urges). This theory would suggest that an individual's consciously stated reason for buying a product may hide a more fundamental unconscious motive. An individual proposing to purchase an executive car may claim that this decision is based on the need for quality and reliability, whereas the unconscious desire may be for status.
- **Maslow's theory of motivation**. Maslow claimed that individuals have a hierarchy of needs. At the lowest level individuals are driven by basic physiological needs. When individuals are able to satisfy the needs at one level they will be motivated by the needs at the next level in the hierarchy (see Figure 4.3). The implication of the theory for marketers is that individuals will seek different products and services as they move up this hierarchy.

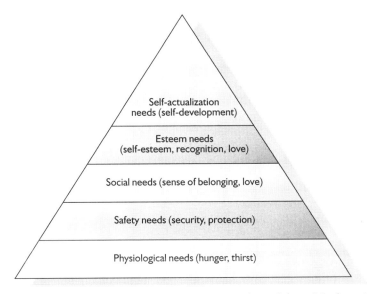

Figure 4.3 Maslow's hierarchy of needs. (*Source* : Adapted from Maslow, 1970)

This theory is not universal and is biased towards Anglo-Saxon cultural values, in particular individualism and need for self-development. These needs would not have the same prominence in Japan or Germany where, for example, the need for personal security and conformity take a higher priority.

Motivation theories relate to consumer needs and satisfying consumers' needs is a central tenet of marketing. These motivation theories therefore have influenced approaches to market segmentation. It should be noted that although Freud and Maslow's theories have been very influential in management and marketing theory and practice, they have been challenged on the grounds that the research evidence to support their utility as a psychological theory of motivation is weak (Steers *et al.*, 1996). However, they are useful for marketers as they help to categorize consumers into groups based on needs.

Perception

The way an individual perceives an external stimulus will influence their reaction. Individuals can have different perceptions of the same stimulus due to the process of selective attention, selective distortion and selective retention:

- **Selective attention**. Individuals cannot observe all the potential stimuli in the external environment. Selective attention refers to the tendency of individuals to screen out the majority of stimulants to which they are exposed.
- **Selective distortion**. Individuals process information within the confines of their current set of attitudes and beliefs. The tendency to adjust perceptions to conform to their current mindset is called selective distortion.
- **Selective retention**. Individuals do not remember everything they perceive. Information that reinforces their attitudes and beliefs is more likely to be retained.

Perceptual behaviour is relevant to the segmentation process because of its links with learning, attitudes and beliefs.

Learning, attitudes and beliefs

Learning relates to any change in the content of an individual's long-term memory and is associated with how information is processed (covered above under Perception). There are various ways in which learning can take place, including conditioning, social learning and cognitive learning:

- **Conditioning**. This learning theory proposes that reinforcement is necessary for individuals to develop attitudes and beliefs. Therefore if an individual's experience of a particular product is positive this will reinforce their positive attitudes and beliefs about the brand. If the experience is negative it is unlikely that the consumer will buy the product again. The negative attitude that has been formed towards the product could also affect the individual's attitude to other products and services offered by the company or linked to the brand.
- **Social learning**. This theory suggests that learning can take place without direct personal reinforcement. Individuals may remember the slogan associated with a brand name and form an attitude about its attributes without any direct reinforcement. An individual may learn from observing the behaviour of others and the recognition or rewards they receive.
- **Cognitive learning**. In high involvement purchases an individual may use their own powers of cognitive reasoning to develop their attitudes and beliefs about a product.

Forming attitudes and beliefs about products effectively creates a position for the product or brand relative to other products and brands in the mind of the consumer. This lies at the heart of product positioning which is central to the successful implementation of segmentation strategy (see Chapter 9).

The buying situation

The buying process (see Figure 4.4) an individual goes through when making purchasing decisions is affected by the particular situational factors surrounding the activity.

High involvement purchases refer to situations where both the information search and the use of referent group consultation and post-purchase evaluation is extensive. It occurs when the following factors are involved:

- **Self–image**. The purchase has a major effect on an individual's self-image, such as the purchase of a car.
- **Perceived risk**. The impact of a mistaken purchase would have a dramatic effect on the consumer. Expensive purchases would fall into this category, where any mistake could have a major effect on an individual's financial position.
- **Social factors**. An individual's level of social acceptance may depend on the right purchasing decision.

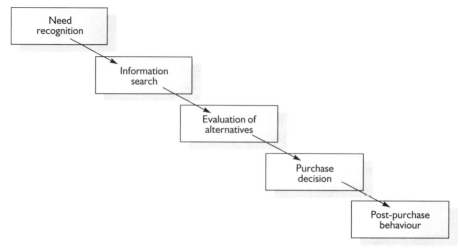

Figure 4.4 The buying process

- **Hedonistic factors**. The purchase is concerned with products or services that are linked to providing personal pleasure.

Consumer behaviour theory is a complex area and only a brief overview has been provided here. Consumer behaviour is central to the segmentation, targeting and positioning process, in particular in establishing useful segmentation criteria.

Consumer segmentation criteria

Segmentation criteria can be divided into three main categories:

- **Profile variables** are used to characterize the consumer but in terms that are not expressly linked to, or predictive of, an individual's behaviour in the specific market.
- **Behavioural variables** relate to the behaviour of the consumer. Thus behavioural factors such as benefits sought, usage, and the purchase occasion all come under this category.
- **Psychographic variables** identify an individual's attitudes, opinions and interests to build up a lifestyle profile that includes the consumer's consumption patterns. Thus these profiles are inextricably associated with specific purchasing behaviour.

Segmentation is a creative process and can be conducted using a range of different variables each bringing a particular perspective to the dynamics of the market. The air travel market could be segmented according to the benefits sought (value or status), or usage occasion (business or holiday), or stage in the family life cycle (young and single or middle-aged, married with kids). On occasion it may be relevant to use a single variable to segment a market, but more often than not variables will be used in combination. For instance, a potential market segment in the air travel market could be middle-aged consumers with children who seek status benefits for business travel. Innovative combinations of variables from across the range can uncover new market segments, even in supposedly traditional markets.

There is no hierarchy to these variables. Marketers can use any variable as a starting point (first-order variables), and then add further variables (second-order variables) to give the grouping a clearer definition. Thus a segment of consumers seeking physical fitness may initially be determined using benefit segmentation. Profile variables may then be added such as age, gender, geodemographics etc., to identify more clearly the consumer in order to allow the company to develop specific media communication and distribution plans.

Profile variables

There is a range of demographic, socio-economic and geographic segmentation variables in this category.

Demographic segmentation

The key demographic variables consist of age, gender and the family life cycle.

Age

Consumers' purchasing decisions will change with age. Older people are likely to be looking for different benefits from a holiday than younger people. However, age by itself may not be a sophisticated enough variable to help identify a consumer segment. Using the age range of 25- to 35-year-old individuals to identify a consumer group results in a rather unclear grouping. 25- to 35-year-old women will have different needs from 25- to 35-year-old men in certain markets. A 30-year-old women who is single and has a professional job is likely to have different needs from a 30-year-old women who is married with three children and has chosen not to work outside the home. Both will have different needs from a 30-year-old unemployed woman who is single with a child.

There is also the issue of psychological age to be considered when using this variable. That is, consumers may perceive themselves to be in a different age group to their true chronological age. Therefore a product or service aimed at 35-year-olds may attract older customers who still see themselves in this age range.

Age alone therefore has limitations as a method of breaking a market down into useful segments.

Gender

Sex, as a variable, has similar limitations to age. Clearly there are differences between consumer groups based on gender. However, this variable by itself only narrows the market down by 50 per cent. There are still major differences within the gender category. Younger women may have different needs from older women. Cadbury's, when designing a box of chocolates called Inspirations, which was aimed at the female market, found that older women did not like the contemporary design used on a prototype, while younger women like the modern packaging (Ensor and Laing, 1993).

Obviously age and gender variables can be used together to help define a segment. Therefore we can define segments in terms of 25- to 35-year-old females, or 55- to 65-year-old males. However, this still gives us quite broad customer groupings that do not take into consideration wider factors that may affect consumers in these particular age and sex groupings. One way of attempting to overcome these deficiencies is to look at consumer life cycles.

Life-cycle segmentation

The essence of the family life cycle is that consumers are likely to go through one of the alternative routes in it (see Figure 4.5). The classic route would be for a consumer to move from young and single to young married without children, to young married with children, to middle-aged married with children, to middle-aged married without dependent children, to older married, ending up finally as older unmarried.

At each stage a consumer's needs and disposable income will change. Someone who is young and single has very few commitments so, although their income in real terms may be low, they have high disposable income. Once an individual is married with children, commitments have increased. They are likely to have to move into the housing market, and in addition they are now buying products for young babies and children. The couple may well start to take out savings and insurance policies to protect their children's future. In

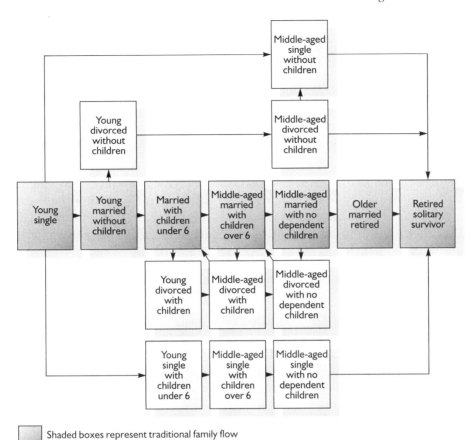

Shaded boxes represent traditional family flow

Figure 4.5 A contemporary Family Life cycle (*Source*: Adapted from Murphy and Staples, 1979)

middle age they will begin to be more interested in pension arrangements. Quite obviously, as an individual moves through these stages, their propensity to buy certain types of products will change. This approach is therefore useful in identifying these consumer groupings.

In Western cultures there has been speculation that the family as a unit is of decreasing importance; however, there is contradictory evidence on this issue. In 1985 a Family Policy Studies Centre report looking at the UK claimed that:

- Nine out of ten people will marry at some time in their lives.
- Nine out of ten married couples will have children.
- Two in every three marriages are likely to be ended by death rather than divorce.
- Eight out of ten people live in households headed by a married couple.

There was one key change from earlier studies, however. This was a growing trend for individuals to go through the cycle belonging to more than one family group, with individuals divorcing and remarrying. Therefore both parental figures in a family grouping may not be blood relatives of the children. Also the siblings may not be blood relatives. From a marketer's point of view, however, it is the fact that family groupings are still a key feature in society that is important. These family life-cycle stages are therefore still relevant for segmentation purposes.

Another trend that Lawson (1988) identified after analysing demographic trends in the UK was that the stages have altered in both length and importance. Full-nest stages, when children live with their parents, are shorter due to the fact that couples are having fewer children and that these children are being born closer together. This means that individuals spend more time in the bachelor and empty-nest stages and there are more people in these groups.

As a result of this study Lawson updated the family life cycle using the 1981 census, claiming this modernized version covers over 80 per cent of the population (see Figure 4.6).

The 18.68 per cent of households excluded from this table are made up of young people living in joint households, households with residents other than family and households with more than one family.

Indeed, households can be a useful way of looking at social grouping. Individuals sharing a flat have to take part in group decision making for

Stage	Percentage of households
Bachelor	1.42
Newly married couples	3.11
Full nest 1 (with pre-school children)	11.91
Full nest 1 (lone parent)	1.26
Middle-aged no children	1.19
Full nest 2 (school age children)	16.97
Full nest 2 (lone parent)	1.92
Launching families (with non-dependent children)	6.3
Launching families (one parent)	1.45
Empty nest 1 (childless, aged 45–54)	9.45
Empty nest 2 (retired)	9.51
Solitary survivor under 65	2.66
Solitary survivor retired	14.17
Total	**81.32**

Figure 4.6 **The modernized family life cycle** (*Source*: Lawson, 1988)

products such as furniture, electrical appliances etc. Lawson claims, when discussing the 18.68 per cent of the population that do not fit into the family life cycle, that households are likely to be a better unit with which to analyse consumer behaviour than the family.

Illustrative Example 4.1: The OXO Family

In September 1999 Brooke Bond ended a 16-year advertising campaign for OXO cubes featuring a 'traditional family' group. What became known as the 'OXO family' campaign developed to become almost a mini soap opera. The OXO family represented a white middle-class husband and wife with three children living in suburbia. Brooke Bond's decision to change its advertising reflects the fact that this traditional family group is increasingly seen as an ineffective advertising tool. Many advertisers are now creating advertisements with more social realism, replacing images of the traditional family by representing a more diverse range of specific household types and lifestyles.

Socio-economic segmentation

In socio-economic segmentation factors such as occupation, educational background, place of residence, and income are used to classify individuals into larger 'social class' groupings.

In the UK, JICNARS' classification of social class has been a common tool to categorize an individual's social class (see Figure 4.7). JICNARS' approach is heavily dependent upon income and occupation as the key factors which are used in determining its six major social groupings.

This is the traditional type of socio-economic classification system that has been used in the UK for censuses since 1911. The UK National Statistics Office, however, is planning to use a new categorization system for the 2001 census (Rose and O'Reilly, 1999). This is as a result of the major shifts in make-up of the UK population. Currently 60 per cent of the population are deemed to be middle class compared with 51 per cent in 1984. The new categories also take account of the increased role in the workplace of women who now occupy 18 per cent of all professional posts compared with 4 per cent in 1984. Women, under the new system, will be categorized in their own right rather than according to their husband's occupation. The new classification was based on a survey of 65,000 people across 371 occupations (see Figure 4.8).

Social grade	Social status	Occupations	Examples	Approx. % of households
A	Upper middle class	Higher managerial/ professional	Doctors, lawyers, professors, directors	3
B	Middle class	Intermediate managerial	Managers, teachers, computer programmers	10
C1	Lower middle class	Junior managerial, supervisory, clerical administrative	Foreman, shop assistants, office workers	24
C2	Skilled working class	Skilled manual labour	Electricians, mechanics, plumbers and other crafts	30
D	Working class	Semi-skilled and unskilled manual labour	Machine operators, assembly workers	25
E	Subsistance	None	Pensioners, casual workers, unemployed, students	8

Figure 4.7 JICNARS' social grade definitions

New social class	Occupations	Examples
1	Higher managerial and professional occupations	
1.1	Employers and managers in larger organizations	Bank managers, company directors, financial managers, senior local government officers
1.2	Higher professional	Doctors, lawyers, dentists, higher civil servants, academics, engineers, teachers, airline pilots, social workers, librarians, personnel officers, computer analysts
2	Lower managerial and professional occupations	Police officers, fire-fighters, prison officers, nurses, physiotherapists, journalists, actors and musicians
3	Intermediate occupations	Secretaries/PAs, airline flight attendants, driving instructors, computer operators, clerical workers, computer engineers, dental technicians, precision instrument makers
4	Small employers and own-account workers	
5	Lower supervisory, craft and related occupations	Electricians, TV engineers, car mechanics, train drivers, printers
6	Semi-routine occupations	Drivers, hairdressers, bricklayers, plasterers, welders, cooks, shop assistants, garage forecourt attendants, supermarket check-out operators
7	Routine occupations	Car park attendants, cleaners, road workers, refuse collectors, labourers, road sweepers

Figure 4.8 New Classes for 2001 UK Census. (*Source*: Adapted from Rose and O'Reilly, 1999)

Despite this new classification there are still several problems with socio-economic approaches to segmentation for marketing managers:

- Social class is not an accurate gauge of disposable income. An electrician or a plumber who would be classified as social class C2 may well have a higher income than a junior manager who would be classified as social class C1.
- In Western societies there has been a major trend toward women working. Social classification has used the head of household's occupation to define social class; however, if both adults are working defining the head of household becomes more difficult. Earlier in this chapter we also saw that family structures themselves have become more complicated in the West. The new classification does attempt to address this issue but 'how does the new classification help to predict family purchasing behaviour?' Individuals from the same household may be in two completely different social classes.
- The variety and the changing nature of people's occupations make it increasingly difficult to apply social class categories consistently.

Most importantly, in today's society social class is a less important predictor of behaviour than other methods of segmentation. For instance, an individual whatever their social class who is interested in sport is more likely to buy products and services in the sporting area than an individual in the same social class who is not interested in

---

Illustrative Example 4.2: The ethical consumer

In autumn 2000 the Co-operative Bank published a report claiming that 'ethical' consumers extend across most socio-political boundaries, and cannot be defined by social class, age or gender. Although consumers are still predominantly concerned with quality and value when making purchasing decisions, other factors, such as an organization's treatment of its workforce or its concern for the environment, are becoming more influential. The Co-operative Bank's report speculates that the potential for ethical products could be as high as 30 per cent in consumer markets. The Bank has developed an ethical position in the financial services market in order to address this growing customer segment. Other UK companies are also appealing to the ethical customer: B & Q only offers for sale wood grown from sustainably managed forests, The Body Shop will not sell products tested on animals, and Iceland only sells food free of genetically modified ingredients. All these companies are addressing the newly emerging 'ethical consumer'.

---

sport. It may therefore be more important for marketers to identify individuals who share a common interest (e.g. sport) rather than identify social class groupings.

Geographic segmentation

Geographic

This variable was used more extensively in the past. There used to be clear consumer patterns in product areas such as food and alcohol across Europe, or even within a market such as the UK. Although some of these patterns still show through, mass communication and wider access to travel has tended to erode these regional differences. In the UK individuals are eating a much more cosmopolitan diet than thirty years ago. Pizzas and pasta dishes are common in many homes. Where geographic variables are used they tend to be used to reflect some wider cultural differences between markets. However, geographic variables can be useful if they are used in conjunction with other factors.

Geodemographics

Geodemographic segmentation combines information on household location with certain demographic and socio-economic data. This approach relies on information that is gathered in census returns. In the UK the census information on family size, household size, occupation, and ethnic origin can be used to group residential housing into geographic areas that display similar profiles. There are several geodemographic forms of classification, one of the best known in the UK being ACORN (A Classification Of Residential Neighbourhoods). The ACORN classification identifies six major categories (one group is unclassified) that can be further subdivided into seventeen groups (see Figure 4.9).

These seventeen groups can be further subdivided into fifty-four neighbourhood types. For instance, ACORN category C (Rising), group 7 (Prosperous Professionals, Metropolitan Areas) is made up of two neighbourhood types. One of these is neighbourhood type 19 that is categorized as 'Apartments, Young Professional Singles and Couples'. These types of neighbourhood areas are heavily concentrated in London. Outside London these neighbourhoods are found in such places as Edinburgh, St Albans and Cambridge.

These neighbourhood areas allow specific patterns of consumption to be identified. For instance, ACORN type 5, 'Mature, Well-off Suburbs', is a sub-group of category A, group 1, 'Wealthy Achievers, Suburban

Category	% Pop.	Groups	% Pop.
A – Thriving	19.8	1. Wealthy achievers, suburban areas	15.1
		2. Affluent greys, rural communities	2.3
		3. Prosperous pensioners, retirement areas	2.4
B – Expanding	11.6	4. Affluent executives, family areas	3.8
		5. Well-off workers, family areas	7.8
C – Rising	7.8	6. Affluent urbanites, town and city areas	2.3
		7. Prosperous professionals, metropolitan areas	2.1
		8. Better-off executives, inner-city areas	3.4
D – Settling	24.0	9. Comfortable middle-agers, mature home-owning areas	13.4
		10. Skilled workers, home-owning areas	10.6
E – Aspiring	13.7	11. New home-owners, mature communities	9.7
		12. White collar workers, better-off multi-ethnic areas	4.0
F – Striving	22.7	13. Older people, less prosperous areas	3.6
		14. Council estate residents, better-off homes	11.5
		15. Council estate residents, high unemployment	2.7
		16. Council estate residents, greatest hardship	2.7
		17. People in multi-ethnic, low-income areas	2.2
Unclassified	0.5		0.5

Figure 4.9 The ACORN consumer targeting classification (*Source*: CACI Limited, 1993. ACORN is a registered trademark of CACI Limited)

Areas'. This group is made up of mature suburbs found all over the UK, particularly in Surrey, Hertfordshire, South Glamorgan and Outer London. Individuals in this group buy above average levels of fresh and dried pasta, ground coffee, fresh fish and fruit. Ownership of most financial products in this group is above the national average except for personal pensions. This type of detailed profile allows for highly sophisticated targeting.

This segmentation approach can be used to aid decision making in a variety of areas:

- Identifying favourable retail locations for a specific retail format.
- The specific mix of products and services delivered in a particular retail location.
- Decisions on direct mail campaigns.
- The boundaries of specific sales territories.
- Location of poster sites.
- Selection of media.

There are criticisms of this approach. It is claimed that all these geodemographic systems contain inaccuracies because of the difficulties in lining up the census enumeration districts with postal codes. There are also problems in reflecting the changes in housing that take place between each census.

The geodemographic systems referred to so far are used at a relatively local level. There have been developments to try to use this approach at a much larger regional level. Geodemographic techniques have been used on a European scale to identify consumers who have common characteristics but who may live in different countries. Using demographic (age), economic (income), cultural (language), and geographic (longitude and latitude) factors, six Euro-consumer segments can be identified (see Figure 4.10).

Segment	Geographical boundaries	Description	Pop.
1	UK and Ireland	Average age and income profile; English as a common language	60.3m
2	Central Germany, Central and Northern France, Southern Belgium and Luxembourg	High proportion of older people and low proportion of middle-aged; average income; German and French languages	54.5m
3	Portugal and Spain	Young population; below average income; Portuguese and Spanish languages	50.4m
4	South-eastern France, Southern Germany, Northern Italy	High proportion of middle-aged people; above average income; French, German and Italian languages	71.5m
5	Southern Italy and Greece	Young population; below average income; Italian and Greek languages	31.2m
6	Northern Germany, the Netherlands, Northern Belgium, Denmark, Sweden, Finland, Norway, Iceland and Switzerland	High proportion of middle-aged people; very high income; multilingual; German, French Italian and Scandinavian languages	57.6m

Figure 4.10 Euro-consumer segments using geodemographic segmentation (*Source*: Adapted from Vandermerwe and L'Huillier, 1989)

This approach illustrates the point that consumers in different countries can share similar characteristics. For instance, the consumers in segment 4 show more similarities to each other than to other consumers from their own country. This is the first step towards European segmentation, and may well lead to the identification of subsegments within these larger groups and to the ability for marketers to target relatively large geodemographic segments that transcend national boundaries.

Behavioural variables

The segmentation approaches that have been discussed so far are all using characteristics of the consumer as a way of identifying clear groupings. However, identifying consumer behaviour rather than personal attributes can be a more effective way of identifying market segments.

The main behavioural variables in this category are benefits, usage and purchase occasion.

Benefit segmentation

Benefit segmentation uses the underlying reasons why an individual purchases a particular product or service, rather than trying to identify an individual's particular personal attributes.

Benefit segmentation is based on the concept that the key reason a consumer buys the product or service is for the benefit that product or service gives them. Identifying groups of consumers that are seeking a common benefit in a particular market allows a producer to develop specific products or service offerings. An example of benefit segmentation would be in the management education market. A survey in the USA found that there were several benefit segments in the market for MBA qualifications (see Figure 4.11).

The advantage of benefit segmentation is that it is a market-orientated approach which, by seeking to identify consumers' needs, allow organizations to set about satisfying them.

Usage segmentation

The characteristics and patterns of consumer usage are the essence of this segmentation approach. Consumers will generally fall into categories of heavy users, medium users, occasional users and non-users of a particular product or service. Identifying heavy users can be useful as they are likely to consume a larger percentage of an organization's sales than other groups, as the Pareto Effect would suggest (see Figure 4.12). This can lead to the identification of new segmentation opportunities for an organization.

Quality seekers wish to have the highest quality education available. They believe a top ranked education will benefit them during their entire business life, and will lead to job advancement or a career change.

Speciality seekers wish to have a specialized education and to become experts in their areas of particular interest. Concentrated courses tend to fit their needs, and they will search for institutions that offer them.

Career changers are seeking new jobs or employers and believe an MBA qualification will open up opportunities for career advancement and mobility. They have several years' work experience and feel that they are in a career cul-de-sac.

Knowledge seekers wish to learn and feel increased knowledge will lead to power. They believe that an MBA will be an asset not only in their career but also in all aspects of their life.

Status seekers feel an MBA will lead to increased income and prestige.

Degree seekers believe that a first degree is no longer sufficient and that an MBA is needed in order to be competitive in the contemporary job market. These individuals tend to be active, self-orientated and independent.

Professional advancers are striving to climb the corporate ladder. They are looking for professional advancement, higher salaries and job flexibility. They are upwardly mobile, serious, future orientated and wish to build a career within the current corporate structures.

Avoiders look for MBA programmes that require the least effort to complete. They believe that all Business Schools will provide essentially the same education. Their motivation is 'other directed' and they will seek low cost, 'lower quality' programmes.

Convenience seekers will join MBA programmes that are located near their homes or places of work and which have simple entry procedures. They are interested in any Business School which provides these conveniences and are low cost.

Non-matriculators wish to undertake an MBA course without completing any formal application procedures. They are therefore attracted to a Business School that allows them to begin an MBA programme without any formal application.

Figure 4.11 MBA benefit segments (*Source*: Adapted from Miaoulis and Kalfus, 1983)

For example, Mangers relaunched their cleaning product Sugar Soap, which was a universal non-silica based household cleaner, by identifying that the heavy users of this product were professional household painters and decorators. In fact, the reason this group were heavy users of the product was because it could be used to clean surfaces that needed to be painted and because it was a non-silica based cleaner they could paint straight onto the surface. Once managers had identified this

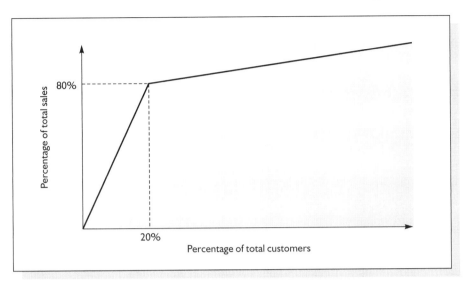

Figure 4.12 The Pareto Effect, also known as the 80/20 rule

group of heavy users they relaunched the product to the Do It Yourself market for individuals wishing to decorate their own houses.

Airlines use frequent-flyer programmes to retain the heavy user of their services. Many other companies in other sectors use incentives to retain this important customer grouping.

Banks and building societies may wish to have charging scales on their accounts that give incentives for heavy users while at the same time increasing relative charges for light users as they are relatively more expensive to manage.

Purchase occasion

Consumer groups can be identified on the basis of the type of occasion for which they buy a particular product or service. Some products may be bought as gifts, or for specific formal social occasions such as weddings or New Year celebrations. The convenience store concept is an example of occasion segmentation, where individuals can make purchases at a time and place that are agreeable to them.

Psychographic variables

The techniques that have been discussed so far have used either consumer characteristics or behavioural variables as the basis for

identifying consumer groupings. Psychographics is a more recent
approach that attempts to identify segments based on lifestyle characteristics, attitudes and personality. Rather than concentrating on single
factors such as age, sex and marital status, it attempts to build a broader
picture of consumers' lifestyles based on their activities, interests and
opinions. Asking a series of questions about consumers' activities,
interests and opinions as well as questions about product and service
usage identifies these lifestyles (see Figure 4.13).

Activities	Interests	Opinions	Demographics
Work	Family	Themselves	Age
Hobbies	Home	Social issues	Education
Social events	Job	Politics	Income
Vacation	Community	Business	Occupation
Entertainment	Recreation	Economics	Family size
Club membership	Fashion	Education	Dwelling
Community	Food	Products	Geography
Shopping	Media	Future	City size
Sports	Achievements	Culture	Stage in life cycle

Figure 4.13 Questions posed in lifestyle studies (*Source*: Plummer, 1974)

Several models have been developed using this approach, all having
broad similarities, and two will be discussed in more detail.

The VALs framework

This model was developed in the USA by asking 2713 individuals 800
questions. The VALs framework identified nine lifestyle groups in the
American population. The model also identified three developmental
stages that individuals may pass through. Normally individuals would
move from one of the need-driven stages to either an outer-directed or
an inner-directed stage. This is a hierarchical model and relatively few
would reach the integrated stage (see Figure 4.14).

The framework is divided into a series of segments:

- The needs-driven segment identified by this model has relatively
  little purchasing power and is therefore of marginal interest to profit-
  making organizations. This is a declining group in Western societies.

Developmental stage	Grouping (% of US population)
Need-driven	**Survivors.** This is a disadvantaged group who are likely to be withdrawn, despairing and depressed (4%). **Sustainers** are another disadvantaged group, but they are working hard to escape poverty (7%).
Outer-directed	**Belongers** are characterized as being conventional, nostalgic, reluctant to try new ideas and generally conservative (33%). **Emulators** are upwardly mobile, ambitious and status conscious (10%). **Achievers.** This group enjoys life and make things happen (23%).
Inner-directed	**'I-am-me'** tend to be young, self-engrossed and act on whims (5%). **Experientials** wish to enjoy as wide a range of life experiences as possible (7%). **Societally conscious** have a clear sense of social responsibility and wish to improve society (9%).
Nirvana	**Integrateds** are completely mature psychologically and combine the positive elements of outer and inner directedness (2%).

Figure 4.14 The VALs framework developed by Arnold Mitchell at the Stanford Research Institute

- The outer-directed groups are more affluent and are interested in status products that other individuals will notice. They are therefore interested in brand names such as Rolex and Cartier.
- Inner-directed individuals in contrast are more concerned with their individual needs rather than external values. This is an important sector as they tend to be trendsetters. This group is also the fastest growing group in Western societies.
- Very few individuals reach the integrated group.

The Monitor framework

This framework was developed by the Taylor Nelson research agency. The model similarly divides consumers into three main groups each with its own sub-groups (see Figure 4.15).

The advantages of this lifestyle approach are:

- It takes into account factors other than status and class.
- Purchasing patterns are encompassed in the lifestyle profile.
- Well-defined communication channels may emerge as part of the lifestyle.
- Brand personalities can be built to appeal to specific lifestyles.

Groups	Sub-groups (% of UK population)
Sustenance-driven are concerned about material security	**Aimless.** Includes the young unemployed and elderly drifters (5%). **Survivors** are working class people who retain traditional attitudes (16%). **Belongers** straddle the sustenance-driven and outer-directed groups. They are a conservative family-orientated group. (The sub-group is 18% of the UK population in total, with 9% in the sustenance-driven group.)
Outer-directed	**Belongers.** This half of the sub-group are still conservative and family-orientated but are also status-driven (9%). **Conspicuous consumers** are driven by a desire for status (19%).
Inner-directed	**Social resisters** are caring and tend to hold doctrinaire attitudes (11%). **Experimentalists** are individualistic and are interested in the good life (14%). **Self explorers** hold less doctrinaire attitudes than the social resisters and are less materialistic than the experimentalist sub-group (17%).

Figure 4.15 The Monitor Framework developed by the Taylor Nelson research agency

These models allow a more rounded view of consumer groups to emerge. Identifying the lifestyle of potential consumer segments allows the marketer to develop sophisticated marketing mixes that tie in with a particular lifestyle group. The lifestyle profile may highlight the type of retail outlets that the consumer group is attracted to, or the publications they are more likely to read. This allows managerial decisions to be made about the distribution and promotional aspects of the mix.

Weaknesses with psychographical models are that they currently tend to reflect a Western social hierarchy and culture. As a result these frameworks are not always easily transferred to different social settings. Cultural values may mean that aspirations are different from those represented by Western values of individualism, self-development and status. These models also do not easily represent the flatter social class structures that occur in certain cultures such as Scandinavia.

Some critics of the approach would also argue that these broad lifestyle profiles are not accurate predictors of consumers' purchasing behaviour in any particular market sector. An outer-directed individual who may in general buy status products may not buy branded goods in a market area where there is very little risk of damage to their self-image. The soap powder they buy is unlikely to be of major significance to the way they feel about themselves or about the way other people see them. However, the car they drive or the clothes they wear are likely to be much more significant indicators of their status to both themselves and others.

Lifestyle segmentation has led to the proliferation of acronyms to describe consumer groupings (see Figure 4.16).

Yuppies	Young upwardly mobile professionals
Dinks	Dual income no kids
Bumps	Borrowed-to-the-hilt, upwardly mobile professional show-offs
Silks	Single income lots of kids
Glams	Greying leisured affluent middle-aged
Jollies	Jet-setting oldies with lots of loot

Figure 4.16 Acronyms developed from lifestyle groupings

Organizational/industrial segmentation techniques

So far this chapter has concentrated on segmentation of consumer markets. Obviously many companies' main markets lie in the organizational or industrial sphere. In these markets companies have to sell products and services directly to organizational purchasers. There are differences between the type of segmentation variables used in an organizational market and the ones that have so far been outlined for consumer markets. The difference in approach lies in the nature of organizational buyer behaviour.

Organizational buyer behaviour

An organization's purchase decisions are likely to be more complex because of the number of individuals and groups involved in the purchase decision and the possibility of the actual product/service being more expensive and sophisticated. All the individuals that participate in the decision-making process will have interdependent goals and share common risks although they may face different systems of reward. What emerges is a decision-making unit (DMU) made up of all these individuals and groups. Individuals in the DMU will play one of six main roles:

- **Initiator.** Identifies a problem that can be overcome by the purchase of a product or service. An individual in a retail company may, for instance, identify a problem in the merchandising function of the company that could be resolved by a new piece of software. (The merchandise function develops the buying plan for a retail company, monitors sales and product margins amongst other things.)
- **User.** Will be the actual user of the product in the merchandising function of the company in this case. They may well be the initiator, although this role may be someone outside the user group.
- **Buyer.** Actually undertakes the negotiation with potential suppliers. The brief for the technical requirements of the software needed, however, is likely to come from one of the other areas of the DMU.
- **Influencer.** Does not directly make the product or supplier choice but has a major impact on the decisions made. In this case an individual from the computer services unit in the organization will lay down the technical requirements of the software based on the need for it to integrate with the current hardware system.
- **Decider.** This is the individual who actually makes the decision to purchase. This individual may not have direct line management control of the merchandise or IT areas of the business but occupies this role because of the power and influence they have over the area being investigated. This is a crucial position in the DMU and yet it can be the most difficult to identify because several individuals may potentially play this role. In this case it may be the merchandise director, the finance director (many finance directors are responsible for IT functions) or the managing director.
- **Gatekeeper.** Determines the flow of information within the DMU without being directly involved in the buying decision. They control whether a potential supplier gains access to other individuals in the DMU. The flow of promotional material and information about suppliers is also under their guidance. Secretaries are very obvious gatekeepers but any individual in the DMU can potentially play this role. A technical person may favour one particular supplier and pass only their promotional material to other members of the DMU.

The size of the DMU will depend in part on the type of purchase decision being undertaken. Where a simple low-risk purchase is being made one or two individuals could undertake all the roles in the DMU. A high-risk expensive purchase may involve a large number of people from different functional areas in the company. Organizational purchases can be classified in terms of their level of risk as follows:

- **Routine order products**. These are used and ordered on a regular basis. The products or services are unlikely to pose any problems regarding their use or performance and are therefore low risk (e.g. office stationery).
- **Procedural problem products**. These products may involve some level of training in order for individuals to adopt them successfully. This will increase the risks associated with the successful introduction of the purchase to the company (e.g. personal computers or word processors).
- **Performance problem products**. The risks here lie with the question of whether the product can perform at the necessary level to meet the user's requirements. There may also be concerns about the product's ability to be compatible with the company's existing resources and current equipment (e.g. introducing new technology).
- **Political problem products**. Political problems could arise where a purchase takes away resources from another area within the organization. A high investment in a product for one area of the business may mean that another area has to forgo investment. Political problems can also take place where it is planned that the same product will be used by several different units, each having their own requirements (e.g. a new information system).

Political pressures also build up in the DMU because individuals look for different attributes from a particular product. This is partly based on the operational needs of their department. Individuals also pursue their own self-interest and are motivated by the formal rewards available to them. Individuals in different areas of the company may be given incentives in different ways. Buyers may be evaluated and/or given incentives to save the organization money. Production managers may be given quality and output targets. This can lead to strange effects. Bonoma (1982) talks of an organization that reduced its list price to well under its competitors', but gave only small discounts off this list price. All the competitors charged higher prices but gave larger discounts. Even though the company had lower prices organizations favoured the competitors. The main reason for this turned out to be that the buyers were evaluated and given incentives based on the price concessions they were able to obtain during negotiations rather than on the end price paid.

Figure 4.17 shows how each unit may have its own set of rewards. These disparate incentives can also lead to conflict within the DMU. Buyers may feel they cannot save money because the production engineers are setting technical specifications on a product that are too high. Alternatively, production engineers may not be able to reach their output targets because the buyer has bought a cheaper product from a supplier who has less dependable delivery times.

Figure 4.17 Rewards/incentives as a source of conflict in organizational decision-making units (*Source*: Adapted from Morris, 1988)

This demonstrates that organizational buying decisions are more complex than general consumer buyer behaviour. Frameworks have been developed to give a more comprehensive view of the complex factors involved. These also act as a foundation for developing meaningful segmentation criteria in organizational markets. The Webster–Wind and the Sheth frameworks both try to develop logical models of this process.

The Webster–Wind framework

This framework identifies four categories of variables that have an influence on organizational buying decisions (see Figure 4.18).

- **Environmental**. Any aspect of the external environment that may affect the organization buying behaviour is embraced under this

Figure 4.18 The Webster–Wind framework (*Source*: Adapted from Webster and Wind, 1972)

heading. This includes political, economic, cultural, legal, technological and physical environments. Competitors' marketing actions are also deemed to be in the external environment.

● **Organizational**. There are several organizational factors that affect behaviour. The company's goals and objectives set parameters on activity. The organization's structure and resources act as constraints on its culture in terms of the type of policies and procedures that are followed. These all affect buying behaviour.

- **Interpersonal**. The relationships between the individuals in the buying centre are an important determinant of how decisions are reached. How coalitions are formed and where loyalties lie within an organization will be dependent on these relationships.
- **Individual**. Attitude to risk, creativity, competitiveness, style of problem solving and locus of control will all be unique in each individual. The individual's personal goals, past experience and training will inform their way of operating. Each individual will influence the DMU's decisions to a greater or lesser extent.

Each of these categories has two subcategories of task and non-task related variables. Task related variables are directly related to the buying decision being undertaken; non-task related variables are not directly concerned with the buying decision but nevertheless affect the decisions made (see Figure 4.19).

	Task Influences *(Relate directly to the buying problem)*	**Non-task Influences** *(Extend beyond the buying problem)*
Individual influences	Goal of obtaining the best price	Beliefs, values and needs of the individual
Interpersonal influences	Group dynamics during meetings to agree specifications	Informal off-the-job social interactions
Organizational influences	Company policies restricting supplier choice	Criteria used for personnel evaluation
Environmental influences	Potential changes in prices	Economic and political climate in an election year

Figure 4.19 Examples of task and non-task influences on organizational buying decisions (*Source*: Adapted from Webster and Wind, 1972)

The Sheth framework

The Webster–Wind framework identifies and helps to assess key variables that influence an organization's purchasing decisions, but does not concentrate on the process to any great degree. Sheth (1973) developed a model that has some elements in common with the Webster–Wind framework but also has more of an emphasis on the psychology of the decision-making process.

He identified the importance of four main factors that influence organizational buyer behaviour:

- The expectations of the members of the DMU.
- The factors influencing the buying process.
- The character of the decision-making process.
- Situational factors.

The model is constructed so that the flow of the actual decision-making process can be illustrated (see Figure 4.20).

Figure 4.20 A model of organizational buyer behaviour (*Source*: Adapted from Sheth, 1973)

The expectations of the members of the DMU

Every individual in the DMU will have their own attitudes and particular background that shapes the way in which they judge a supplier. An engineer will use different criteria from an accountant. Individuals' expectations will be determined by their educational background, their job or task orientation and their lifestyle in general.

Individuals will also be influenced by information from a range of sources. When the purchase being considered contains a high level of risk to the organization it is likely that a rigorous process will be undertaken to identify as many sources of information as possible. This information search is likely to be undertaken by the professional buyers and can lead them to play an important gatekeeping role by choosing what information is passed on to other members of the DMU.

The information provided, as with any communication, will be subject to perceptual distortion by the individuals in the DMU. Individuals' expectations will also be influenced by their previous experience of the product or service.

The factors influencing the buying process

The Sheth model outlines two sets of factors that will determine the particular buying process for a specific product or service. The first set of factors relates to the product itself:

- **Perceived risk**. If the purchase is high risk then a detailed search for information will take place, drawing more individuals into the DMU. This could occur if the purchase was a major capital expenditure.
- **Time pressure**. If a decision has to be made under time pressure a smaller number of individuals will be drawn into the DMU. The fewer people involved the quicker the decision.
- **Type of purchase**. A routine repurchase of a product is likely to be undertaken by an individual who has been delegated the responsibility.

The second set of factors that influence the buying process is related to the organization itself:

- **The organization's orientation**. An organization may be, for example, engineering orientated or marketing orientated. This orientation will, to an extent, reflect the balance of power within the DMU and have an important influence on its attitude to a purchase decision. An organization that has a dominant engineering orientation will perceive a purchase by using engineering values.
- **Size of the organization**. A small organization may have only one individual responsible for buying. This individual may undertake all the information searches themselves. Large organizations are likely to have more individuals involved in purchase decisions.

- **Degree of centralization/decentralization**. A central buying department would be common in a strongly centralized organization. A much greater spread of individuals would be involved in a decentralized company.

Character of the decision-making process

Sheth's model identifies two types of decisions:

1 Autonomous decisions are taken by an individual and are relatively straightforward.
2 Joint decisions are undertaken by more than one individual. As the model has already indicated each individual has a unique set of factors influencing them and therefore some level of conflict is likely.

The manner in which these conflicts are resolved affects the final decision. The model outlines four approaches to making decisions:

- **Problem solving**. This involves gathering information and using a systematic approach to weighing up the alternative options. A disadvantage of this approach is that it inevitably takes time.
- **Persuasion**. Time is taken in order to get everybody to put the organizational needs and objectives above personal agendas. Again the disadvantage is that this can slow the decision process down.
- **Bargaining**. This is used in order to reach a compromise. Individuals in the buying centre trade concessions. This may result in a sub-optimal decision. Individuals may be satisfied but the decision may not be in the best interest of the organization as a whole.
- **Politicking**. Power and influence are used to coerce individuals into supporting majority positions within the DMU.

The model would suggest problem solving and persuasion are the most rational approaches to decision making. Many practising managers will be well aware that the bargaining and politicking options are common practice in many organizations.

Situational factors

Finally, the model highlights situational variables that are outside the control of the organization but influence the DMU. These variables would be such things as:

- A strike at a key supplier.
- A supplier suddenly taken over by a competitor.
- Financial problems.
- Production breakdown.
- Changes in corporate taxation.

These two models illustrate the complexity of the buying process in organizations. They also give some insights into potential factors that can be used to identify organizational market segments.

Approaches to organizational market segmentation

Organizational markets can be segmented according to the characteristics of the organization. This is sometimes referred to as the macro level. Factors that would be analysed at this level would be:

- **Industry sector**. Standard industry classification codes (SIC codes) will identify an organization's primary business activity. Different industry sectors may have unique needs from a product or service. In the computer hardware and software market the needs of retailers, financial services companies and local government will be different.
- **Size of the organization**. This can be judged using several variables such as the number of employees, volume of shipments and market share. This method of segmentation has to be used with caution – just because an organization is large does not mean that it will be a large purchaser of your product. However, larger organizations will differ from smaller companies by having more formalized buying systems and increased specialization of functions.
- **Geographic location**. Traditional industries can tend to cluster geographically, an example being the car industry in Detroit, USA. However, even emerging technologies show a tendency to locate in the same geographical area. The UK computer industry has clusters in central Scotland ('Silicon Glen') and along the M4 motorway in southern England. Internationally there may well be different regional variations in purchasing behaviour, for example between Western and Eastern Europe.
- **End use application**. The way in which a product or service is used by a company has an important effect on the way the organization views its value. A truck used twelve hours a day by a quarrying company may represent great value. But for a construction company that only uses the same piece of equipment for two hours a day it may represent a much lower value-for-money purchase. Establishing

end-use application can help establish the perception of value that will be used in particular segments.

Organizational markets can also be segmented according to the characteristics of the decision-making unit; this is sometimes called micro segmentation. The factors used include:

- **The structure of the decision-making unit**. This is directly related to the models covered earlier in this chapter on organizational buyer behaviour. The type of individuals involved in the DMU of an organization will vary, as will its size and complexity.
- **The decision-making process**. This can be short and straightforward or complex and time-consuming. This will largely be dependent on the size and complexity of the DMU.
- **Structure of the buying function**. The buying function can be centralized or decentralized. Centralized buying allows an individual buyer to specialize in purchasing particular types of product categories. An individual is responsible for buying much larger volumes per purchase than under a decentralized structure. This allows them to negotiate larger discounts. In centralized structures the professional buyer has much greater influence within the DMU over technical advisers compared with buyers in decentralized systems.
- **Attitude towards innovation**. There may be specific characteristics that mark out innovative companies. Identifying companies that exhibit this profile will allow a segment to be established at which new products can be initially targeted. There are organizations that are followers and only try a product once innovators have already adopted it. Identifying these companies can also be useful to a marketer.
- **Key criteria used in reaching a decision on a purchase**. These can include product quality, price, technical support, supply continuity and reliability of prompt deliveries.
- **Personal characteristics of decision makers**. Factors such as age, educational background, attitude toward risk and style of decision making can potentially be used to segment the market.

Figure 4.21 (page 80) summarizes macro and micro segmentation.

A more systematic method of organizational market segmentation has been developed called the nested approach. This method moves through layers of segmentation variables, starting with the demographics of the organization (the macro level) down through increasingly sophisticated levels, reaching the complex areas of situational factors and personal characteristics. This approach effectively establishes a

Variables	Examples
Macro segmentation	
■ Size of organization	■ Large, medium or small
■ Geographical location	■ Local, national, European Union, worldwide
■ Industrial sector	■ Retail, engineering, financial services
■ End market served	■ Defined by product or service
Micro segmentation	
■ Choice criteria	■ Quality, delivery, value in use, supplier reputation, price
■ Structure of decision-making unit	■ Complexity, hierarchical, effectiveness
■ Decision-making process	■ Long, short, low or high conflict
■ Buy class	■ New task, straight or modified re-buy
■ Importance of purchasing	■ High or low importance
■ Type of purchasing organization	■ Matrix, centralized, decentralized
■ Innovation level of organization	■ Innovative, follower, laggard
■ Purchasing strategy	■ Optimizer, satisficer
■ Personal attributes	■ Age, educational background, risk taker/adverse, confidence level

Figure 4.21 Organizational macro and micro segmentation

hierarchical structure in which to undertake the segmentation process (see Figure 4.22, page 81).

There is a balance to be struck with this approach between the macro level, which is generally inadequate when used in isolation, and the micro level, which may be too time-consuming and expensive to establish and operate in markets with limited potential.

Summary

This chapter has illustrated how an in-depth knowledge of both consumer and organizational buyer behaviour is needed to identify successfully useful segmentation criteria. This led to an exploration of a wide range of criteria that can be used to segment both consumer and organizational markets. This is the first step in the critical strategic process of establishing market segments that are available for a company to serve. Companies have to evaluate the potential of these segments and to make choices about which groups to serve (targeting) and on what competitive basis (positioning). The next steps to successful segmentation will be explored in detail in Chapter 9, Targeting, positioning and brand strategy.

Figure 4.22 The major factors for segmenting organizational markets (a nested approach) (*Source*: Adapted from Bonoma and Shapiro, 1983)

References

Bonoma, T.V., 'Major sales: Who really does the buying?' *Harvard Business Review*, 60, May–June, pp. 111–19, 1982

Bonoma, T.V. and Shapiro, B.P., *Segmenting the Industrial Market*, Lexington Books, D.C. Heath and Company, 1983

CACI Limited, (Data source BMRB and OPCS/GRO(s)), © Crown Copyright (1991). All rights reserved. ACORN is a registered trademark of CACI Limited.

De Mooij, M.K. and Keegan, W., *Advertising Worldwide: Concepts, Theories and Practice of International, Multinational and Global Advertising*, Prentice Hall, 1991

Doyle, P., *Marketing Management and Strategy*, Prentice Hall, 1994

Ensor, J. and Laing, S., *Cadbury's Project Gift*, European Case Clearing House, 1993

Family Policy Studies Centre Report, cited in Rice, C., *Consumer Behaviour*, Butterworth-Heinemann, 1993

Lawson, R.W., 'The family life cycle: a demographic analysis', *Journal of Marketing Management*, Vol 4, No. 1., 1988

Maslow, A.H., *Motivation and Personality*, 2nd edition, Harper & Row, 1970

Miaoulis, G. and Kalfus, D., '10 MBA benefit segments', *Marketing News*, 5 August, 1983

Morris, M.H., *Industrial and Organizational Marketing*, Merrill Publishing Company, 1988

Murphy, P.E. and Staples, W., 'A modernised family life cycle', *Journal of Consumer Research*, June, 1979

Plummer, J.T., 'The concept and application of life style segmentation', *Journal of Marketing*, Vol. 38, January, 1974

Rose, D. and O'Reilly, K. (eds), *Constructing Classes: Towards a New Social Classification for the UK*, ESRC/ONS, 1999

Sheth, J.N. 'A model of industrial buyer behaviour', *Journal of Marketing*, Vol. 37, No. 4, pp. 50–6, 1973

Steers, R.M., Porter, L.W. and Bigley, G.A., *Motivation and Leadership at Work*, McGraw Hill, 1996

Tinson, J., *Customer Service Interface: Implications for Maternity Service Provision*, Conference Paper, Academy of Marketing, 1998

Vandermerwe, S. and L'Huillier, M., 'Euro-consumers in 1992', *Business Horizons*, Jan.–Feb., pp. 34–40, 1989

Webster, F.E. and Wind, Y., 'A general model of organizational buying behaviour', *Journal of marketing*, 36, April, pp. 12–17, 1972. © American Marketing Association

Further reading

Hooley, H.J., Saunders, J. A. and Piercy, N.F., *Marketing Strategy and Competitive Positioning*, 2nd edition, Chapters 9 and 10, Prentice Hall, 1998

McDonald, M., *Marketing Plans. How to Prepare Them: How to Use Them*, 4th edition, Chapter 4, Butterworth-Heinemann, 1999

Rice, C., *Consumer Behaviour: Behavioural Aspects of Marketing*, Butterworth-Heinemann, 1993

Chapter 5

Internal analysis

About this chapter

The internal analysis of an organization's resources is the final stage of the auditing process. It creates the information and analysis necessary for an organization to identify the key assets and competencies upon which a strategic position can be built. The chapter explores the nature of organizational assets, competencies and capabilities. The auditing process used to identify these assets and competencies includes the elements of an innovation audit. The use of various auditing tools to facilitate this process, in particular the portfolio models and the SWOT analysis, are also covered.

Introduction

So far in Part 1 the external environment, the market and the customer have been analysed. However, before an organization can begin to review its strategic options it has to evaluate the enterprise's relative ability to compete and satisfy customer needs in attractive market areas. The organization's current and potential capabilities have to be identified and this can be achieved by evaluating the assets and competencies that make up the company's resources. Once this has been undertaken an organization can begin to develop a competitive position that matches organizational capabilities to the needs of consumers in market sectors identified as attractive (see Figure 5.1). This approach builds on two sources: a resource-based view of the firm, and market orientation. A resource-based view of the firm emphasizes the need for an organization to exploit its distinctive capabilities, whereas market orientation emphasizes the need to be responsive to market needs.

Figure 5.1 Matching organizational capabilities to market needs through competitive positioning

This chapter will explore aspects of an organization's capabilities, before illustrating the component parts of an audit and the tools available to facilitate the audit process.

Organizational capabilities

In this chapter resources are defined as all the assets and competencies to which the organization has access. Assets are given a broad definition to include both the tangible and intangible capital of the organization. Competencies are the skills that are contained within the organization. The application of these skills to deploy the available assets effectively delivers the organization's strategic capabilities in the market. Corporate capabilities are therefore defined as the combination of assets and competencies that denote the organization's competitive capacity.

Establishing an organization's current and potential capabilities is therefore reliant upon an evaluation of two aspects of its resources: assets and competencies.

Organizational assets

Organizational assets are the accumulated capital, both financial and non-financial, that a company has at its disposal. These assets are both tangible and intangible (Hooley *et al.*, 1998) and include:

- **Financial assets** – such as working capital, or access/availability of investment finance, and creditworthiness.
- **Physical assets** – ownership or control of facilities and property. In the retail sector ownership of an outlet in a prime location could be a significant asset.

- **Operational assets** – production plant, machinery and process technologies.
- **People assets** – the quantity of human resources available to the organization and the quality of this resource in terms of their background and abilities.
- **Legally enforceable assets** – ownership of copyrights and patents, franchise and licensing agreements.
- **Systems** – management information systems and databases and the general infrastructure for supporting decision-making activities.
- **Marketing assets** – of particular concern in the development of marketing strategy are of course marketing assets.

These marketing assets fall into four main categories:

- **Customer-based assets**
  These are assets that the customer perceives as being important such as:
  - **Image and reputation**. These relate to the company and the recognition of its corporate identity.
  - **Brand franchises**. These are important because of the time and investment required in building them. Once established effective brands have high levels of customer loyalty, create competitive positions that are defendable and obtain higher margins because customers feel a higher price is merited by the added value that the brand provides for them. Weak brands of course show the opposite characteristics.
  - **Market leadership**. A strong brand may not be the market leader but a brand leader enjoys distinct advantages such as excellent market coverage, widespread distribution and beneficial shelf positions in retail outlets.
  - **Country of origin**. Consumers associate particular attributes with different countries; these then become associated with an organization or a brand that derives from that particular state. So for instance Germany is associated with efficiency and quality. Products like Mercedes and BMW benefit from this perception of their country of origin and it reinforces their quality positioning in the market.
  - **Unique products and services**. These are key assets. Their distinctiveness in the market can be built on a number of attributes such as price, quality, design or level of innovation.
- **Distribution-based assets**
  Distributing a product or service successfully into the market is a critical marketing activity. Therefore a number of potential assets lie in this area such as:

- **The size and quality of the distribution network**. The size of the distribution network should be seen in terms not only of geographic spread but also of the intensity of that coverage on the ground. An organization may only distribute over a specific geographic region of a national market, but has built up a strong presence in that area and is locally dominant. Quality should be seen in terms of fitness for purpose. There are a range of factors that could be used to judge quality, such as ability to guarantee supply, lead times, or ability to react quickly.
- **Level of control over distribution channels**. An organization that can exert control over the main channels of distribution in a market is at a huge advantage, making control a key marketing asset. For example, Irn-Bru is the market leader in the soft drinks market in Scotland. However Coca-Cola successfully stopped Irn-Bru being distributed through McDonald's fast food restaurants in favour of Coca-Cola. Coke were able to apply control over that channel of distribution due to their global relationship with McDonald's.

● **Internally-based assets**
There are a number of internal organizational assets that lie outside the marketing function but can be deployed to give advantages to marketing activities. It is important to identify the underlying asset rather than just the activity. It is the asset that has the potential to be deployed in new ways to create additional advantages. There is a range of organizational assets that may give advantages to marketing activities:

- **Cost structure**. The organization may be able to achieve lower costs than competitors through higher capacity utilization, better economies of scale, or by applying newer or more innovatory technology. This could allow marketing to set lower prices for their products and services than the competition. The asset is the manufacturing cost base; this can be deployed to give advantage to the marketing activity of pricing.
- **Information systems**. These can be applied to marketing research activities to collect and analyse customer, competitor and market information. These systems could also be used to create customer databases, a marketing asset that can be exploited.

There are also some organizational competencies that lie outside the marketing function that can be used to create advantages in marketing activities such as:

- **Innovatory culture**. The ability to be able to create and maintain a culture for innovation is an important competence. This competence facilitates activities such as new product development, customer service through empowering front-line staff to develop creative solutions to customers' problems, and advertising through a willingness to adopt creative ideas.

- **Production skills**. These may allow an organization's production to have more flexibility, higher quality or shorter lead times, all of which can be used to advantage by the marketing function.

- **Alliance-based assets**

  There are a number of areas where the asset is linked to a formal, or informal, external relationship. These agreements with third parties can allow an organization to gain:

  - **Access to markets** – through local distributors that the organization could not cover with its existing resource base.
  - **Management expertise** – from outside agencies not available within the company.
  - **Access to technological developments or processes** – through licensing or joint ventures.
  - **Exclusive agreements** – with third parties, such as Coca-Cola and McDonald's already mentioned above, that effectively exclude competitors.

Organizational competencies

These are the abilities and skills available to the company to marshal the effective exploitation of the company's assets. The combination of assets and these skills allows an organization to undertake specific activities. Activities such as producing innovative products are a capability that arise out of the underlying assets and competencies of the organization. These competencies can lie at the three decision-making tiers: strategic, functional and operational; and at three levels in the organization's structure: corporate, team and individual (Hooley *et al.*, 1998):

- **Strategic competencies**. These relate to the management skills, the drive and the strategic direction of the organization. Skills should be assessed in a range of areas, including ability to create strategic vision, communicate, motivate, implement strategy, assess changing circumstances, learn and innovate.
- **Functional competencies**. These refer to the skills available to the organization to manage its activities in the various functional areas such as finance, operations and marketing. The marketing function should be assessed on its skills such as handling customer relationships, channel management, product management, product innovation and new product development.
- **Operational competencies**. These skills are necessary to run the day-to-day operations across the functional areas of the organization. As

an example, in the marketing function these would include skills of co-ordinating and implementing sales force activities, promotional campaigns, public relations activities, special offers and discounts, updating product packaging and labelling. Where these activities are subcontracted to third parties such as PR agencies, the skills that need to be assessed are the abilities of co-ordinating and controlling these external relationships.

● **Individual competencies**. These are the abilities and skills that lie with individuals in the organization. These competencies are based not on individuals' skills in isolation, but on whether individuals have the required skills to execute the tasks they face in their area of responsibility, whether at strategic, functional or operational level.

● **Team competencies**. It is necessary for individuals in organizations to work together in teams. These may be teams formed on a formal or informal basis. Despite the specific skill base of the individuals involved, a group also requires the skills necessary to work together as a team. A key element of successful project management relies on these team competencies.

● **Corporate-level competencies**. These are the skills, that apply to the organization in its entirety, to execute tasks at strategic, functional and operational level. This could relate to the ability to foster innovation throughout the organization, or the ability to exploit and continually update the organizational knowledge base, by effective communication of critical learning throughout the business.

Once the assets and competencies of an organization have been identified there are likely to be some assets that are more important than others. The relationship between these assets and competencies can be mapped to uncover the key relationships (see Figure 5.2).

Initial corporate-wide internal audit

As has already been stated, some assets and competencies that can be deployed to create advantage in marketing activities are found in other functional areas besides marketing. Any audit will therefore need to carry out a thorough analysis of the company's resources to establish assets and competencies that either currently, or potentially, could assist the marketing function and support strategic marketing developments. Hooley *et al.* (1998) suggest that these wider non-marketing assets and competencies will fall into five categories: financial resources, managerial skills, technical resources, organization and information systems. Once this overview has taken place the specific marketing activities of

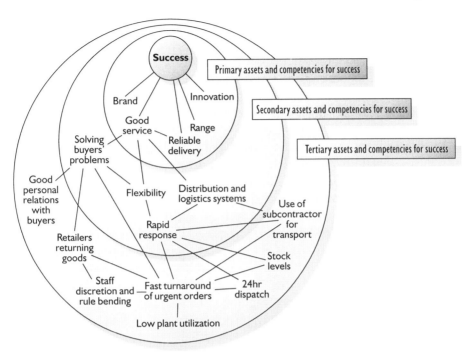

Figure 5.2 Hierarchy of assets and competencies for a consumer goods company supplying major retail outlets (*Source*: Adapted from Johnson and Scholes, 1999)

the organization should be evaluated. This can be undertaken by an internal marketing audit.

The internal marketing audit

The internal marketing audit is specifically aimed at reviewing the marketing activities of the enterprise and is split into five distinct areas (Kotler *et al.*, 1996):

- **Marketing strategy audit**. This analysis examines the organization's current corporate and marketing objectives to establish if they are relevant and explicit. The current strategy is evaluated in terms of its fit with the set objectives. This element of the audit also highlights whether adequate resources have been allocated for the successful implementation of the strategy.
- **Marketing structures audit**. This examines the structure of the marketing function and its relationship with other areas of the business. In particular, the profile that the marketing function has within the business is reviewed. For instance, is the head of

marketing a member of the board of directors? This is an indicator of how influential marketing considerations are in strategic decisions. Communication both within the marketing function and between marketing and other functions should also be analysed to see how effective the function is at co-ordinating its activities. The internal structure should be examined to establish whether marketing activities are carried out efficiently.

- **Marketing systems audit**. This part of the audit inspects the planning systems, control measures and new product development processes in the organization, as well as examining the information systems that support these activities.
- **Productivity audit**. This element of the audit examines the organization's activities using financial criteria such as profitability and cost-effectiveness applied to assess the relative productivity of products, market sectors, distribution channels and geographic markets.
- **Marketing functions audit**. This element of the audit looks in detail at all aspects of the marketing mix: the products and services the organization produces, pricing policy, distribution arrangements, the organization of the sales team, advertising policy, public relations and other promotional activities.

One other area that should be examined is the organization's innovation activities. These abilities may have been identified at the initial stage in the audit when wider organizational resources were reviewed. However, this area is of increasing importance to organizations and deserves further attention.

The innovation audit

This part of the auditing process reviews how effectively the organization is able to deliver the level of innovation necessary to create new products, new services, and new ways of undertaking activities. Success in these activities is likely to depend on the company successfully harnessing the latent creativity in individuals at all levels in the organization. The innovation audit examines whether the necessary assets and competencies are present and examines four key areas:

- The current organizational climate with regard to innovation.
- Hard measures of the organization's current performance in innovation.
- The organization's policies and practices that are currently used to support innovation.
- The balance of the cognitive styles of the senior management team.

The organizational climate

There are two components to the audit of the organization's climate: an attitude survey, and the technique of metaphorical description.

An attitude survey of key areas of the organizational climate that affect creativity

The aim of this component of the audit is to discover the current feelings of staff about the organizational climate. There are eight influential factors that are crucial in supporting innovation and four areas that act as constraints (Burnside, 1990). Support for creativity and innovation include:

- **Teamwork** – the level of commitment to the current work, the level of trust between team members and the willingness to help each other.
- **Resources** – the amount of access to appropriate resources in terms of facilities, staff, finance and information.
- **Challenge** – the challenge involved in the work undertaken in terms of its importance and the very nature of the task. Is it intriguing in itself?
- **Freedom** – the amount of control individuals have over their work and ideas. How much freedom are they allowed to decide how a project or task will be undertaken?
- **Supervisor** – managerial support in terms of clear goals, good communication and building morale.
- **Creativity infrastructure** – level of senior management support and encouragement of creativity and the structures necessary for developing creative ideas.
- **Recognition** – the level of recognition and the type of rewards given for innovative ideas.
- **Unity and co-operation** – factors such as a collaborative and co-operative atmosphere and the amount of shared vision in the organization.

Factors that act as constraints on innovation in an organization include:

- **Insufficient time** – there is a lack of time in which to consider alternative approaches to undertaking work.
- **Status quo** – a traditional approach, an unwillingness of managers and other staff to change the current way of doing things.
- **Political problems** – battles over areas of responsibility and lack of co-operation between different areas of the organization.
- **Evaluation pressure** – the evaluation or feedback systems are perceived to be inappropriate. The environment is focused on criticism and external evaluation.

Two other areas should be included in the audit of the staff's perceptions on organizational climate:

● **Creativity.** How creative is the organization perceived to be overall?
● **Productivity.** How productive is the organization perceived to be?

Metaphors

This audit is about innovation and it should therefore use proven creativity tools as part of the process; the second part of the evaluation of the organizational climate therefore uses the technique of metaphorical description (Morgan, 1993).

The power of the metaphor approach is that it can overcome the limitations of literal language and describe far more complex relationships and connections.

Individuals are asked to describe their organization in terms of a metaphor. For example: 'This organization is like a well-oiled machine. It runs well and doesn't make too much noise', or 'This organization is like a supertanker – it takes a long time to change direction'. These metaphors can then be analysed. They are likely to be either positive or negative observations based around seven organizational practices:

● managerial skills
● organizational structure
● operations
● organizational life cycle
● strategic orientation
● people orientation
● power orientation

This method allows a more rounded perspective of the organizational climate to emerge.

Hard measures

There is a range of hard measures that can be reviewed to establish the current organizational performance in the areas of creativity and innovation:

● Rate of new product development in the last three years. Davidson (1997) suggests that both total innovation development and percentage success rate are analysed (see Figure 5.3).

Innovation criteria	3 years ago	This year
Number of significant innovations in the past 5 years	11	6
Number successful	4	4
% Success rate	36%	66%
% Total sales in product/ services launched in past 5 years	16%	28%
% Incremental sales	11%	14%
Average annual sales per new product/service (£m)	6	12.5
Incremental payback per new product/service (years)	3	4

These product and service innovation performance measures show the following:

■ New product and service developments are lower in the last five years, but the rate of successful market launches has risen from 36 per cent of developments to 66 per cent.

■ Sales per new development have risen from £6 m to £12.5 m.

■ Although 28 per cent of sales in the last twelve months are from products launched in the last five years (up from 16 per cent three years ago) only 14 per cent of these sales are new (incremental) sales. The remaining 14 per cent are sales that have cannibalized current products. This is an indication of poor planning.

■ The payback period for new developments is also lengthening.

One action the organization could take is to have more effective segmentation and targeting processes, so that new product sales are developmental rather than cannibalizing existing sales. This type of analysis allows an organization to explore its current performance using hard output measures

Figure 5.3 Product and service innovation performance measures (*Source*: Adapted from Davidson, 1997)

● Customer satisfaction ratings. These should be reviewed not just in terms of the actual core product but across all areas of customer service.
● Staff turnover.
● An innovation/value portfolio analysis (see Figure 5.4) should be undertaken on the organization's strategic business units or products to establish whether they are:
  – **Settlers**. Businesses or products that offer the normal (me-too) market value.
  – **Migrators**. Businesses or products that offer value improvements over competitors.
  – **Pioneers**. Businesses or products that represent value innovations, such as the Dyson vacuum cleaner or the Sony Walkman.

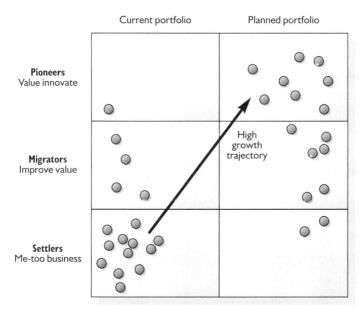

Figure 5.4 **The innovation/value matrix (*Source*: Kim and Mauborgne, 1998)**

Research undertaken on a hundred new business launches (Kim and Mauborgne, 1998) discovered that 86 per cent of them were standard market value (me-too) launches, or only offered incremental improvements. These businesses only generated 62 per cent of launch revenues and 39 per cent of profits. The remaining 14 per cent of launches were businesses that created markets or recreated markets that were already in existence. These 'pioneering' businesses, although only 14 per cent of the sample, generated 38 per cent of revenues and a massive 61 per cent of profits. The clear implication of this study is that organizations that are driven by future profitability need to have a spread of business across the portfolio. Companies that find the majority of their businesses or products are in the settler area are paying insufficient attention to the innovation process.

The organization's policies and practices that are currently used to support innovation

This review consists of identifying current policies that may be in place to support innovation. It would also review whether any structures or procedures have already been developed to try and facilitate creativity and innovation.

Cognitive area	Concerned with...	Handles these with...	Tends to be...
Intuition	Possibilities, patterns and ideas	Metaphors and symbols	Ingenious and integrative
Feeling	People and values	Force of personality	Enthusiastic and insightful
Thinking	Cause and effect	Regulations and language	Reliable and orderly
Sensation	Activities, events	Spontaneity and action	Adaptable and practical

Figure 5.5 Cognitive styles (*Source*: Adapted from Hurst *et al.*, 1989)

The balance of the cognitive styles of the senior management team

The final part of the innovation audit is to evaluate the cognitive preference and behaviours of the management team. Although individuals have the capacity to make use of all their cognitive functions, one area tends to dominate. The four cognitive preferences are shown in Figure 5.5.

Cognitive composition	Time orientation	Strategy orientation
Mainly intuitives with some feelers	Future	Prospecting
Mainly thinkers with some sensors	Near term, future and past	Analytical
Mainly sensors	Current	Reflective
Mostly feelers with some intuitives	Past	Preserving
Mix of intuitives, feelers, thinkers and sensors	Future through to the past	Renewing

Figure 5.6 The senior management's cognitive composition and its likely relationship to business strategy (*Source*: Adapted from Hurst *et al.*, 1989)

It is important to have a mix of cognitive styles in the senior management team that will influence the business's orientation towards creativity and innovation. Researchers have hypothesized the likely influence of a range of senior management teams' potential cognitive profiles as illustrated in Figure 5.6.

The whole issue of the nature of groups and the need for balanced teams is considered further in Chapter 6.

Auditing tools

There is a range of tools that can be applied during the auditing process that are capable of providing useful insights into the company's situation.

Value chain

The value chain is an obvious analytical tool to use in the internal audit. This tool looks specifically at the primary and support activities of an organization and therefore directly relates to identifying organizational capabilities. A full explanation of this tool is given in Chapter 8.

Portfolio analysis

There are a number of portfolio models that are used to identify the current position of business units or products. This position will be the result of the organization's current resources and can be seen as a symptom of the competencies and assets of the organization. They reflect the organization's current performance and identify strengths on which the marketing strategy can be built, or weaknesses that the strategy is required to overcome.

The Boston Consultancy Group (BCG) growth share matrix

This is one of the most well-known portfolio models. The growth share matrix is concerned about the generation and use of cash within a business and can be used to analyse either strategic business units (SBUs) or products. The two axes on the model represent relative market share and market growth (see Figure 5.7). Relative market share is seen as a predictor of the product's capacity to generate cash. The proposition is that products with a dominant position in the market will achieve high sales, but will need relatively less investment as they are already an established brand and should have lower costs through economies-of-scale advantages. Market growth, on the other hand, is seen as a predictor of the product's need for cash. Products in high growth sectors require investment to keep up with the increased demand.

The model uses market share relative to competitors as an indication of the product's relative strength in the market. To do this the axis uses a log

Relative market share
(ratio of company share to share of largest competitor)

Figure 5.7 The Boston Consultancy Group's growth share matrix (BCG)

scale. At the mid-point of the axis, represented by 1.0 (or 1×) on the scale, the product's market share is equal to its largest competitor's market share. At the extreme left-hand side of the axis, represented by 10.0 (or 10×) a product has ten times the market share of the largest competitor. At the other extreme of 0.1, on the axis, the product would only have a tenth or 10 per cent of the largest competitor's market share.

Products or SBUs are represented on the model by circles and fall into one of the four cells into which the matrix is divided. The area of the circle represents the product's sales relative to the sales of the organization's other products. The four cells in the matrix represent:

- **Cash Cows**. These products have high profitability and require low investment, due to market leadership in a low-growth market. These products are generating a high level of cash. They should be defended to maintain sales and market share. Surplus cash should be channelled into Stars and Question Marks in order to create the Cash Cows of the future. Current Cash Cows will inevitably lose their position over time as their market changes.
- **Stars**. These are market leaders and so are generating high levels of cash, but are in areas of rapid growth which require equally high levels of cash (investment) to keep up with the growth in sales. Cash

generated by the Cash Cows should be channelled to support these products.

- **Question Marks**. These are also sometimes referred to as Problem Children or Wildcats. Question Marks are not market leaders and will have relatively high costs. At the same time these products require large amounts of cash as they are in high-growth areas. An organization has to judge whether to use cash generated by the Cash Cow to try and develop this product into a Star by gaining market share in a high-growth market or to invest in other areas of the business.

- **Dogs**. These are products with low levels of market share in low-growth markets. Products that are in a secondary position to the market leader may still be able to produce cash (Cash Dogs). For others the organization's decision is likely to be a choice between moving the product into a defendable niche, harvesting it for cash in the short term, or divestment.

The overall aim of an organization should be to maintain a balanced portfolio. This means investments should flow from Cash Cows into Stars and Question Marks in an effort to make products move round the matrix from Question Marks into Stars and from Stars into Cash Cows. This movement of cash and products round the matrix thus ensures the future cash flows of the business.

There have been a number of revisions and adaptations to this basic model in order to accommodate different factors. Figure 5.8 highlights the fact that products in the research and development stage also need investment which cash generation provides, an issue the standard BCG overlooks. Figure 5.9 applies the basic portfolio analysis technique but in the context of the public sector. On one axis of this matrix is the organization's ability to deliver a service effectively within the constraints of current resources, on the other is the level of the political requirement to offer the service. This allows a key consideration of the public sector bodies, the need to provide services to satisfy political objectives, to be accommodated within a portfolio analysis approach.

The BCG model is criticized for having a number of limitations. Amongst these are:

- Market growth is seen as an inadequate measure of a market or of an industry's overall attractiveness. This measure does not consider such issues as barriers to entry, strength of buyers or suppliers or investment levels.

- Market share is an inadequate measure of a product's relative ability to generate cash. Other factors such as product positioning, brand image and access to distribution channels may allow an organization to gain higher margins and strong cash flows as a result.

Our competitive position

High ←   → Low

Market attractiveness (vertical axis: High ↑ to Low)

Stars	**Question marks**	**Research and development**
Cash generated + + +	Cash generated +	Cash generated 0
Cash used – –	Cash used – – –	Cash used – . – . – .
+	– –	– – –

Cash cows	**Dogs**
Cash generated + + +	Cash generated +
Cash used –	Cash used –
+ +	0

Figure 5.8 Matrix to accommodate research and development (*Source*: McDonald, 1985)

Ability to deliver the service effectively

High ←   → Low

Level of the political requirement to offer the service (vertical axis: High ↑ to Low)

Public-sector star	Political hot box
Golden fleece	Back drawer issue

Figure 5.9 Public sector portfolio matrix (*Source*: Adapted from Montanari and Bracker, 1986)

- The focus on market share and growth ignores fundamental issues such as developing sustainable competitive advantage.
- Not all products face the same life cycle. Therefore for some stars facing a short life cycle it may be better for the organization to harvest them, rather than committing further investment.
- Cash flow is only one factor on which to base investment decisions. There are others to consider, such as return on investment, market size, and competitors.

There are a number of models that use a range of weighted criteria in place of relative market share and growth in order to overcome some of the limitations of the growth share matrix.

The General Electric multifactor portfolio matrix

This model has two axes: market attractiveness on one axis and competitive strength on the other. Industry/market attractiveness is assessed on a range of weighted criteria including:

- market size
- market growth rate
- strength of competition
- profit potential
- social, political and legal factors

Competitive strength is also assessed on a range of weighted criteria such as:

- market share
- potential to develop differential advantage
- opportunities to develop cost advantages
- channel relationships
- brand image and reputation

On the basis of these criteria and on an agreed weighting scheme, the SBU or product is then positioned on the matrix, which is divided into nine separate cells, three on each axis (see Figure 5.10). The SBU or product is represented on the matrix by a circle. The circle's area represents the sales volume of the business/product as a percentage of the overall business. On occasion the circle represents the size of the market and a slice of the circle is shaded to represent the business's share of that market.

Figure 5.10 The General Electric multifactor matrix

The Shell directional policy matrix

This takes a similar approach to the General Electric multifactor matrix (see Figure 5.11). In both models the cells contain policy recommendations for businesses/products that fall within their boundaries. For instance, for products that fall in the cell that represents high industry attractiveness and strong business strength, on the GE multifactor model the policy recommendation is to invest for growth.

In both these models the number of factors, considered as important on either axis, and their relative weighting, are based on managers' subjective judgements. This is a major criticism of these more sophisticated portfolio models. However, this ability to use judgement, based on their knowledge of their markets and industry, does allow managers to adapt each model to an organization's specific situation. The models are also criticized as being more difficult for managers to use and more time-consuming than the BCG matrix.

There are also wider criticisms of portfolio models in general:

- They are based on an analysis of current areas of business and are therefore an inappropriate tool to employ in tackling the issue of new business development.

Prospects for sector profitability

	Unattractive	Average	Attractive
Weak	Disinvest	Phased withdrawal	Double or quit
Average	Phased withdrawal	Custodial growth	Try harder
Strong	Cash generation	Growth leader	Leader

(Row labels Weak / Average / Strong are grouped under the vertical axis label "Enterprise's competitive capabilities")

Figure 5.11 The Shell directional policy matrix (DPM) (*Source*: Shell, 1975)

- They place too much emphasis on growth, either through entering high growth markets, or through gaining high market share, whereas there are virtues in entering stable markets that have lower growth rates.
- These models require information that can be difficult to obtain and are complex and time-consuming to execute successfully.

In response to these criticisms, it should be pointed out that organizations should already be collecting much of the information required for portfolio analysis, in order to support strategic decisions.

The reality is also that all models have weaknesses – their very role is to try and simplify relationships in order to foster understanding. Managers should be using a range of portfolio models along with other analytical tools in order to establish a rounded and comprehensive view of their organization's performance.

SWOT analysis

The SWOT (strengths, weaknesses, opportunities and threats) analysis is another tool that is commonly used during the auditing process. The SWOT draws together the key strengths, weaknesses, opportunities and threats from the audit. This tool should be used to distil the critical factors that have been identified during the auditing process. It is a summary of the audit not a replacement. The strengths and weaknesses of the organization have to be judged in relation to the opportunities and threats identified in the external environment. The list should therefore be limited rather than extensive. The aim of the SWOT is to highlight the critical issues in order to focus attention on them during the strategy development.

Summary

The internal analysis aims to identify the organization's key resources which are its assets and competencies. Out of these arise organizational capabilities. There are a number of tools to help with this process. The aim at this stage is to identify these assets and competencies. Their current usage will already have been identified, the next stage is to decide how they may be potentially applied. This requires managers to develop a view of future changes in the environment that these assets and competencies can effectively address. The next stage before developing a marketing strategy is to generate a view of the future.

References

Burnside, R., 'Improving corporate climates for creativity', in M.A. West and J.L. Farr (eds), *Innovation and Creativity at Work*, Wiley, 1990

Davidson, M., *Even More Offensive Marketing*, Chapter 2, Penguin, 1997

Hooley, G.H., Saunders, J.A. and Piercy, N.F., *Marketing Strategy and Competitive Positioning*, 2nd edition, Prentice Hall, 1998

Hurst, D.K., Rush, J.C. and White, R.E., 'Top management teams and organizational renewal', *Strategic Management Journal*, 10, pp. 87–105, 1989

Johnson, G. and Scholes, K., *Exploring Corporate Strategy*, 5th edition, Prentice Hall, 1999

Kim, C.W. and Mauborgne, R., Pioneers strike it rich, *Financial Times*, 11 August, 1998

Kotler, K., Armstrong, G., Saunders, J. and Wong, V., *Principles of Marketing: The European Edition*, Prentice Hall, 1996

McDonald, M., Seminar Notes, Cranfield MBA Programme, 1985

Montanari, J.R. and Bracker, J.S., Article in *Strategic Management Journal*, Vol. 7, No. 3, pp. 251–65, 1986

Morgan, G., *Imaginization, the Art of Creative Management*, Sage, 1993
Shell Chemical Company, *The Directional Policy Matrix: a New Aid to Corporate Planning*, Shell, 1975

Further reading

Davidson, M., *Even More Offensive Marketing*, Chapter 2, Penguin, 1997
Macdonald, M., *Marketing Plans: How to Prepare Them, How to Use Them*, 4th edition, Chapter 5, Butterworth-Heinemann, 1999
Wilson, R.M.S. and Gilligan, C., *Strategic Marketing Management: Planning, Implementation and Control*, 2nd edition, Chapter 9, Butterworth-Heinemann, 1997

Chapter 6

Developing a future orientation

About this chapter

So far in Part 1 the strategic analysis has focused on establishing the current situation. Any strategy has to address the future, and therefore forming a perspective on possible developments is necessary. This chapter explores a range of forecasting techniques, trend extrapolation, modelling, individual forecasting, consensus forecasting and scenario planning. Information requirements and the make-up of teams undertaking forecasting are also covered.

Introduction

In Part 1 of this text we have been analysing the situation that any organization currently faces and identifying current issues that may have an impact on the company's operations. However, in order to make plans that are of a long-term nature an organization has to develop a view of the future in which it will have to compete. One of the major mistakes that an organization can make is to base decisions on the logic that explained yesterday's market. To quote L.P. Hartley (1953), 'The past is a foreign country: they do things differently there'. The future is not a replication of the past and an organization cannot develop strategy based on a historical perspective. Over a five-year period there can be dramatic shifts in a whole range of areas that can have a major impact on an organization, for example aspects of consumer behaviour, distribution channel arrangements or advances in technology. An organization that has anticipated these changes can take advantage of any opportunities they offer and establish a far stronger competitive position as a result.

It is important that organizations are creative in the manner in which they address these changes. Yesterday's view of what worked is unlikely to be appropriate in the changed environment of the future. Drucker (1980) states, 'The greatest danger in times of turbulence is not the turbulence: it is to act with yesterday's logic'. The first step an organization has to take is to form a view as to what may occur in the future – the second step is to address creatively the issues that arise.

The role of forecasting is therefore crucial to developing strategy. New product development depends on forecasts of technological developments. Selecting target markets is reliant upon forecasts of their attractiveness on a range of factors. Plans have to be developed to address the future not to suit the past. How then can organizations form this view of the future?

Forecasting

Forecasting the future is a different activity from market research. Market research can identify the current activities and perceptions of consumers. At an operational level relevant marketing information is likely to be readily available to support the activities that have to be undertaken. At the marketing management level marketing information which is relevant to the supported activities will not be so easily available. At a strategic level marketing information to support decisions is likely to be largely unavailable and the reliability of that information questionable (see Figure 6.1).

On what basis can a manager judge the quality of marketing information relating to the future? To give an example: market research could be undertaken to establish consumers' current perceptions of the future. However, consumers' views of the future are based on what they currently know and they may not be in a position to take an informed view. Indeed, there is no reason to believe that the view of the average customer is relevant. Is this view any more realistic than the view of a single expert in the area?

More and more marketing information can be produced but at a strategic level this is unlikely to be reliable. There is no useful benefit in acquiring more and more marketing information in order to support strategic decisions. It is typical that only 1–10 per cent of a company's resources and effort in gathering marketing information is useful in supporting the strategic decision-making process which is

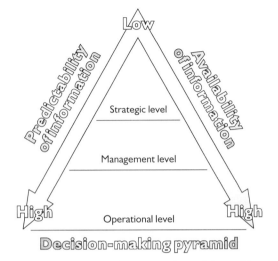

Figure 6.1 **Decision-making pyramid** (*Source*: **Adapted from Piercy, 1997**)

likely to generates 90–99 per cent of the value in an organization (Diffenbach, 1983).

What is critical is for managers to form a fully developed understanding of the market they are in and to establish the strategic issues that could have an impact on the business in the longer term. This will allow them to establish the key areas where changes in the environment could affect critical factors such as the industry's structure, market demand, or competitive reactions. Effectively this entails establishing the key questions that need to be answered in order to form a view of the future. These questions are unlikely to be important in terms of the day-to-day operation of the business but will be crucial to its long-term direction. Forecasting can be an effective way of identifying these strategic questions.

There are various forecasting techniques that can be used by an organization (see Figure 6.2).

Trend extrapolation

A simple forecasting technique is trend extrapolation. This technique simply takes a historical trend over time and extrapolates where the trend line will be if extended into the future. The general assumption is that whatever happened in the past will continue in the future.

In some areas this may be an entirely suitable way to establish what the situation will be. For instance, demographic trends are slow moving and therefore more predictable. However, trend lines can mislead

Technique	% of companies reporting use of techniques
Expert opinion	86
Trend extrapolation	83
Alternate scenarios	68
Single scenarios	55
Simulation models	55
Brainstorming	45
Causal models	32
Delphi projections	29

Figure 6.2 Forecasting techniques used by large industrial organizations (*Source*: Adapted from Diffenbach, 1983)

planners if they fail to understand the underlying nature of a market. Car ownership in the UK has been on an upward growth curve for years. The assumption is that this will continue, causing escalating problems in terms of congestion and pollution. However, it is unlikely that these growth estimates will be fulfilled precisely because roads will become more overcrowded and less easy to use. Consumers will switch to other forms of transport.

Even where trends can provide reasonable forecasts it is usually in areas that are not of major strategic importance. Issues that have a major impact on the organization's strategy are likely to occur where a development in the future causes the trend line to change. Identifying these discontinuities is a critical activity, which this simple technique ignores.

Modelling

Modelling techniques have a generally more sophisticated approach to forecasting than trend extrapolation. The technique is to identify the key variables in a situation and to model how they interact with each other. In this way the key inputs to a particular market can be modelled. Once the model is created variables such as quantity of supply or consumers' level of disposable income can be altered to see what effect this has on the market as a whole. These variables tend to be those that can be easily quantified. The problem with this approach, when applying it to futures forecasting, is that what appear to be key variables in the current market may not be the key variables in the market of the future. The relationship between these variables may also change in the future.

To enable managers to form a more challenging view of the future other techniques have to be used that foster a more creative approach.

Individual forecasting

There can be some merit in an individual forecast or 'Genius' forecast. If an individual is an expert in a specialist area they are able to form a comprehensive overview of their area of activity. This can allow them to see potential patterns or relationships emerging that very few other individuals or groups have the perspective to contemplate.

In the 1930s military planners believed that any future war in Europe would be a repeat of the type of war fought between 1914 and 1918, with armies facing each other over fortified defences. One individual wrote a book called *The Army of the Future* in France in the early 1930s forecasting that any future war would be dominated by highly mobile tanks supported by aircraft. The British and French high commands rejected this forecast. The Americans believed they understood how a mobile war should be fought due to their experiences in the 'non-mechanized' American Civil War and rejected the book's view of the future. Adolf Hitler read this book and as we now know realized the strength of the ideas it contained. The book was written by a certain Charles de Gaulle, then a little-known French army officer. This is a dramatic illustration of the power of an individual genius forecasting the future.

However, the dangers of individual forecasts are obvious. An individual forecast is a personal judgement and is open to idiosyncratic interpretations of an individual's observations.

In reality, though, many company forecasts are reliant on an individual. This may be the owner of a small company or the marketing manager in a larger organization. Organizations also use forecasts published by an individual expert as the basis of their planning. The techniques we are going on to discuss try to address the weaknesses of this individual approach. However, it needs to be stressed that, while there are obvious problems with relying on a single individual, futures forecasting is largely more of an art than a science.

Consensus forecasting

To overcome the limitations of individual forecasting the obvious step is to involve a group of individuals in the forecast. These individuals will develop a forecast by reaching some sort of consensus. There are different methods available to reaching this consensus: a straightforward jury system or the Delphi technique.

Jury forecasting

According to Dalrymple (1989) and Mentzer and Cox (1984), a jury of executive opinion is one of the most popular forms of forecasting used by organizations. Effectively a group of company executives (or it could be a panel of experts external to the company) are brought together to discuss their respective views of events that may occur in the future. A group forecast emerges that is the consensus view of the group. Any forecast will depend on the quality of the individuals within the group. There are several problems with a jury method. Decisions about the composition of the jury will have a major impact on the judgements the group will derive. The consensus reached by a jury, as it attempts to reach an accommodation all members can live with, may diminish the input of the more talented forecasters. An even greater threat is that persuasive individuals, or those with greater status, rather than those with the most knowledge dominate the group. The greater the cohesiveness of the group the more likely it is that they will be unwilling to listen to a dissenting individual within the group. This tendency is called 'groupthink' and can have major implications for management groups in general and jury forecasting in particular. Groupthink tends to occur with groups of individuals that know each other well, enjoy being together and belong to the same 'ingroup' (Janis, 1972; Janis and Mann, 1982). These ingroups are widespread in organizations.

Four key factors affect the way ingroups work and the level of groupthink that develops:

- **High cohesiveness**. Ingroups display the tendency to have a high degree of cohesiveness among their members. There is a great feeling of harmony among members of the group and a mutual self-support of fellow members. This results in members of the group increasingly comforming and complying to group norms. Members are less willing to show dissent during group meetings as a result.
- **Strong leadership**. Strong group leaders carry enormous influence within the group and this can lead to increased pressure for a unanimous group position to be taken in order to show solidarity with the leader.
- **Lack of objective search and evaluation**. Groups develop their own way of reaching decisions, which tends to be informal because of the

level of trust between members. The result is that alternative courses of action are not explored. When alternative actions *are* identified they are only considered at a superficial level.

- **Insulation of the group**. As the group bonds increase members tend to have fewer interactions with members outside the group. Alternative viewpoints therefore are not heard on a regular basis. When they are heard they are largely rejected because the individual proposing them is not a member of the group and therefore not a reliable source.

Groupthink causes six different types of problem for jury forecasting:

- **Illusions of invulnerability**. Because the responsibility for a decision is shared in a group, individuals don't feel the same level of responsibility for the outcome. Groups therefore are more willing than an individual to take decisions that carry a higher level of risk. This is exacerbated by the fact that the individual group members have confidence in the combined wisdom of the group and feel the group's deliberations will have identified all the potential dangers. The reality is that ingroups tend to be over-optimistic and ignore warning signs, taking more risky decisions as a result. Research also shows that groups tend to become more extreme, whatever they are like, so for example conservative groups become more conservative.
- **Collective rationalization**. Ingroups tend to develop a collective rationale to discredit any evidence that may act as a warning or a threat. Elaborate reasons are developed to explain why events did not happen as predicted. The group will find a rationale that will allow it to defend itself from criticism, especially from outside individuals or groups. The overall effect is to reassure the group that its decisions are legitimate.
- **Belief in the inherent morality of the group**. All members of the group are presumed to have a set of high moral and ethical standards. Group decisions as a result are seen as unquestionably morally right. Ingroups therefore fail to pay rigorous attention to the moral consequences of their decision making.
- **Pressure on dissenters**. Both direct and indirect pressure to conform is applied to members of the group. A member who shows signs of dissent may be excluded from a select inner circle unless they return to the conformist view. Ultimately they may be ejected from the group altogether if their dissent continues.
- **The illusion of unanimity**. Individuals who may hold opposing opinions to other members of the group on an issue tend to practise self-censorship. They will give voice to mildly opposing views or

keep quiet altogether as a way of avoiding the hostile reaction of the rest of the group. Group members may stay quiet merely because they believe that no one else shares their views, which further reinforces self-censorship.

- **Self-appointed mind guards**. Members of the group take on the role of guarding against incoming information that may threaten the group's position. Thus information is effectively filtered to stop any opposing evidence from being considered during group discussions. The absence of any contradictory evidence reinforces the unanimity of view amongst group members.

Janis regarded decisions such as the Bay of Pigs crisis, escalation of the Vietnam War and the lack of preparation for an air attack on Pearl Harbor as illustrations of the effect of groupthink. A more contemporary example would be the disaster of the Challenger space shuttle There are obvious commercial examples as well, including perhaps the Sinclair C5.

Ingroups cause obvious problems for organizations as they curtail critical evaluation, limit the serious reflection of alternative courses of action and foster acquiescent behaviour in individuals. However, they are virtually impossible to eradicate. Ingroups exist precisely because they offer security to individuals and a sense of belonging. There are ways to minimize groupthink behaviour during forecasting and planning activities. The aim of these curtailing actions is to enforce a critical evaluation of the decision-making process without destroying the group. Fostering a critical evaluation can be facilitated by instituting several procedural measures (Makridakis and Wheelwright, 1989):

- A member of the group can be assigned the role of the 'Devil's advocate' when specific decision-making activities are taking place. The individuals undertaking this role will obviously work in rotation.
- The group leader is not allowed, at least at the early stages of the discussion, to advocate a particular point of view. They have to take an impartial role and allow the group to develop its own opinions.
- The group can invite outside independent individuals to attend group discussions when critical decisions are being made. Their role could be precisely to raise alternatives or to provide alternative evidence not considered by the group.

Given that group forecasting is prevalent in organizations it is crucial that companies recognize the dangers of groupthink in their forecasting and planning activities.

Delphi forecasts

One technique that has been developed to overcome the problem with group forecasts is the Delphi forecast. A Delphi forecast purposely keeps the panel of experts involved physically apart. In many studies they will remain unknown to each other. Communication is undertaken by letter or e-mail directly to each individual from the Delphi study co-ordinator. This approach is taken in order to remove the social pressures and other undesirable aspects of group interaction. If a study examining what technological breakthroughs are desirable and achievable in the next twenty years was commissioned the following procedures would be executed. Once a panel of experts has been formed by the co-ordinator the Delphi study will have at least four phases:

- **Phase 1**
  A letter is sent to each of the experts asking them to state the scientific breakthrough and technological developments that they feel are firstly beneficial and secondly could be attainable in the next twenty-five years. Each expert will send his or her independent judgement back to the co-ordinator. From these lists the co-ordinator will create a comprehensive list or choose those items of particular concern to the organization undertaking the study.
- **Phase 2**
  In the second phase each expert is sent the list and asked to judge for each item the probability of when each potential development will take place. The timescale would normally be broken down into five-year bands.
  Therefore one expert may reply to a question as follows:

Year	By 2005	2006–2010	2011–2015	2016–2020	2021–2025	Never
Probability	0.0	0.15	0.25	0.35	0.25	0.00

A second expert's judgement, however, may be different:

Year	By 2005	2006–2010	2011–2015	2016–2020	2021–2025	Never
Probability	0.5	0.10	0.15	0.25	0.45	0.00

The co-ordinator will then collate all the replies and draw up charts displaying the distribution of experts' responses for each potential development.

- **Phase 3**

  The co-ordinator will then write to each panel member enclosing the charts that have been developed as a result of the second phase. These results will, however, be broken down into two areas. One set of results will have a very small spread of responses and therefore a near consensus. The other set will have a wide spread of responses and therefore be clearly non-consensus items. On each question the expert can see how far they are away from the average. They are then asked to reassess their responses. Experts that are at an extreme position from the mean can be asked to give a rationale for their prediction if they continue to maintain their position.

- **Phase 4**

  This is a repeat of the third phase except that the experts will now consider revised charts that have been developed as a result of the reconsideration that individuals have undertaken in the previous round. Panel members can adjust their judgements in the light of the previous round. In particular, they may change their view once they have seen the reasoning given by the experts who took an extreme position.

Delphi forecasts aim to arrive at a consensus position and can go beyond a fourth phase in order to do so. Once a consensus has been achieved an organization can then begin to weigh up the impact the forecasted events will have on their operations.

There are several problems with this forecasting technique:

- The process consumes a lot of time, as there can be considerable delays waiting to receive a full set of replies every round.
- The time delays cause organizational problems as panel members begin to drop out or become less motivated.
- Delphi forecasts appear to be heavily influenced by the ideas in fashion at the time of the survey.
- Experts on these studies have invariably been over-optimistic on the timescales involved in developments coming to fruition.
- There are also issues about the membership of the panel in the first place. Panel decisions, and who is involved in making those deliberations, can be subject to all the problems outlined in the jury method discussed earlier.

The advantages of the Delphi method should not be dismissed, however – the technique does attempt to remove some of the problems related to group decision making. The Delphi method is also a move away from striving to form a single view of the future. Although the aim is to narrow down the responses to as much of a consensus as possible this may not be achieved. When the process does not reach a clear consensus it can still be useful as it has identified the spread of opinion among experts in the field. A planning team can therefore consider a series of potential outcomes.

Illustrative Example 6.1: The Copenhagen Institute

The Copenhagen Institute, an academic group specializing in futures forecasting, undertook a scenario planning exercise for a Danish bank. Three discrete scenarios emerged from this process of developing a view of the future of banking over a ten-year period. The first scenario saw banks offering a wide range of standard computerized products and services. The second scenario envisioned banks offering different products and service levels to each customer group across a range of market segments. The final scenario saw banks operating as financial consultancies offering individualized value-added products and services. These scenarios were then used as useful ingredients to add to the process of developing a strategic marketing plan for the bank.

Scenario planning

This idea of identifying a diverse range of potential futures lies at the heart of the scenario planning process. Scenarios are normally developed by a whole management group, although they can be undertaken by a cross-section of people from across an organization. They may also include specially invited outside guests who may be able to offer an alternative perspective. It is important that all members of the group are familiar with the environmental analysis that has already taken place.

There are several techniques available to develop scenarios, some much more sophisticated and thorough than others. Here we only explore the development of simple scenarios. There are four key stages in the development of simple scenarios:

- **Identify the critical variables**. The first step is to use a brainstorming session to establish the factors that will drive changes in the future environment. Longer-term time horizons should be used so that participants do not simply extrapolate from present trends. The focus is on the external environment not the organization and its current relationships. Once these drivers for change have been identified they should be evaluated on the basis of their importance to the organization and the level of certainty associated with the manner in which that driver of change will actually develop (see Figure 6.3).

Figure 6.3 The importance/uncertainty matrix (*Source*: Adapted from Van Der Heijden, 1997)

- **Develop possible strings of events**. The key drivers of change will be ones that are identified as being important but not predictable in which way they will develop. There will be more than one view or interpretation on which way these drivers will manifest themselves in the future. These will form the building blocks for the scenarios. The important drivers that are certain to develop may also appear in the scenario but these will appear in every scenario on the same timescale. The next step is again to have a brainstorming session that puts these drivers into alternative sequences of events over time. One way of operating is to write each driver of change on a separate sheet of paper. These can then be moved to change their position as each alternative scenario is developed. The whole aim is to build scenarios that start from the situation today and develop into a future position that was not pre-planned, by the planning group, at the beginning of the scenario's development.
- **Refine the scenarios**. Once a whole range of scenarios have been developed using the same key drivers for change they will need to be evaluated. Scenarios have to be challenging and have an internal consistency. A scenario would not, for example, be internally consistent if it had the UK government cutting interest rates

dramatically below the rate of other European countries, while at the same time the pound (sterling) was dramatically strengthening against the euro. Scenarios also should be credible and recognizable. Once the weakest scenarios have been discarded it is important to test the remainder for their robustness. One useful approach is to test the scenario from the perspective of organizations or individuals that are actors in the story line. Do their actions appear to be compatible with the logic of that actor's position?

- **Identify the issues arising**. The robust scenarios that have survived the evaluation process should then be reviewed to see whether any critical event or outcomes have been identified that would have a major impact on the organization.

There is no reason to assign a probability of the likelihood of a scenario actually happening. If the reasoning behind a scenario is sound then it is a potential future that could happen and management needs to be aware of the impact that future could have on their organization.

The technique was used to great effect by Shell in the early 1980s. Shell evolved a range of scenarios aimed at developing a view of economic development and the demand for oil that would accompany them covering the period 1980 to 1985. One scenario created a surprise result that demand for oil would fall as consumers began to implement conservation measures to lower energy use as a result of the second oil shock (OPEC's second oil price increase). The general consensus in the oil industry was that demand would be sustained at normal levels. At the time there were worries about the outbreak of the Iran–Iraq war, customer orders were strong, and therefore the general feeling in the industry was towards expansion. Oil companies in 1980–81 competed heavily to win supply contracts and increase drilling activity massively. However, early in 1981 there were the first signs that the scenario of less demand for oil was beginning to develop in the real economy. Further scenario work led Shell to refine this scenario to include more detail.

With the benefit of hindsight, in 1980–81 oil companies clearly overestimated future demand. The scenario technique allowed Shell to see this early and to prepare appropriate plans if this scenario actually started to develop. In 1981 Shell reduced oil stocks much earlier and at a greater level than the industry as a whole. This had the added benefit of allowing them to sell before prices decreased (Wack, 1985).

The scenario technique is obviously open to similar group dynamic problems as the jury method. It may also be open to the problem of currently fashionable ideas being given too high a profile. There are, however, clear benefits to the scenario planning process:

- It is a useful technique to help managers understand the critical issues that lie at the heart of the future of the organization. It can help create a framework within which to understand events as they evolve.
- It prepares managers for the possibility that there may be discontinuities in the external environment.
- Critically, it helps to place fundamental strategic issues on the management agenda.

The key dimension of scenario writing is not so much forecasting the future but helping managers to understand the factors that could have a major impact on their business. Graham Galer of Shell states, 'Accuracy has to be judged, I think, in terms of whether the scenarios got the right things on the management agenda' (Galer, 1998).

Illustrative Example 6.2: New Solutions

New Solutions is one of a number of consultancy practices that employ scenario planning as a method of creating perspectives on the future consumer environment. In one exercise the consultancy explored the emerging pattern of consumer behaviour using a model with two key dimensions. On one axis was a range with 'work dominated life' and 'a balanced life' at either extreme, and on the other axis was a range from 'acceptance of risk' to 'aversion to risk' at either extreme. Four scenarios were thus developed using these consumer characteristics, as shown in Figure 6.4.

Scenario title: The Kaleidoscope

In this scenario consumers are more self-assured and are happy to experiment and lead non-conformist lifestyles. Success is a matter of achieving a balance in the activities of one's life. In this environment a diverse range of highly differentiated brands emerges to satisfy the wide spectrum of disparate consumers.

Scenario title: The Fast Show

In this scenario consumers attempt to squeeze as much into life as possible. They are extremely committed to both work and play. In order to achieve this full lifestyle they need domestic services such as those offered by nannies and cleaners. The scenario envisages the Victorian world re-emerging with a rich

Figure 6.4 New Solution's four scenarios

middle and upper class dominating society supported by a domestic service class ('below stairs').

Scenario title: The Fortress Society

This is a society marked out by anxiety. Individuals with employment find work is an unrelenting treadmill. Those without employment are marginalized and have no relevant role in society. The price of a brand becomes the major factor in consumer choice as lifestyle brands become the domain of a shrinking social elite.

Scenario title: The Virtual Village

Here personal identification is tied to a sense of community. Consumers work only in order to live rather than work for its own sake. Virtual as well as real markets are vehicles in which to trade skills. Successful brands in this environment have to earn the trust of stakeholders by portraying a commitment to community values.

This is one example of scenario planning allowing organizations to explore visions of the possible consumer environments that might emerge in the future.

Market sensing

There is some overlap between the aims and operation of scenario planning and market sensing as an approach. With market sensing the emphasis is on the need for managers to understand the market (Piercy, 1997). The role of individuals who co-ordinate marketing planning is to develop a process whereby managers can gain a more in-depth understanding of the fundamental dynamic forces in their industry. The emphasis with market sensing is similar to scenario planning and is to establish the impact on the organization of critical events that may take place in the environment and decide upon the probability of that event occurring.

Strategic questions

Whichever approach is taken to developing a view of the future, one key feature is that the critical strategic questions facing the organization have to be identified. There has been a range of studies by psychologists that show that in judgmental situations predictive ability does not improve as the amount of information increases (Alpert and Raiffa, 1982). The main effect of additional information is to lead to an overconfidence in the judgements made. In fact the studies show that the optimum amount of information reaches a plateau reasonably early in the process (Makridakis and Wheelwright, 1989). Once past this point additional information only increases the confidence of those involved in the judgement but does nothing further to enhance the quality of the forecast. Thus increasing amounts of marketing research beyond the threshold is wasting the resources of an organization.

Forecasting activities help identify the key factors underpinning an organization's position in the market. The follow-up is to monitor and evaluate developments in those areas on an ongoing basis. This allows an organization to focus the marketing research requirements and planning efforts into the critical areas for strategic development (see Figure 6.5). Where an event has a high impact on the organization and the probability of it happening in the near future is high, then the company needs to undertake more in-depth analysis and develop a strategy that addresses the impact of the development. Where the impact of an event is high but the probability of it happening is low, or the event is only likely to happen far into the future, then the organization should monitor and analyse data and begin developing contingency plans. Events that have only a low impact will be given a much-reduced emphasis in terms of monitoring and analysis undertaken by the company.

Figure 6.5 Categories of responses to strategic events forecast in the external environment (*Source*: Adapted from Aaker, 1995)

People involved

The mix of people involved in the forecasting process will have an impact on the effectiveness of the exercise. Part of the essence of the environmental analysis and futures forecasting is to build an understanding across the organization of the issues that it faces. Therefore this has to be a team activity that is widely spread. There are a number of issues that have to be considered when creating this team:

- **Ownership**. The managers that will be responsible for creating and delivering the strategy that flows from any analysis have to be involved in the process. If they are involved in developing the forecasts there is a higher likelihood that they will take ownership of resolving the issues that the process raises.
- **Subordinates' inputs**. A study by Aguilar (1967) illustrated that 23 per cent of information about the external environment came from subordinate executives. Alternatively only 9 per cent came from superiors and meetings. The clear implication is that lower status executives have to be involved in the process. Some forecasters also believe it is easier for younger people to envision the future because

Conformity to structure

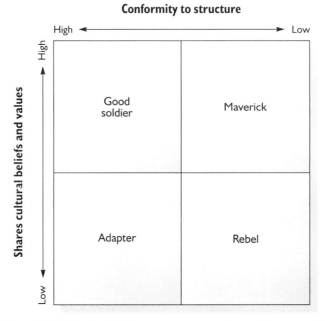

Figure 6.6 How Individuals fit into corporate culture (*Source*: Adapted from Sathe, 1988)

they have been brought up and socialized in the latest social, technical and political environment. Older individuals have come to the current situation holding values and beliefs developed when a different environment existed. Therefore an individual brought up with e-mail and CD-ROM technology may have a clearer perception of the technologies' potential than an individual whose formative education was centred on paper-based information sources. These individuals again are likely to come from more junior executive positions in an organization. Although there should not be too much emphasis placed on this issue, having a group of individuals of mixed experience could help provide a more rounded perspective.

- **Challengers**. Creating a team that all have the same values and attitudes to the company is likely to develop a view of the future that does not challenge the status quo. Individuals who do not conform to the company stereotype are more likely to challenge and test the conventional attitudes and beliefs that predominate (see Figure 6.6). Mavericks and rebels are the type of nonconformists that will challenge conventional wisdom, and are of course the very individuals that ingroups tend to exclude.
- **Cross-functional teams**. Any team is obviously stronger if it is made up of individuals from across the company's operations. Not only

does each individual bring an in-depth knowledge of their particular area of expertise but it also helps to build support for marketing plans within other functional areas.

- **Outsiders**. As has already been mentioned under scenario planning there can be advantages in including outside experts in any team. This can be widened to include representatives of both customers and suppliers.

Obviously there are likely to be weaknesses with any group that is formed. It is unlikely that all the above factors can be covered in any particular team. However, consideration of the above issues should be undertaken by anyone who is responsible for co-ordinating forecasting activity.

Summary

Developing a view of the future is a clear step in the development of strategy. Without it we are merely planning for the past. There is a range of forecasting techniques available to planners. Scenario planning is a useful way of identifying the important issues facing a company. It can also help managers achieve a greater understanding of how the market they operate within actually works. This ties in well with the idea of market sensing. The crucial step is then to motivate managers to develop creative approaches to deal with future issues the organization may face. Formulating elegant strategies to address the possible future that this part of the strategic analysis has identified is the next significant step in the planning process.

References

Aaker, D., *Strategic Market Management*, 4th edition, Wiley, 1995

Aguilar, F.J., *Scanning the Business Environment*, Macmillan, 1967

Alpert, M. and Raiffa, H., 'A progress report on the training of probability assessors', in D. Kahneman, *et al.* (eds), *Judgement under Uncertainty: Heuristic and Biases*, Cambridge University Press, 1982

Dalrymple, D.J., 'Sales forecasting practices from a United States survey', *International Journal of Forecasting*, 3, pp. 379–92, 1989

Diffenbach, J., 'Corporate environmental analysis in large U.S. corporations', *Long Range Planning*, Vol. 16, No. 3, p. 111, 1983

Drucker, P., *Managing in Turbulent Societies*, Heinemann, 1980

Galer, G., *Shell Group Planning*, cited in D. Mercer, *Marketing Strategy: The Challenge of the External Environment*, Sage, 1998

Hartley, L.P., *The Go-Between*, Hamish Hamilton, 1953

Janis, I.L., *Victims of Group Think*, Houghton Mifflin, 1972

Janis, I.L. and Mann, I., *Decision Making: A Psychological Analysis of Conflict, Choice and Commitment*, 2nd edition, Free Press, 1982

Makridakis, S. and Wheelwright, S.C., *Forecasting Methods for Management*, 5th edition, Wiley, 1989

Mentzer, J.T. and Cox, J.E., 'Familiarity application and performance of sales forecasting techniques', *Journal of Forecasting*, Vol. 3, pp. 27–36, 1984

Piercy, N., *Market-led Strategic Change*, 2nd edition, Butterworth-Heinemann, 1997

Sathe, V., *Culture and Related Corporate Realities*, Irwin, 1988

Van Der Heijden, K., *The Art of Strategic Conversation*, Wiley, 1997

Wack, P., 'Scenarios: shooting the rapids', *Harvard Business Review*, Nov./Dec. pp. 139–50, 1985

Further reading

Mercer, D., *Marketing Strategy: The Challenge of the External Environment*, Chapters 2, 5–8, The Open University/Sage, 1998

Piercy, N., *Market-led Strategic Change*, 2nd edition, Chapter 10, Butterworth-Heinemann, 1997

Part 2

Formulation of strategy

- ■ Strategic intent
- ■ Strategy formulation
- ■ Targeting, positioning and brand strategy
- ■ Product development and innovation
- ■ Alliances and relationships
- ■ The strategic marketing plan

Part 1 examined the elements that make up a strategic analysis. This analysis is the foundation upon which strategic decisions are constructed. Part 2 explores the process involved in formulating strategy.

Chapter 7 examines the strategic intent of an organization. The influences on an organization's mission and the creation of a mission statement are explored. The development of specific goals and objectives are then discussed.

Strategy is formulated to achieve the mission and objectives of an organization. Chapter 8 explores the process of strategy formulation: competitor advantage, industry position and product/market strategies. A number of strategic models are also covered.

Chapter 9 explores the issues concerned with developing a specific competitive position, through targeting, positioning and branding strategy.

Chapter 10 examines the crucial areas of product development and innovation. Specifically, product development strategy and the new product development process is discussed. The chapter then examines management methods that can facilitate innovation in an organization.

Chapter 11 considers the increasing importance of alliances and joint ventures. Relationship marketing is also examined.

Chapter 12 examines the strategic marketing plan, and focuses on corporate and marketing planning. The analytical, behavioural and organizational aspects of planning which help overcome the barriers to success are also discussed.

Chapter 7

Strategic intent

About this chapter

An organization has to have key objectives that define the aims that any strategy attempts to fulfil – this is the realm of strategic intent. This chapter explores the issues surrounding an organization's mission, goals and objectives. The hierarchy of objectives in an organization is discussed, as is the use of the balanced scorecard approach.

Introduction

Before an organization starts to make judgements about how it is going to compete, fundamental decisions about the organization's overall method of operation and the areas it wishes to serve have to be articulated. A conscious statement of the primary direction and purpose of the organization has to be the key foundation upon which objectives and strategy are based. This rationale behind the company's existence usually comes in the form of a mission statement and is meant to act as a guiding light to all personnel within the organization.

Mission

The mission of the organization is the unique purpose that distinguishes it from other companies and defines the boundaries of its operations. The mission statement is a proclamation of the organization's primary objective that encapsulates its core values. The organization's aims and aspirations are the result of a series of influences (see Figure 7.1).

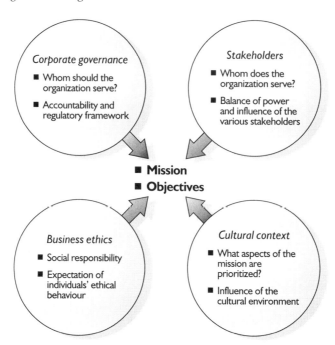

Figure 7.1 Influences on an organization's mission and objectives (*Source*: Adapted from Johnson and Scholes, 1999)

There are four major sources of influence acting upon the core meaning behind an organization's existence. Johnson and Scholes (1999) refer to these as:

- **Corporate governance**. To whom should the organization be accountable and within what regulatory framework should executive decisions be overseen and reviewed? With any organization these issues which relate to accountability will have an influence on the overall direction of the institution. Some groups that the organization is meant to serve, such as small shareholders, can be very removed from the managers actually running the company. Thus the regulatory framework acts to constrain management freedom and protect the rights of stakeholders.
- **Stakeholders**. Stakeholders in an organization include such groups as customers, suppliers, shareholders, employees, financiers, and the wider social community. In reality, even operating within the corporate governance framework, organizations may be inclined to further the interests of particular stakeholder groups according to the power and influence the groups actually wield.

- **Business ethics**. An ethical dimension also affects the mission and objectives that an organization should fulfil. This mainly relates to the corporation's social responsibility to stakeholder groups, in particular those whose power and influence is marginal, such as a local community. Although expectations of an individual's ethical behaviour has a significant influence, this ethical domain is subject to cultural attitudes and beliefs.
- **Cultural context**. The aspects of mission that are prioritized will reflect the cultural environment that surrounds the corporation. This influence will occur at several levels: at a broad level wider national cultures will be influential; individuals in functional areas will be influenced by the culture of their professional reference groups, and there will also be internal subcultures operating at divisional or functional level within the company.

A mission statement then is subject to these influences and needs to address their interests in a manner that allows it to satisfy their diverse demands. In essence the mission statement ought to characterize the organization's principles and priorities and define the broad product, market and technologies that are core to the business. Missions can be framed with a very narrow view of the business or be given a much broader frame of reference.

- **Narrow focus**. Some organizations choose to frame a mission statement with a very narrow focus. An example is Newport News Shipbuilding. The advantage is that it gives a very clear description of the organization's primary business. However, creating a narrow focus may set unnecessary constraints on the company's activities in terms of the markets served, the product/service offered or the technology employed.

Newport News Shipbuilding

Mission statement – unchanged since the company was founded in 1886

We shall build good ships here – at a profit if we can – at a loss it we must – but always good ships.

(*Source*: Cosco, 1995)

The Scottish Power Mission Statement

To be recognized as a highly rated utility based company trading in electricity, other utility and related markets providing excellent quality and service to customers and above average total returns to investors.

- **Broad focus**. The use of a broad mission statement is fairly common and generally refers to all the various stakeholders in the business: shareholders, customers and employees as well as the area of business to be served. Scottish Power's mission statement has this broader focus, although it has a reasonably defined business scope. One noticeable stakeholder group not referred to in this mission statement is, surprisingly, the employees.

In general, broad mission statements can address the problem of giving too narrow a focus on the business's area of operation, but can fall into the trap of failing to define clearly the market and product areas that are core to its operation. Richer Sounds is a company that retails hi-fi equipment; however, its mission statement makes no reference to the product or market areas it is concerned with as a business. It does, though, engender a clear vision on the way that business should be undertaken.

Mission Statement of Richer Sounds

The Richer Way

In our business, our aim is to give customers friendly, efficient service and value for money second to none. We believe that by giving excellent customer service we will earn their loyalty and word of mouth recommendation to others. This is the only way to ensure our future success and so, looking after the customer must be an absolute priority at all times, and we really do expect our colleagues to give above average service.

We also believe that work should be fun. We believe that if people enjoy what they do, they will do a better job. We also believe at all times in aiming to be the best. This means that we expect and demand superior performance from our people with both quality of service, attention to detail in the presentation of our stores and in everything we do. We believe that if customer service is the top goal, this will create loyalty, and long-term revenue and profitability will naturally follow.

(*Source*: Drummond and Ensor, 1991)

Successful mission statements have to demonstrate the following characteristics:

- **Credibility**. The mission statement has to set realistic ambitions for the organization. In particular they have to be believable in the eyes of stakeholders, and especially the employees.
- **Uniqueness**. The mission has to relate to the particular organization. It should not be a statement that could be generically applied to a range of other organizations. The mission has to relate to the company and its stakeholders in a unique fashion.
- **Specific capabilities**. The mission should also embrace the core capabilities of the organization and emphasize their core role in the future of the organization.
- **Aspirational**. The mission needs to motivate individuals by giving them a statement that has significance to the work they undertake – a vision that is meaningful in terms of more than just making profits. It should engender a vision to which individuals feel they wish to contribute.

A mission statement should also define the boundaries of the business's ambitions. What is the territory that the business wishes to operate within? This is commonly referred to as the scope of the business or the competitive domain. There are several dimensions that have to be considered when defining the organization's scope:

- **Product scope**. This is defined in terms of the goods and services the enterprise supplies to customers. A critical aspect of defining product scope is deciding how to categorize the organization's products. Some products may fit into a collective category easily, some more important products may be better served listed separately. The product could be defined in terms of its technology.
- **Market scope**. Market scope can be difficult to define but it is an important exercise. Market scope should depict the consumers and customers who utilize the company's products. There are a number of criteria that are helpful in defining market scope, such as:
  - type of industry sector targeted
  - channels of distribution
  - demographics
  - salient features of the consumer
- **Geographical scope**. This should be defined at an appropriate level of aggregation – in strictly local terms, for a small business, through to national and international regions for large organizations.

Definitions of the scope of the business based on markets are likely to be safer than a product definition. Particular products and technologies ultimately become obsolete but the consumer's needs addressed by those products or technologies may endure. There is a danger of marketing myopia developing (Levitt, 1960) if a business's competitive domain is defined solely according to a product type rather than a market need. Pharmaceutical companies are beginning to redefine their competitive domain in terms of the customer benefits of 'good health' rather than in purely product terms of 'drugs' (Green, 1995). SmithKline Beecham now sees the scope of its business covering four key areas of the healthcare market: prevention, diagnosis, treatment and cure, rather than just research and development of drugs. Products and services that address these primary market needs may change but the underlying market areas are likely to remain.

Stakeholders also have to be considered when developing a mission statement. Stakeholders are individuals or groups who rely on an organization to achieve some of their own personal objectives. At the same time the organization is reliant on these individuals (Johnson and Scholes, 1999). There are a number of different stakeholders that companies try to address and accommodate in a mission statement:

- **Internal**. These are the people most directly involved with the organization, therefore the values and attitudes of these groups are a key influence on the aims and objectives of the organization. Internal stakeholders include owners or shareholders, managers, employees and unions.
- **External**. These groups do not have the same close relationship with the organization as internal stakeholders do, nevertheless they can be a major source of influence over the direction of an enterprise. External stakeholders can be split into two groups:
  - **Primary external stakeholders**. These are external groups that have a direct relationship with the organization. They include crucial groups such as customers, suppliers, financiers and competitors.
  - **Secondary external stakeholders**. These have a less direct relationship with the company and include groups such as government agencies (local, national or international), political pressure groups, the financial community at large and society in general. These groups can exercise influence over the organization through such things as legislation and ethical campaigning.

Criticisms of mission statements are that many are too bland and ill-defined and therefore fail to give clarity to the business's endeavours. This could well be the result of the development of a statement that attempts to satisfy the interests of all stakeholders in the business. On the other hand, mission statements are sometimes too brief to depict clearly the organization's strategic intent.

Statement of strategic intent

Some writers see strategic intent, or the corporate vision, as a concept separate from the mission. They would argue that a mission statement merely states what the organization is currently doing and that a statement of intent, or a vision statement, is also needed. A statement of strategic intent describes what the organization aspires to become. However, many companies strive to achieve both objectives within the single mechanism of the mission statement.

Nature of support for the mission statement

Mission statements can be put to use in different ways depending on which stakeholders have the dominant influence and what the nature of their support for the vision is. The dominant stakeholder will either be internal or external to the organization. Stakeholders' attitudes can range from passionate support for the mission to those who will afford more equivocal support (see Figure 7.2).

- **Faint support**. A mission statement is likely to be paid lip service where strategic decision making is dominated by internal managers that view other stakeholders and corporate governance in general merely as constraints. In these circumstances a mission statement has little influence on the strategic developments of the organization.
- **Passionate support**. Where the strategic process is dominated by internal managers who have a close identification with the values and philosophy of the organization, the mission statement will be central to their actions. These managers use the mission statement as a vehicle to drive the corporate aims and aspirations through the organization.
- **Dissipated mission**. If strategic decisions are the territory of external stakeholders, whose overriding concerns are to do with corporate governance, then regulation and process will dominate the enterprise. The mission will become lost in the day-to-day routines of

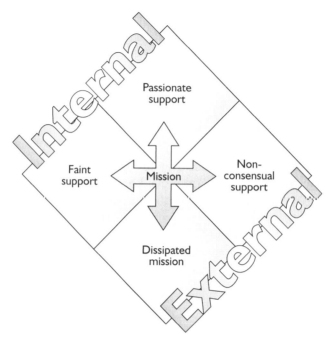

Figure 7.2 Level of adoption of a mission statement (*Source*: Adapted from Johnson and Scholes, 1999)

compliance with the regulations. Bureaucracies are classic examples of this type of organization, where the original mission of the organization is lost in the day-to-day paperwork and strict regulations that have to be adhered to at all times.

- **Non-consensual mission**. The opposite of the previous situation is where external stakeholders that hold passionate ideological views dominate the strategic process. When this occurs it can become difficult to develop a mission statement that is acceptable to the different stakeholder groups. Alternatively the mission becomes a highly political one. One example is of state-owned industries that needed to shed production capacity and jobs in order to become competitive. These industries suffered because stakeholder groups, such as governments, could not support the organization's strategic decisions because of their own political/ideological position. European governments and unions currently feel unable to support the closure of car plants even though there is clear over-capacity and therefore lack of profitability in the industry.

In summary, the mission statement, or mission and statement of strategic intent, operates as a guiding light that acts as a reference point when making strategic decisions in general and when forming objectives in particular.

Goals and objectives

The mission statement acts as a guide and leads to the development of a hierarchy of objectives. Objectives are the specific intended outcomes of strategy. There are differing views on the definition of goals and objectives. Some writers see goals as being less specific than objectives. Strategic goals are general aspirations that the organization needs to achieve but are difficult to measure or put within a specific timescale. Objectives therefore are more specific than goals and state what is to be achieved; they are given a quantifiable measure and a specific timescale. These objectives are seen as needing to be:

- **Specific**. Objectives that are specific should be set so that there is clarity throughout the organization as to what is to be achieved.
- **Measurable**. Objectives should state clearly, with tangible targets, what is to be achieved. Objectives can then be measured over time.
- **Aspirational**. Objectives should be set at a level that provides a high enough challenge to motivate individuals although not so high that they are demoralized. Different groups or functions will have various perceptions of the level of challenge set by the objectives. One way to address this problem is to set distinct objectives for each specific group.
- **Realistic**. Objectives should be achievable, based on a thorough strategic analysis. Companies can fall into the trap of developing objectives that reflect an unrealistic, but desired for, position that does not reflect the current reality of their situation.
- **Timescaled**. A timescale should be put on the achievement of an objective. This again allows the organization to measure its performance against a set deadline.

These quantifiable objectives are normally referred to by their acronym SMART. Examples of SMART objectives are 3M's financial objectives.

Minnesota Mining & Manufacturing's Financial Objectives

- To achieve 10% annual growth in earnings per share.
- To achieve 20–25% return on equity.
- To achieve 27% return on capital employed.

(*Source*: Wheelen and Hunger, 1998)

Other writers, however, argue that both quantifiable and non-quantifiable objectives can be set. They would argue that some important objectives such as technology leadership might be impossible to quantify (Johnson and Scholes, 1999). Obviously with specific objectives it is easier for an organization to gauge whether those objectives have been achieved. However, a less specific objective, such as technology leadership, can still be assessed by comparing the organization with the performance of competitors. There are dangers, though, if all objectives are couched in such qualitative terms, in that it becomes difficult to know whether they have been achieved or not.

Whichever perspective is taken on this matter, successful objectives also need to demonstrate the following characteristics:

- **Acceptability**. Internal managers are more likely wholeheartedly to support objectives that are in line with their own inclinations. As with the mission statement, some of the organization's long-term objectives are drawn up to be acceptable to groups external to the organization.
- **Flexibility**. Objectives have to be flexible enough to be adaptable when discontinuities in the external environment occur (see Chapter 6). Here again is the issue of a trade-off between flexible and SMART objectives.
- **Comprehensibility**. Managers and staff at all levels have to understand what is to be achieved and know the main criteria by which their performance will be judged.

Drucker (1954) suggests that there are a number of key areas within which organizations should develop objectives:

- **Market standing**. This relates to the organization's success in the market. Objectives can be a statement of the total sales or the market share the organization seeks.
- **Innovation**. Targets can be set for innovation in product and service development, cost reduction, financing, operational performance, human resources and management information.
- **Productivity**. Objectives can be set for the productive use of resources. A common approach is to state the number of items produced or the number of services performed per unit of input. Sometimes productivity can be stated in terms of decreasing inputs whilst retaining the same outputs. For example, an objective could be to decrease overtime while at the same time maintaining production levels.
- **Physical and financial resources**. An organization can state objectives about the acquisition and use of resources.
- **Profitability**. A range of targets can be established for financial returns including earnings per share or return on equity.

- **Manager performance and development**. Objectives can be framed to set performance criteria for managers.
- **Employee performance and attitude**. Specific performance criteria can be set against which actual achievements can be measured. Objectives relating to aspects of employee relations are seen as beneficial in gaining employees' loyalty.
- **Public responsibility**. Objectives can be set for an organization's wider social responsibilities – in particular an effort could be made to be seen as responsible corporate citizens. The organization may establish objectives for contributions to charities, community action, urban renewal, or other forms of public and political activity.

There are dangers for organizations that see objectives in one of these areas as overriding. Komatsu concentrated so much on competitive positioning objectives that its main concern became its position relative to its main competitor, Caterpillar. As a result Komatsu ignored emerging areas where there were opportunities for growth. This began to lead to a decline in the organization's profitability until corrective action was taken (Pearce and Robinson, 1997).

Hierarchy of objectives

Objectives are not only developed across a range of key areas, they also exist at a number of levels within an organization. Objectives cascade down through an organizational structure effectively forming a hierarchy. The fictitious Edinburgh Hotel is given as a useful example to illustrate this hierarchy of objectives (see Figure 7.3).

Edinburgh Hotel's objectives include:

- **Corporate objectives**. Objectives at a corporate level relate to the organization's overall direction in terms of its general attitude towards growth. At this higher level, managers of the Edinburgh Hotel are likely to be concerned with long-term profitability. (*Note*: In a not-for-profit organization the key objectives are more likely to relate to the efficient use of resources rather than profitability.) In this case the hotel management wishes to increase operating profit by 30 per cent over three years. The method proposed to achieve this objective is by growing market share to 25 per cent of the Edinburgh market. At this corporate level expanding market share becomes a strategy for achieving the organization's principal objective.
- **Functional objectives**. At a functional level expanding market share becomes an objective. Each functional area – finance, human

	Objectives	**Strategy**
Corporate (over 3 years)	■ Increase gross operating profit by 30%	■ By becoming market leading luxury hotel in Edinburgh with 25% share
Marketing (over 3 years)	■ Achieve 25% share of Edinburgh luxury hotel market	■ By providing best facilities for key market segments ■ By providing best standards of service ■ Promote it
Marketing Mix (1–3 years) Product	■ Provide best facilities for key market segments	■ Build more informal restaurant ■ Refurbish hotel to higher standard ■ Add fitness club ■ Improve bus facilities
Service	■ Provide best service standards	■ Retrain staff etc.
Promotion	■ Create awareness of improved facilities, service, etc.	■ Promote new restaurant ■ 'Relaunch' hotel

Figure 7.3 The Edinburgh Hotel's hierarchy of objectives *Source*: Adapted from Revuelta, 1996)

resources, operations and marketing – will develop a strategy to support this objective. In terms of the marketing function it is concerned about which products/services should be sold into which markets. At a fundamental level marketing strategy is about products and markets. In this example the strategy at the marketing function's level is to provide the best facilities in Edinburgh for key market segments, provide the best standards of service and ensure that they are adequately promoted.

● **Operational objectives**. At this level the functional level marketing strategy becomes the objective. Strategies have to be developed for each element of the marketing mix to support these operational objectives.

This hierarchy ensures that at each level the objectives developed are consistent with the objectives that lie at the level above them. However, there has to be strong co-ordination between functional areas otherwise conflicting actions may be taken as each functional area conducts independent actions in order to fulfil their objectives. The key corporate objective could be to increase profitability by 10 per cent over the next three years. If independent actions are taken, marketing could develop strategies to increase sales in order to meet this objective. At the same time production could be operating at optimum capacity so that any increase in throughput would increase its costs. Without co-ordination and communication functional areas can effectively be working against each other.

In many situations there will be more than three levels to this hierarchy, increasing the complexity of the situation even more:

- **Strategic business unit (SBU) objectives**. In an organization with a divisional structure this hierarchy will have an additional level of the business (or SBU) level objectives. These will be derived from the corporate level objectives and strategy and then feed into the functional level objectives.

Long-term versus short-term goals

There is some tension between long-term and short-term objectives. Long-term objectives are an integral part of the planning horizons of up to five years ahead. Shorter-term objectives for twelve months are more likely to drive the activities at the operational level. However, short-term objectives have to fall within the overall direction of the longer-term objectives. Budgets and targets generally are based on these short-term objectives and are essential for management control. But unless they are developed within a long-term framework they are not strategic in nature.

According to Aaker (1995), short-term financial measures such as sales, return on investment and market share are the dominant objectives in businesses. Even where other objectives exist they are eclipsed by these quantitative ones. This often leads to a bias in strategic choice towards squeezing a business and starving it of investment in order to improve the short-term financial performance. One way to avoid this bias is to use the balanced scorecard approach – this would also have helped Komatsu to avoid their concentration on one key objective.

The balanced scorecard

Objective setting is not an isolated process. As has already been discussed, there is a need for managers to know the key criteria by which their performance against objectives will be measured. There is a clear link between setting objectives and the setting of performance measures. The balanced scorecard (Kaplan and Norton, 1992, 1993) is an approach that more clearly links these two activities. Kaplan and Norton suggest that a balanced set of objectives should be created and at the same time a coherent set of performance measures should be developed alongside them.

At the core of the balanced scorecard approach is the belief that managers have to be able to look at a business from four key perspectives:

- **Customer perspective**. How customers see a business is critical, but financial measures alone do not provide this view. Customers are generally concerned with quality, performance, service and time. For each of these categories the organization should develop objectives and performance measures. Obviously how these categories are defined has to be from the customer's perspective. This will allow the organization to track how customers view the business over time.
- **Internal perspective**. Managers have to identify the critical internal processes that will allow them to satisfy customer needs. Identifying the processes that are important to customer satisfaction allows managers to identify the functions and competencies in which they need to excel.
- **Innovation and learning perspective**. An organization's ability to create value is inextricably linked to its capacity continually to improve through innovation and learning.
- **Financial perspective**. This allows the organization to see how the business looks from the shareholders' point of view. This financial performance measures the success not only of an organization's strategy but also of its implementation.

The balanced scorecard widens the view managers have of the business rather than concentrating purely on financial criteria. For each of these perspectives the organization has to create distinct objectives and at the same time develop the accompanying performance measures. This process also forces managers to understand many complex relationships and to surmount some of the traditional functional barriers that hamper strategic development (Figure 7.4).

The balanced scorecard approach also addresses one other potential problem – that of ensuring consistency between objectives. This can be difficult in practice because objectives are formed in a range of areas, at different levels and on different timescales (effectively objectives are formed both horizontally and vertically through the organization).

Gap analysis

The process of strategic analysis explored in Part 1 of this book effectively establishes the current situation that the company finds itself

	Strategic objectives	**Strategic measures**
Financial	F.1 Return on capital F.2 Cash flow F.3 Profitability F.4 Profitability growth F.5 Reliability of performance	➡ ROCE ➡ Cash flow ➡ Net margin ➡ Volume growth rate vs. industry ➡ Profit forecast reliability ➡ Sales backlog
Customer	C.1 Value for money C.2 Competitive price C.3 Customer satisfaction	➡ Customer ranking survey ➡ Pricing index ➡ Customer satisfaction index ➡ Mystery shopping rating
Internal	I.1 Marketing ■ Product and service development ■ Shape customer requirement I.2 Manufacturing ■ Lower manufacturing cost ■ Improve project management I.3 Logistics ■ Reduce delivery costs ■ Inventory management I.4 Quality	➡ Pioneer percentage of product portfolio ➡ Hours with customer on new work ➡ Total expenses per unit vs. competition ➡ Safety incident index ➡ Delivered cost per unit ➡ Inventory level compared to plan and output rate ➡ Rework
Innovation and learning	IL.1 Innovate products and services IL.2 Time to market IL.3 Empowered workforce IL.4 Access to strategic information IL.5 Continuous improvement	➡ Percentage revenue from pioneer products ➡ Cycle time vs. industry norm ➡ Staff attitude survey ➡ Strategic information availability ➡ Number of employee suggestions

Figure 7.4 The balanced scorecard (*Source*: Adapted from Kaplan and Norton, 1992, 1993)

in and allows forecasts to be made of how the company will perform in the future. The objectives that are set by the organization allow it to project what the company's actual performance will need to be to achieve those objectives. It is at this point that the organization can calculate the gap between these two positions. This is commonly referred to as the gap analysis (see Figure 7.5).

The gap between these two positions represents the divide that the marketing strategy has to address. The rest of Part 2 of this book addresses how an organization can develop strategy to allow it to meet its objectives by crossing this gap.

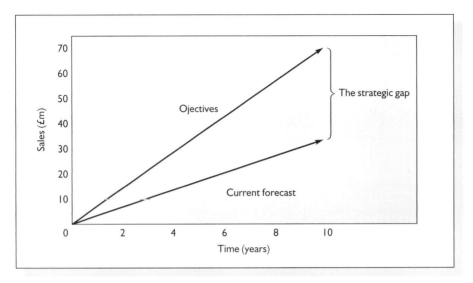

Figure 7.5 **The gap analysis**

Summary

This chapter has explored the issues surrounding corporate mission, in particular influences acting upon the development of an organization's mission statement. The nature of strategic objectives was discussed, as well as the hierarchy of objectives and strategies. The possible tensions between functional objectives and strategies were highlighted. Strategies are developed to achieve the mission and objectives of the organization. The next step in the process is for the organization to formulate strategies to ensure that it can cross the gap between its current position and the fulfilment of its primary objectives.

References

Aaker, D.A., *Strategic Market Management*, 4th edition, Wiley, 1995

Cosco, J., 'Down to the sea in ships', *Journal of Business Strategy*, Nov./ Dec., p. 48, 1995

Drucker, P., *The Practice of Management*, pp. 65–83, Harper & Row, 1954

Drummond, G. and Ensor, J., *Teaching Note for the Richer Sounds Case Study*, European Case Clearing House, 1991

Green, D., 'Healthcare vies with research', *Financial Times*, 25 April, p. 34, 1995

Johnson, G. and Scholes, K., *Exploring Corporate Strategy*, 5th edition, Prentice Hall, 1999

Kaplan, R.S. and Norton, D.P., 'The balanced scorecard: measure that drive performance', *Harvard Business Review*, Vol. 70, No. 1, pp. 71–9, 1992

Kaplan, R.S. and Norton, D.P., 'Putting the balanced scorecard to work', *Harvard Business Review*, Vol. 71, No. 5, pp. 134–47, 1993

Levitt, T., 'Marketing myopia', *Harvard Business Review*, July/Aug., pp. 45–56, 1960

Pearce, J.A. and Robinson, R.B., *Strategic Management*, 6th edition, Irwin, 1997

Revuelta, J., Seminar, Napier Marketing Group, 1996

Wheelen, T.L. and Hunger, J., *Strategic Management and Business Policy*, 6th edition, p. 11, Addison-Wesley, 1998

Further reading

Johnson, G. and Scholes, K., *Exploring Corporate Strategy*, 5th edition, Chapter 5, Prentice Hall, 1999

McDonald, M., *Marketing Plans: How to Prepare them, How to Use Them*, 4th edition, Chapter 6, Butterworth-Heinemann, 1999

Chapter 8

Strategy formulation

About this chapter

Marketing strategy aims to generate sustainable competitive advantage. The process is influenced by industry position, experience curves, value effects and other factors such as product life cycle. In any given market place, businesses must adopt defensive and attacking strategies. Such actions aim to maintain and/or increase market share. Organizations need to ensure their strategic position is relevant to current/future market conditions.

Strategy formulation – an overview

Chapter 7 outlined the basic principles of setting objectives. It is important to recognize that alternative methods of achieving objectives exist. The ability to identify and evaluate these alternatives forms the essence of strategy development. The goal is to obtain sustainable competitive advantage within predetermined markets. Figure 8.1 summarizes the process.

Competitive advantage

The notions of competitive advantage and marketing strategy are intrinsically linked. Competitive advantage is the process of identifying a

Figure 8.1 The formulation of strategy

fundamental and sustainable basis from which to compete. Ultimately, marketing strategy aims to deliver this advantage in the market place.

Porter (1980) identifies three **generic strategies** – fundamental sources of competitive advantage. These are: cost leadership, differentiation and focus. Arguably, these provide a basis for all strategic activity and underpin the large number of marketing strategies available to the organization. Additionally, management needs to define the competitive scope of the business – targeting a broad or narrow range of industries/customers (see Figure 8.2), essentially either

Figure 8.2 Competitive advantage (*Source*: Adapted from Porter, 1980)

operating industry-wide or targeting specific market segments. Each generic strategy is examined in turn.

Cost leadership

One potential source of competitive advantage is to seek an overall cost leadership position within an industry, or industry sector. Here the focus of strategic activity is to maintain a low cost structure. The desired structure is achievable via the aggressive pursuit of policies such as controlling overhead cost, economies of scale, cost minimization in areas such as marketing and R&D, global sourcing of materials and experience effects. Additionally, the application of new technology to traditional activities offers significant opportunity for cost reduction.

Difficulties can exist in maintaining cost leadership. Success can attract larger, better resourced competitors. If market share falls, economies of scale become harder to achieve and fixed costs, such as overheads, are difficult to adjust in the short-to-medium term. Additionally, cost leadership and high volume strategy are likely to involve high initial investment costs and are often associated with 'commodity' type products where price discounting and price wars are common.

Remember, low cost does not need to equate automatically to low price. Products provided at average, or above average, industry price (while maintaining cost leadership) can generate higher than average margins.

The basic drivers of cost leadership include:

- **Economy of scale**. This is perhaps the single biggest influence on unit cost. Correctly managed, volume can drive efficiency and enhance purchasing leverage. Additionally, given large-scale operations, learning and experience effects (see later) can be a source of cost reduction.
- **Linkages and relationships**. Being able to link activities together and form relationships can generate cost savings. For example, a 'just-in-time' manufacturing system could reduce stockholding costs and enhance quality. Forging relationships with external organizations is also vital. If industry partners were to share development and distribution costs, or activities were 'outsourced' to specialist operators, a substantial reduction in overheads is possible.
- **Infrastructure**. Factors such as location, availability of skills and governmental support greatly affect the firm's cost base. Given the

development of information technology and the global economy it is possible to have a worldwide infrastructure and selectively place activities in low-cost areas.

Differentiation

Here the product offered is distinct and differentiated from the competition. The source of differentiation must be on a basis of value to the customer. The product offering should be perceived as unique and ideally offer the opportunity to command a price premium. Will customers pay more for factors such as design, quality, branding and service levels?

The skills base for a differentiation strategy is somewhat different from a cost leadership strategy and will focus on creating reasons for purchase, innovation and flexibility. Remember, often it is the perception of performance as opposed to actual performance that generates differentiation.

There are several 'downsides' to this type of strategy. Firstly, it can be costly with associated costs outweighing the benefits. Secondly, innovation and other initiatives can be duplicated by competitors. Thirdly, customer needs change with time and the basis of differentiation can become less important as customers focus on other attributes. For example, in the car market, safety may now be seen as more important than fuel economy.

Common sources of differentiation include:

- **Product performance**. Does product performance enhance its value to the customer? Factors such as quality, durability and capability all offer potential points of differentiation. Performance is evaluated relative to competitors' products and gives customers a reason to prefer one product over another.
- **Product perception**. Often the perception of a product is more important than actual performance. Hopefully, the product has an enduring emotional appeal generating brand loyalty (see Chapter 8). This is commonly achieved via marketing communications (advertising, branding, endorsement, etc.) and direct experience of customer groups.
- **Product augmentation**. We can differentiate by augmenting the product in a way that adds value. For example, high levels of service, after-sales support, affordable finance and competitive pricing all serve to enhance the basic product offering. It is common for distributors, such as retailers, to provide the added-value augmentation. Product augmentation is dealt with in Chapter 10.

Focus

The organization concentrates on a narrower range of business activities. The aim is to specialize in a specific market segment and derive detailed customer knowledge. This focus, or niche, strategy can also generate the benefits of cost leadership or differentiation within a defined market segment (see Figure 8.2). For example, it may be possible to obtain cost leadership within a chosen segment or that segment may regard your product offering as differentiated.

Success within a specialist niche can attract competitors – perhaps much better resourced. Additionally, the narrow business base means more susceptibility to downturns in demand from key customer groups.

A focus strategy is based on factors such as:

- **Geographic area**. Using geographic segmentation allows a product to be tailored to local needs. The local association may offer the potential to differentiate the offering (e.g. Champagne comes from a specific French region) and protect the market from larger predators. Another rationale for such segmentation is to serve markets too small or isolated to be viable on a large scale (e.g. rural communities).
- **End-user focus**. It is possible to focus on a specific type of user as opposed to the entire market. Specialization offers the opportunity to get 'close' to customers and have a better understanding of their needs (e.g. specialist hi-fi manufacturer). Additionally, within a narrow segment the focused organization may be able to offer the choice, service and economy-of-scale not available to more broadly-based competitors. This strategy often works by selecting specific points on the price/quality spectrum within a given market (e.g. discount food retailer).
- **Product/product line specialist**. The organization focuses on a single product type or product line. Value is derived from the specialization in terms of skills, volume and range (e.g. industrial power supplies).

Consistency and the alternative view

The Porter (1980) view of generic strategy supports the need for consistency of approach. The organization needs to adopt a definite generic strategy. Attempting to mix the above strategies, within a defined market place, may result in failing to achieve the potential benefits and result in the organization being 'stuck in the middle' of either low cost, differentiated or focused strategies. Figure 8.3 illustrates this.

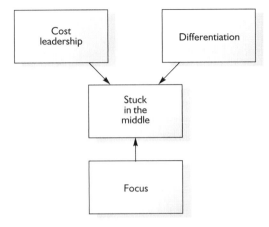

Figure 8.3 Inconsistent strategy

Illustrative Example 8.1: SimplyOrg@nic Food Company Ltd – A niche 'e-tailor'

The food retailing business is highly competitive, with large supermarket chains (e.g. Tesco) dominating the market place. However, potential exists for specialist retailers. The SimplyOrg@nic Food Company stocks a range of over 1500 organic products. These include fruit and vegetables, meat, fish, wine and beer, groceries, dairy and infant products. Telephone and internet home shopping allow easy ordering, with products delivered to UK customers before noon on a day of their choice. The company has recently expanded its organic range to cover non-food products – gifts, fabrics and home care items.

While the large supermarket chains offer a range of organic goods, they operate on a broad retail basis as opposed to SimplyOrg@nic's specific focus. As a home shopping 'e-tailer' – a dot.com company selling to the general public – focusing on organic goods, the potential exists to create and sustain competitive advantage.

Porter's concept of competitive advantage advocates pursuing one generic strategy and thus avoiding a low profit 'stuck-in-the-middle' position. However, alternative views exist. The adoption of common production, quality, marketing and management philosophies by industry competitors may mean that effective differentiation or absolute cost leadership is rarely achieved. Additionally, what managers are not concerned with controlling costs? Therefore differentiation strategies need a cost focus. It is also possible to follow 'hybrid strategies' aiming to offer added value and lower cost. Indeed, Fulmer and Goodwin (1988) point out that the two strategies (cost leadership and differentiation) are not mutually exclusive. For instance, total quality management programmes have resulted in superior quality and cost reductions.

The reality of modern business is that many successful organizations are 'stuck in the middle' within their competitive environments. This is not to decry the importance of establishing competitive advantage and consistency of approach. It merely serves to illustrate the competitive nature of modern business and the importance of uncovering and optimizing all available sources of competitive advantage. It is a question of how best to add value within the context of the strategic business environment.

Identifying sources of competitive advantage

Once the generic strategy is understood, it is possible to consider how it can be translated into specific competitive advantage. A prerequisite to competitive advantage is sustainability. The organization must be able to sustain its competitive advantage over the long term. In order to be sustainable the competitive advantage must be:

- **Relevant**. It must be appropriate to current and future market needs. Additionally, it must be relevant to the organization – achievable within the available resource base.
- **Defensible**. There must be barriers to replication, otherwise success will simply be duplicated by competitors. Such barriers tend to be: (i) *asset based* – tangible factors controlled by the organization, such as location, plant and machinery, brands and finance; (ii) *skills based* – the skills and resources required to make optimum use of the assets, such as quality management, brand development, product design and IT skills.

Clearly competitive advantage must be appropriate to the strategic nature of the industry. An interesting template that evaluates the strategic competitive environment has been developed by the Boston Consultancy Group (Hooley *et al.*, 1998). This matrix identifies four types of industry (see Figure 8.4). The industries are classified in terms of: (i) size of competitive advantage, and (ii) number of possible ways to achieve advantage.

- **Stalemate industries**. Here the potential for competitive advantage is limited. Advantages are small and only a few approaches exist to achieving these advantages. Technological advances are commonly adopted by all industry 'players' and we see rapid convergence in product design/performance. Such industries tend to be mature, highly competitive and often akin to commodity-type products

Size of advantage

Figure 8.4 BCG strategic advantage matrix

where price is the key buying criterion (e.g. manufacturing desktop computers).

- **Volume industries**. Here few but highly significant advantages exist. These industries are often capital intensive and are dominated by a few large players who achieve economies of scale (e.g. volume car manufacture).

- **Fragmented industries**. The market's needs are less well defined and numerous ways exist to gain advantage. The industry is often well suited to niche players and profitability may not be linked directly to size. Commonly, organizations grow by offering a range of niche products to different segments – a multi-segmentation strategy (e.g. computer software).

- **Specialized industries**. The potential advantage of differentiation is considerable and numerous ways exist to achieve this advantage. Profitability and size are not automatically related. Such industries include those developing customized solutions to specific problems (e.g. management consultancy) and firms involved in the development/application of innovative technology (e.g. biomedical engineering).

Understanding generic strategies and the application of competitive advantage to the business environment are fundamental to success.

Source of competitive advantage	Examples
1 Actual product performance	Robust, economic, easy to use
2 Perception of product	Brand image, product positioning
3 Low cost operations	Location, buying power
4 Legal advantage	Patents, contracts and copyright
5 Alliances and relationships	Networking, procurement and joint ventures
6 Superior skills	Database management, design skills
7 Flexibility	Developing customized solutions
8 Attitude	Aggressive selling, tough negotiation

Figure 8.5 Sources of competitive advantage (*Source*: Adapted from Davidson, 1997)

Davidson (1997) offers an alternative view and states that competitive advantage is achieved:

> . . . *whenever you do something better than competitors. If that something is important to consumers, or if a number of small advantages can be combined, you have an exploitable competitive advantage.*

Instinctively, this view appeals to the industry practitioner. The most potent sources of competitive advantage can be summarized as shown in Figure 8.5.

Such advantages are underpinned by the previously summarized generic sources of competitive advantage (Porter, 1980) and Figure 8.6 illustrates this concept.

Figure 8.6 Generic strategy and potential competitive advantage

Experience and value effects

Perhaps it is to state the obvious to say experience and ability to create value are closely linked and a major factor in successful marketing strategy. In considering these factors, two useful models are presented here.

The experience curve denotes a pattern of decreasing cost as a result of cumulative experience of carrying out an activity or function. Essentially, it shows how learning effects (repetition and accumulated knowledge) can be combined with volume effects (economy of scale) to derive optimum benefits (see Figure 8.7). With experience, the organization should produce better and lower cost products. The main influence of experience effects has been to promote a high volume/low cost philosophy aiming at a reduction in unit cost. However, in today's competitive business world, organizations cannot simply rely on a 'big is beautiful' strategy based on economy of scale and market share. It is vital to recognize the importance of learning effects on factors such as product quality and service levels. Such factors hold the key to future success and greatly influence the ability to 'add value' to product offerings.

Eventually, cost and learning effects will display diminishing returns and an optimum level is reached. However, the process never stops. The advent of new technologies may mark a shift in experience and offer new challenges. For example, the large monolithic market leader could be in danger as newer, more forward-thinking com-

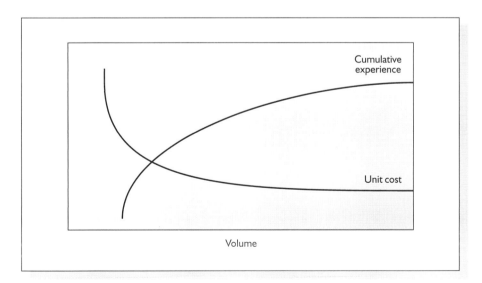

Figure 8.7 Experience curve

petitors readily embrace new technology and the subsequent benefits it brings to today's business environment.

The concept of a **value chain**, developed by Porter (1980), categorizes the organization as a series of processes generating value for customers and other stakeholders. By examining each value-creating activity, it is possible to identify sources of potential cost leadership and differentiation.

The value chain (Figure 8.8) splits activities into: (i) **primary activities** – in-bound logistics, operations, outward logistics, marketing/sales and service, and (ii) **secondary activities** – infrastructure, human resource management, technology development and procurement. These secondary activities take place in order to support the primary activities. For example, the firm's infrastructure (e.g. management, finance and buildings) serves to support the five primary functions. While each activity generates 'value', the linkages between the activities are critical. Consider the interface between in-bound logistics and operations. A just-in-time logistics system, supported by computerized stock ordering (technology development – secondary activity) could reduce stock costs and enhance the quality of products manufactured in the operations phase of the chain, thus enhancing the overall value generated by the process. The value generated is shown as the 'margin of value' in Figure 8.8.

The value chain provides an additional framework to analyse competitive advantage. It helps identify the key skills, processes and linkages required to generate success. Additionally, the concept can link organizations together. A series of value chains can be analysed as one overall process. For example, the value chains of a component manufacturer and equipment manufacturer could be merged into one system, with common support activities. This could have the effect of

Secondary activities

Primary activities

Figure 8.8 The value chain (*Source*: Porter, 1980)

reducing overall costs and improving co-ordination between the companies.

Industry position

Clearly, strategy formulation must consider the position held within a given industry and the organization's resource base relative to competitors. Successful strategy amounts to implementing plans that meet customer need while effectively dealing with rival competitors. This section examines strategies relative to the competition.

Competitive marketing strategy draws heavily on military strategy. Indeed, many strategic principles can be traced to the analogy of the market place as a battlefield with competitors as enemy forces. It could be argued that Sun Tsu's *The Art of War* (a classic work defining ancient military tactics and philosophy) provides as much of an insight into the principles of modern-day strategic marketing as it does to military campaigns.

Market position

The position of the organization (or product) within a given market will clearly influence the strategic options available. For example, when comparing the market leader with a smaller 'niche' competitor, it is likely that marked differences exist in aims, capabilities and resources. When considering a market, competitors break down into four general categories: market leaders, market challengers, market followers and market nichers. Each will be examined in turn.

Market leaders

A market leader is dominant within the given industry or segment. This dominance is normally due to market share. However, some organizations may achieve 'leadership' via innovation or technical expertise. Additionally, the organization may only be a leader in a given segment (e.g. geographic area). Be careful how the term 'market' is defined when talking about market leaders.

The market leader will be a constant target for aggressive competitors and must remain vigilant and proactive. Common strategies include:

- **Expanding the market**. If the total market expands, the leader tends to gain the largest share of this expansion. This can be achieved by finding new users or new uses for the products and by encouraging more use by existing customers.

- **Offensive strategy**. By aggressively pursuing market share, the fight is taken to the competitors.
- **Defensive strategy**. Equally, it is important to protect your existing customer base and ensure that market share is retained.

Offensive and defensive strategies are applicable to all industry 'players' not just market leaders. These strategies are discussed more fully in the next section.

Market challengers

Market challengers will seek confrontation and aggressively pursue market share. Often, such organizations are large and well resourced. They are seeking market leadership and present a long-term sustained challenge to the current leader.

Strategies available to challengers include:

- **Selective targeting**. The challenger can target specific competitors. It may attack smaller (perhaps regional) competitors or firms that are equivalent in size and resources. Basically, the challenger is looking to attack weaker competitors – those failing to satisfy the customer in some way, or those under-financed or under-resourced. By picking off weaker competitors, challengers enhance their market position.
- **Attack the leader**. The challenger can directly challenge the dominant player. This is often a long-term war of attrition and it is unlikely that market leadership will change overnight. Commonly, direct attacks sustained over time erode market share gradually.

Market follower

Being in second, third or even further down the rankings within an industry may still be an attractive position. Market followers tend to 'shadow' the market leader as opposed to challenge them, unless there is a high degree of certainty that a challenge will be successful – they follow the leader. In simple terms, followers duplicate (to a greater or lesser degree) the actions and product offerings of the bigger industry players and avoid 'rocking the boat'.

Typical strategies are:

- **Duplication**. The product offering is duplicated in every possible way, even down to the packaging and promotion. Such strategies are potentially open to legal challenge in the areas of patents and copyright.

- **Adaptation**. Here we adapt the basic product offering. If we can improve on the concept, then potential exists to differentiate ourselves. For example, we may sell the same or similar products but have a reputation for higher levels of customer service.

Market niche

Niche players focus on specific market segments. They are more specialized in nature and seek to gain competitive advantage by adding value in some way appropriate to specific target groups.

Focus strategies, adopted by niche players were outlined earlier in this chapter in the section on Focus (p. 148) and commonly involve geographic, end-user or product line specialization.

Offensive and defensive strategies

Two fundamentals exist in the battle for market share – the ability to gain market share and being able to retain existing market share. To achieve these objectives, organizations need offensive (attacking) and defensive strategies.

Kotler *et al*. (1999) identify a number of attacking and defensive strategies. Such strategies are used in combination by organizations in order to compete successfully in the modern business world.

Offensive strategies, designed primarily to gain market share, are shown in Figure 8.9. Each is summarized in turn here.

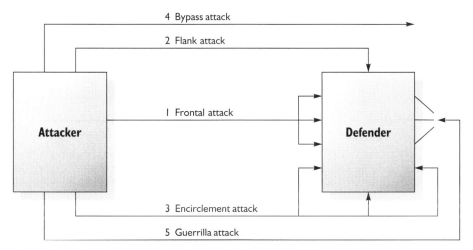

Figure 8.9 Attacking strategies (*Source*: Kotler *et al*., 1999)

1 **Frontal attack**. This is an all-out attack on a competitor. Generally, such an attack requires a sustained effort. Attackers must be certain they have the resources to endure a long hard struggle and survive potentially heavy initial losses. They are likely to face a well-established competitor with broadly the same product offering. Therefore, the attacker needs a clearly defined advantage. For example, the attacker may have a cost advantage or its brands may be perceived more positively.

2 **Flank attack**. This draws on the analogy of the battlefield, where the flanks were always the weakest point of any army. This can be the case in the business world and 'flanking' is achieved by attacking selective market segments where the competitor is relatively weak. By concentrating resources on narrow areas it is possible to achieve superiority. The key to success is to identify worthwhile, under-served segments. For example, a computer manufacturer may feel a rival only offers a limited, and somewhat dated, range of laptop computers. This could be a weak 'flank' vulnerable to attack.

3 **Encirclement attack**. Here we aim to offer a range of products that effectively encircle the competitor. Each of these products will tend to stress a different attribute and leave the competitor's product facing a series of more focused rivals. For example, in marketing soap powder, the market leader could be encircled by three rival products each stressing a different attribute: cleaning power, low cost and environmentally friendly. The combined effect of the three rivals is to undermine the positioning of the market leader.

   One obvious danger of this strategy is that it leads to a proliferation of products. These may compete with each other and are likely to drive up costs.

4 **Bypass attack**. This is perhaps more a policy of avoidance than attack. The attacker moves into areas where competitors are not active. This may involve targeting different geographic areas, applying new technologies or developing new distribution systems. For example, a tour operator could bypass existing retail distribution outlets and sell direct to the public via mail-order.

5 **Guerrilla attack**. Tactical (short-term) marketing initiatives are used to gradually weaken the opposition. Sudden price cuts, bursts of promotional activity or other such tactics are used to create product awareness and slowly erode market share. Such attacks may be a precursor to a longer, more sustained attack. Additionally, guerrilla attacks are not restricted to marketing – legal action such as law suits can be used to harass and restrict competitors. The key to success is the unpredictability of such attacks and their ability to destroy morale and deplete resources, such as management time or finance.

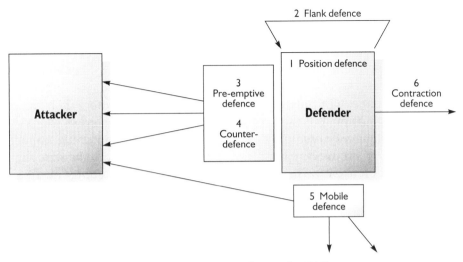

Figure 8.10 Defensive strategies (*Source*: Kotler *et al.*, 1999)

It is true to say that for every offensive move a defensive counter exists. Indeed, the 'backbone' of any marketing strategy must be to maintain market share. Regardless of market position, firms must continually defend their current business against competitors. A strong defence should deter, as well as repel, rivals and allow the organization to build on its strengths. Common defensive strategies are summarized by Kotler *et al.* (1999) in Figure 8.10.

1 **Position defence**. A position defence aims to strengthen the current position and shut out the competition. The aim is to use the distinct competencies and assets of the organization to build an unassailable

---

Illustrative Example 8.2: Marks & Spencer's new style lingerie stores

---

Marks & Spencer aims to maintain its market position within the lingerie sector. By way of a position defence, it plans to offer a value-added product in the women's lingerie market. M&S will open a number of smaller specialist outlets which will only sell ladies' underwear. The stores will be branded as 'msl' (short for M&S Lingerie), and have a different retail format – softer lighting, specialist staff, etc. This move aims to strengthen M&S's current position in the market and make the company less vulnerable to specialist operators and 'designer-label' products. Thus, 'msl' displays the classic characteristic of a position defence.

---

position in the market place. If the defending firm can offer a differentiated, value-added product to customers its market position will be maintained, if not enhanced. Defending a market position is often dependent on brand management, service levels and distribution.

2 **Flank defence**. Not only do organizations need to protect their main areas of operation, but they must also protect any weak spots (flanks). Firstly, managers must identify weak areas and the potential impact of an 'attack' on the core business. Secondly, they need to be sure that the flank defence is sustainable. For example, a food retailer may see its flank as frozen products. Here it competes with specialist frozen food retailers. The flank could be protected by maintaining several 'loss leader' (sold at below cost) products.

3 **Pre-emptive defence**. This involves striking at potential competitors before they attack you. The aim is to pre-empt their actions and reduce the potential competitive threat. This may involve using, or threatening to use, the attacking strategies (e.g. guerrilla attack) shown in Figure 8.9. Large, powerful 'players' deter competitors by routinely threatening, but seldom actioning, price cuts or increased promotional expenditure. They warn others to back off.

4 **Counter-defence**. When attacked, most organizations will respond with a counter-attack. The counter-attack may be immediate or a more considered response might be made once the situation has settled down. By nature, counter-defences are reactive, and if the position defence is strong enough no additional counter may be necessary. For example, a strong well-established brand loyalty may see off a price-cutting competitor.

5 **Mobile defence**. A mobile defence involves a flexible and adaptive response, allowing the defender to switch into new areas of interest as threats or opportunities materialize. It is achieved by broadening current markets or by diversifying into unrelated activities. To illustrate, an insurance company may broaden the range of financial services offered to customers or diversify into areas such as estate agency and property management. The key is to build a strategic presence in a range of lucrative areas/segments.

6 **Contraction defence**. It may prove impossible to defend all operational activities. Therefore, a selective strategic withdrawal could be the best option. By sacrificing some activities, resources are freed to defend core activities. For example, consider a computer company. It could withdraw from the high volume/low margin personal computer market and focus on more profitable areas, such as maintenance and software development.

Product and market strategies

Product/market strategies are detailed in nature. They address the specific market impact of a product or product line. This section examines three concepts useful in formulating such strategies: the product/market matrix, PIMS (product impact of market strategy) analysis and the product life cycle (PLC).

Product/market matrix

Ansoff (1975) developed a policy/market matrix (or 'Ansoff matrix') which provides a useful linkage between products and markets. The matrix (Figure 8.11) considers four combinations of product and market. Each combination suggests a growth strategy.

The organization's potential is determined by the combination of current and new products within current and new markets. Additionally, the element of risk must be considered. As organizations move away from existing markets and products the potential risk factors increase.

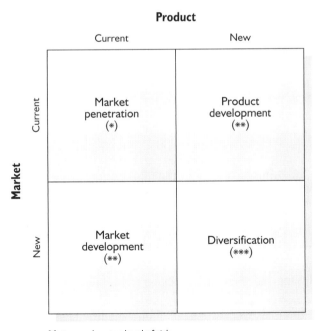

Note: * denotes level of risk

Figure 8.11 Product/market matrix

- **Market penetration**. The aim is to increase sales of existing products in current markets. An aggressive marketing drive, via factors such as competitive pricing, sales promotion or advertising, can expand the share of an existing market. Dealing with familiar customers and products is low risk and provides a starting point to planned growth. However, the potential for market penetration is often limited and strategic plans may require additional options to be pursued.
- **Market development**. Market development aims to find new markets for existing products. This could involve new geographic markets (e.g. exporting), adding distribution channels or finding new market segments. For example, a manufacturer of sports clothing may try to position its products as fashion items and target a different set of retailers.
- **Product development**. Organizations must update their product portfolio to remain competitive. Ideally, a balanced product portfolio should exist, with established products generating funds for product development.
- **Diversification**. This involves moving beyond existing areas of operation and actively seeking involvement in unfamiliar activities. Diversification can be related – having linkages to existing activities – or unrelated – venturing into totally new activities. While unrelated diversification may spread risk, it can be difficult to achieve.

The product/market matrix can be expanded to consider the degree to which new activities are related or unrelated (Figure 8.12) to the core business. As previously stated, it is more difficult to achieve success in unrelated activities. Hence, unrelated diversification of product and/or markets is often tackled via joint ventures, mergers and acquisitions (see Chapter 11).

Figure 8.12 Expanded product/market matrix

Illustrative Example 8.3: Nike – targeting the women's market

Nike recognizes the global importance of the women's sports market. In order to achieve a dominant position in this market, Nike has announced the formation of a new unit. The unit combines design, manufacturing and sales and specifically aims to increase the company's share of the international women's sportswear market.

Nike's strategy can be considered in terms of the 'Ansoff matrix'. The company appears to be looking at a process of market penetration and product development. See Figure 8.11 – The product/market matrix.

PIMS analysis

Many influential marketing studies have examined the link between profit and marketing strategy. These PIMS (profit impact of market strategy) studies aimed to identify the key drivers of profitability and have recognized the importance of market share as such a driver. Generally speaking, profits will increase in line with relative market share. This relationship (Figure 8.13) has influenced marketing thinking, promoting actions aimed at increasing market share as a route to profitability. While such a relationship is often true, it is not universal, and some industries display a 'V-shaped' relationship. Here, profitability

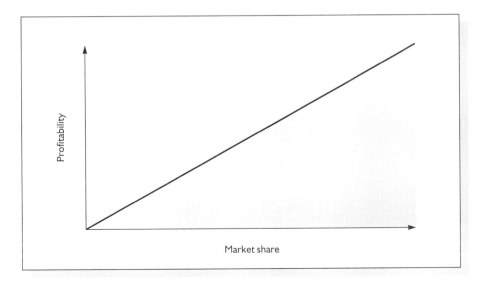

Figure 8.13 Profit related to market share

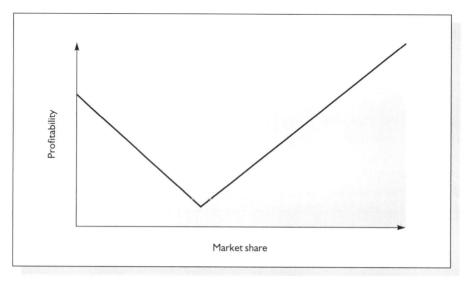

Figure 8.14 'V-shaped' profit/market share relationship

can initially fall until a critical mass, in terms of market share, is reached. The effect of the 'V-curve' is polarization – industries with small niche players and large dominant companies. Medium-sized firms see profits fall until critical mass is reached. This makes it very difficult for small/ medium companies to grow. Figure 8.14 shows the relationship.

Clearly, the marketing strategist must consider the nature of these relationships and not blindly pursue market share. It should be possible to determine the optimum market share/profitability position.

The product life cycle

The product life cycle (PLC) has been described as the most quoted but least understood concept in marketing. Any strategy considering products and markets will be influenced by the PLC. Organizations are advised to ensure that they fully understand the product life cycle for their products *and* industry segments.

The basic concept (Figure 8.15) can be summarized as products passing through four stages: introduction, growth, maturity and decline. Sales will vary with each phase of the life cycle.

- **Introduction**
  It takes time for sales to grow and the introductory phase sees awareness and distribution of the product increasing. Some organizations will specialize in innovation and aim to consistently introduce

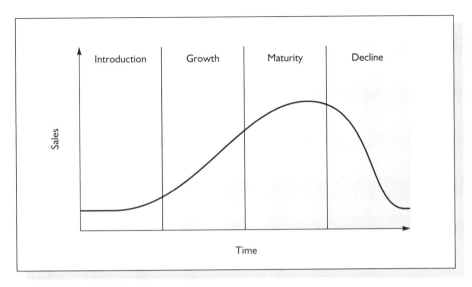

Figure 8.15 Product life cycle

new products to the market place. Common strategies include: (i)
skimming, where a high price level is set initially, in order to
capitalize on the product's introduction and optimize financial
benefit in the short term or (ii) **penetration**, with pricing being used
to encourage use and build market share over time.

● **Growth**
This phase sees a rapid increase in sales. Additionally, competition
begins to increase and it is likely that prices will be static, or fall, in
real terms. The growth stage sees the product being offered to more
market segments, increasing distribution and the development of
product variations.

● **Maturity**
Here product sales peak and settle at a stable level. This is normally
the longest phase of the PLC, with organizations experiencing some
reduction in profit level. This is due to the intense competition
common in mature markets. As no natural growth exists, market
share is keenly contested and marketing expenditure is increased.
Marketers may try to expand their potential customer base by
encouraging more use or finding new market segments.

● **Decline**
The decline stage can be gradual or rapid. It is possible to turn
around declining products and move them back into the mature
phase of the cycle. The alternative is replacement. A residual demand
will exist, with current users needing parts, services and ongoing
support. Often the decline phase offers a choice: reinvesting (turn

around/replace) or 'harvesting' (maximizing financial returns from the product and limiting expenditure).

To utilize the PLC fully, managers need a detailed understanding of the concept and the following points merit consideration.

- **Industry and product line**. The product life cycle concept can also apply to overall industry sales. Clearly, the PLC for individual product lines needs to be considered in relation to this. For example, if an industry is entering the decline phase of its PLC, it may be unwise to launch new product lines. Currently, high technology industries, such as telecommunications, are in the growth phase. However, individual product lines have very short PLCs as they are rapidly replaced by more advanced technology. Make sure you understand where the industry is in terms of overall PLC and how your portfolio of products fits into this overall pattern.
- **Shape of the PLC**. While the PLC normally conforms to the classic 'S-shaped' curve (see Figure 8.15), it is not always the case. Product life cycles can take different forms. They can display: (i) cyclical/ seasonal trends; (ii) constant demand, where a steady level of sales is reached, or (iii) rapid growth and fall, common to fashion or fad products (see Figure 8.16).
- **Volatility**. Any sales person will tell you that sales levels will fluctuate over time. The reality of the PLC is that sales will vary and the smooth graph shown in most textbooks will in fact display considerable volatility. This makes predicting your exact position in the life cycle difficult. Does a fall in sales mean we have reached the point of decline or is it a temporary blip? Only time will tell.
- **Duration of stages**. Some would argue that the length of each PLC phase is closely related to marketing decisions and not simply a

Figure 8.16 Variation in product life cycle shape

natural cycle. Effective marketing should be able to extend and sustain the growth or maturity of a product offering. Equally, ineffective marketing would hasten its decline.

Strategic wear-out

The adage 'nothing lasts for ever' is certainly true of marketing strategy. Care must be taken to avoid strategic wear-out. This occurs when the organization no longer meets customer needs and the pursued strategy is surpassed by competitors. Davidson (1997) summarizes the causes of strategic wear-out as follows:

1 Changes in customer requirements.
2 Changes in distribution systems.
3 Innovation by competitors.
4 Poor control of company costs.
5 Lack of consistent investment.
6 Ill-advised changes in successful strategy.

Future business requires active steps to ensure that the organization's strategy does not 'wear out' and the role of strategy formulation is to develop/maintain a marketing orientation. This is based on the premise of defining customer need and prospering through customer satisfaction and loyalty. Sound general and financial management should underpin this orientation and the entire corporate focus should relate to the key asset of any business – customers.

Difficult market conditions

Marketing strategy is often linked to a premise of favourable market conditions. For example, strategies tend to work well when we are experiencing incremental growth – the market demand grows annually. However, many industries (arguably the majority of industries) are now experiencing static or declining demand. Such markets are hostile in nature and feature factors such as volatility, overcapacity, price discounting, reduced profit margins and 'downsizing'.

Given these conditions, Aaker (1995) advocates a number of strategic options for declining and/or hostile markets:

● **Growth generation**. Can we revitalize the industry by finding growth? This could be possible via: (i) encouraging existing users to increase usage; (ii) developing new markets for our products, and (iii) finding new applications for existing products or technologies/skills. The Ansoff matrix (see Figure 8.11) provides a useful analytical framework for this purpose.

Illustrative Example 8.4: Apple iMAC

Despite increasing levels of sales, the PC market has proved highly hostile. The market has massive price discounting, domination by software suppliers, as opposed to hardware manufacturers, and an increasing number of global competitors. Despite such market conditions prevailing, Apple's iMAC PC went on to become the company's fastest selling product. iMAC achieved a growth rate of over 280 per cent in the UK home market and heralded a dynamic turnaround in the company's fortunes. The product presented a fresh and innovative challenge to existing, slow, boringly styled, difficult to use Windows-based PCs. The product made a virtue of consumer benefits such as speed, ease of use and simplicity. It helped widen the potential user base for Apple products and attract back the software developers so essential to future innovations.

- **Survival**. Organizations can survive by effectively managing cost and clearly signalling their commitment to the industry and its customers. Obviously, there is a need to manage cost structures, with experience effects and economy of scale becoming vital. Organizations may rationalize their product portfolios and focus on larger, more profitable customers. Conversely, perhaps correctly, organizations may actually expand their product range, aiming to cover the maximum number of customers by offering a wide range of price points. We may witness takeovers, mergers and acquisitions, as organizations aim to reduce cost and generate economies of scale. A portfolio approach can be taken, with 'cash cows' supporting operations/products which are currently struggling but are deemed to have long-term potential. A useful strategic option is to reduce industry exit barriers by selectively buying out elements of a competitor's current business. For example, we could take over their commitment to supply spare parts and maintain existing products. This 'shake-out' inevitably leaves the industry with fewer but larger competitors.
- **Exit strategy**. If business conditions are particularly unfavourable, prudence may dictate that we withdraw from the industry. Such action will involve overcoming exit barriers such as the costs associated with downsizing (redundancy, legal costs of breaking contracts, etc.) and handling commitments to existing customers. Exit

strategy can be rapid – withdrawing immediately – or a slow, phased withdrawal with activities being gradually run down. However, exiting a market may have repercussions for other activities and products, as it affects goodwill and customer confidence.

Summary

Strategy formulation offers alternative methods of achieving objectives. The process has three components: (i) competitive advantage; (ii) industry position, and (iii) product/market strategies. The importance of having constant and sustainable strategies cannot be underestimated.

Three generic (fundamental) strategies exist – cost leadership, differentiation and a focused approach. Porter (1980) stresses the importance of adopting one generic source of competitive advantage and thus avoiding the strategic equivalent of being 'stuck in the middle'. These strategies can be expanded upon to generate specific sources of competitive advantage. For example, superior products, perceived advantage or scale of operation are all exploitable competitive advantages. Additionally, it is important to understand the effects of experience curves and value chains within your industry. The primary and secondary activities of a value chain, coupled with experience effects, should support the organization's strategic thrust.

Companies need to examine their position within the market place. They can occupy the role of market leader, challenger, follower or niche player. Marketing strategy needs to be appropriate to the position occupied, relative ambition and resource base. All organizations actively pursue offensive and defensive strategies. The need exists to protect your core business and your flanks (weak areas), while taking the fight to competitors via appropriate offensive options (e.g. bypass or guerrilla attacks).

Ansoff's product/market matrix provides a useful summation of product and market strategies. Organizations can consider market penetration, market development, product development or diversification as key marketing initiatives. Much product/market strategy focuses on gaining market share. PIMS analysis has proved highly influential and has linked market share to profitability. While this relationship is often true, market share should not be blindly chased as the relationship is not universally applicable.

Additionally, an awareness of the product life cycle (PLC) is important. The strategist needs to understand the PLC shape and how the marketing mix varies in the introduction, growth, maturity and decline phases.

Organizations need to be watchful and avoid the pitfall of strategic wear-out and strategies need to address hostile and declining markets.

References

Aaker, D., *Strategic Market Management*, 4th edition, Wiley, 1995
Ansoff, I., 'Strategies for diversification', *Harvard Business Review*, 25(5), pp. 113–125, 1975
Davidson, H., *Even More Offensive Marketing*, Penguin, 1997
Fulmer, W. and Goodwin, J., 'Differentiation: Being with the customer', *Business Horizons*, 31(5), 1988
Hooley, G., Saunders, J. and Piercy, N., *Marketing Strategy & Competitive Position*, 2nd edition, Prentice Hall, 1998
Kotler, P., Armsrong, G., Saunders, J. and Wong, V., *Principles of Marketing*, 2nd edition, Prentice Hall, 1999
Porter, M., *Competitive Strategy: Techniques for Analysing Industries and Competitors*, Free Press, 1980

Further Reading

Aaker, D., *Strategic Market Management*, 4th edition, Chapter 14, Wiley, 1995
Wilson, R. and Gilligan, C., *Strategic Marketing Management*, 2nd edition, Chapters 9 and 10, Butterworth-Heinemann, 1998

Targeting, positioning and brand strategy

About this chapter

The subject of targeting and positioning builds on the segmentation techniques that were covered in Chapter 4. This chapter now explores criteria by which the attractiveness of a market segment can be judged. The targeting process is then examined before a discussion on a range of product positioning techniques is undertaken. Central to this discussion is the issue of brand strategy.

Introduction

At a fundamental level marketing strategy is about markets and products. Organizations are primarily making decisions about which markets to operate in and which products/services to offer to those markets. Once those essential decisions have been taken the company then has to decide on what basis it is going to compete in that chosen market. Segmentation is therefore at the heart of strategic marketing decision making. In essence it is a strategic rather than an operational issue and has to be treated as such.

The previous chapters have been concerned with establishing the organization's strategic intent and formulating the organization's overall strategic approach. Initially any organization has to identify how it can, in general, gain competitive advantage. The stage that we will now explore is concerned with creating a specific competitive position. The first crucial step is to decide in which specific market segments to operate. Chapter 4 examined the criteria that can be used to identify discrete segments within a market. Once segments have been identified they then have to be evaluated in order that an organization can decide which particular segments it should serve. Target marketing, or targeting, is the common term for this process.

Once target markets have been chosen an organization then has to decide how it wishes to compete. What differential advantage can it create that will allow the company's product or service to hold a distinctive place in the chosen market segment? This process is normally called positioning. Targeting and positioning are critical processes that require the attention of senior management.

Evaluating market segments

To evaluate different market segments effectively it is necessary to systematically review two issues: the market attractiveness of the competing segments and the organization's comparative ability to address the needs of that segment. There are a number of criteria that can be used to judge the attractiveness of a market segment. These fall under three broad headings: market factors, the nature of competition and the wider environmental factors. At this point it is important to stress that marketers need to recognize that many of the criteria that can be used to evaluate the attractiveness of a market segment are qualitative rather than quantitative in nature. This has implications for the manner in which the process is managed. We will return to this topic later in the chapter. Firstly we need to review the criteria themselves.

Market factors

When assessing market attractiveness the particular features of a market will affect any evaluation.

- **Segment size**. A large segment will generally have greater sales potential. This in itself will make it more attractive but it may also offer the potential of gaining economies of scale because of the larger volumes involved. Large segments with their potentially larger sales can justify the higher investments that may be necessary for organizations wishing to operate within them. However, large segments may not always be the most attractive. Large segments can be more competitive as their very size will attract other companies into them. Smaller organizations may not have the resources to address a large market and therefore may find smaller segments more appropriate for their attention.

- **Segment rate of growth (measured in terms of real revenue growth after inflation)**. Segments that are growing are normally seen as being more attractive than segments where growth has peaked or even begun to decline. Segments in growth are seen as having a longer-term potential and therefore justify any investment necessary. Once again, however, these segments are likely to be more competitive as other companies also recognize their potential.
- **Segment profitability**. What is the total profitability of the segment? If you are already operating in this segment it is not your organization's profitability alone that should be reviewed. In order that all segments are evaluated on a consistent basis it is the profitability of all companies operating in the segment that should be calculated. This will have to be an estimate based on analysing competitors' activities.
- **Customer price sensitivity**. Segments where consumers have low price sensitivity are likely to be more attractive as higher profit margins can be gained. Consumers will be more concerned about quality and service rather than price alone. Price sensitive segments are more susceptible to price competition, which leads to lower margins.
- **Stage of industry life cycle**. Entering a segment that is in the early stages of an industry's life cycle offers the advantages of potentially high growth in the future. In the early stages there are also likely to be fewer competitors. However, the early stages of the industry life cycle are characterized by the need for high investment in new plant, promotional activities and securing distribution channels. This occurs at a time when there may be only modest sales revenue. There will be a drain on cash into the new area of business that the company has to be able to fund. Businesses that are more interested in cash generation or profits in the short term may consider mature markets more favourable. These markets are likely to require a more modest level of investment.
- **Predictability**. The potential value of a market will be easier to predict if it is less prone to disturbance and the possibility of discontinuities. In the long term a predictable market is likely to be more viable (see Chapter 5).
- **Pattern of demand**. The attractiveness of a segment will be affected by any seasonal or other cyclical demand patterns it faces. A large percentage of sales in the gift and card market take place at Christmas in Western countries. An organization has to be able to withstand the cash flow implications of this skewed demand. The same problem occurs in other industry sectors such as travel and tourism.

● **Potential for substitution**. In any market there is the potential for new solutions to be developed that will address consumers' needs. An organization should review markets to establish whether new innovations could be used in the segment. Where substitutions are likely an organization may decide not to enter on the basis that it makes the segment less attractive. If, however, the organisation has the ability to deliver that innovatory approach it may make the segment a prime target as the company has the skills to change the nature of competition to their advantage.

Nature of competition in the target market and the underlying industry structure

● **Quality of competition**. Segments that have weak competition are more attractive than segments where there are strong and aggressive competitors. It is not the number of competitors operating but the nature of their competition that is critical in judging an opportunity.
● **Potential to create a differentiated position**. A segment will be more attractive if it contains unsatisfied customer needs that allow the company to create a differentiated product or service and gain a higher margin by charging a premium price. If it is a commodity market then competition is likely to be driven by price and the segment will be less attractive.
● **Likelihood of new entrants**. Segments that currently have limited competition may appear attractive. However, the potential for other companies to enter this market has to be taken into account.
● **Bargaining power of suppliers**. An organization will be in a stronger negotiating position where there is a range of potential suppliers. If, however, supply is in the hands of a few dominant companies the balance of power in negotiations will lie with the suppliers, making a segment less attractive.
● **Bargaining power of customers**. Customers may be the end customer but they can also be a customer in the channel of distribution, e.g. a major supermarket. If customers are in a strong negotiating position they will try to push suppliers' prices down, reducing margins. A market segment will be less favourable when a few major customers dominate it or the channels of distribution.
● **Barriers to entry into the market segment**. There may be entry barriers to a segment that will reduce its appeal. These can be in the form of patents, the necessity for new specialized plant or machinery, or the need for high promotional expenditure. It may be that the overall level of investment necessary to enter an area successfully may be unrealistic for some companies. These same barriers may also

put off other potential entrants. Therefore if a company calculates that it can overcome these barriers it may be able to enter a segment where there is little direct competition.

- **Barriers to exiting the market segment**. There may be barriers that make exiting a segment difficult. Expensive facilities may have to be built that can only be used in servicing a particular market segment. Therefore withdrawing from this segment would leave expensive plant redundant. Other barriers could include service agreements to provide spare parts to customers for a number of years into the future, or plant and machinery that would be expensive to decommission. Organizations would have to anticipate the potential barriers to exit when they are initially evaluating a segment's attractiveness.

Environmental factors

- **Social**. Social changes can lead to newly emerging segments that are not currently served by any organization. There can be a significant advantage to companies that are the first to move into these areas. Organizations also need to review the impact that any likely changes in social trends will have on a particular segment.
- **Political**. Changes in the political environment can create new segments in a market. The deregulation of the utilities market created several new market segments that organizations could address. The political environment may also make certain segments less attractive. Segments that are located in particular geographic areas may be affected by political instability. There may also be regulatory changes that will affect a sector such as pharmaceuticals.
- **Economic**. Economic trends may make segments more or less attractive. For example, the growing affluence of older people in Western economies is making them a much more attractive group than twenty years ago.
- **Technology**. Technological changes have to be taken into consideration when evaluating a segment. A judgement will have to be made as to whether new entrants will be able to enter a segment competing on a different basis by using technology to create innovative ways of delivering a product or service.
- **Environmental**. Consumers' and governments' concerns about environmental issues have become much more important in recent years. Therefore an evaluation of the environmental issues that may affect an organization's ability to service a segment will have to be considered.

Establishing organizational capability

Companies will not be capable of supplying every attractive segment that is identified. Having analysed a segment's market attractiveness it is then necessary to compare the needs of that group of consumers with the organization's capabilities. An organization's strengths can be judged by analysing its assets and competencies.

Organizational capabilities will be made up of specific assets and competencies. The key areas to identify are where the organization is superior to the competition. A full discussion on identifying corporate assets and competencies is undertaken in Chapter 5.

In summary, assets are organizational attributes, tangible or intangible, that can be utilized to gain advantages in the market (see Figure 9.1).

Obviously assets should not be viewed in isolation – it is also important to establish any competencies that give the organization advantages. The value chain is a useful framework to use to identify these areas of unique competence (see Figure 8.8 in Chapter 8). Key

Scale advantages	■ Market share ■ Relative and absolute media weight ■ Leverage over suppliers	■ International presence ■ Sales/distribution service coverage ■ Specialist skills due to scale
Production processes (Plant, machinery and information systems)	■ Level of contemporary practice ■ Level of flexibility	■ Economies of scale ■ Capacity utilization ■ Unique items
Customer franchises	■ Brand names ■ Brand franchises ■ Databases	■ Customer relationships ■ Unique products/services ■ Patents
Working capital	■ Quantity ■ Ready access	■ Location ■ Access to credit
Sales/distribution service network	■ Coverage ■ Relationships with external distributors	■ Size ■ Quality
Relationships with other organizations	■ Suppliers ■ Financial institutions ■ Joint ventures	■ Joint exploitation of assets (technology or distribution)
Property	■ Type ■ Location	■ Ability to expand ■ Quality

Figure 9.1 Examples of assets that create a competitive advantage (*Source*: Adapted from Davidson, 1997)

competencies may lie in primary activities. These include activities such as in-bound logistics (e.g. inventory control), operations (e.g. manufacturing), out-bound logistics (e.g. global delivery), marketing (e.g. brand development) and service (e.g. installation). Other key competencies may lie in support activities such as procurement, technology development, human resource management and the organization's infrastructure (refer to Chapter 8 for more detail).

When trying to identify these competencies, rather than using the generic value chain it may be more effective to develop a value chain that reflects the specific operations that face a particular business sector. The primary activities for an organization offering management consultancy are outlined in Figure 9.2.

Figure 9.2 The value chain of a management consultancy practice (*Source*: Adapted from Buckley, 1993)

An organization's key competencies, once identified, will normally fall into the areas of marketing, selling or operations (see Figure 9.3).

Strategic alignment of assets and competencies (targeting)

The critical stage in the segmentation process is matching the capabilities of the organization to attractive market segment opportunities. At a largely operational level management analyses organizational assets and competencies to identify the skills and resources available to build low cost or differentiated positions. Where these assets or competencies currently, or with development could, surpass the competition, they form the basis for creating a specific competitive position in a target market. Company capability should always be judged relative to the competition.

Marketing	■ New product development ■ Business analysis ■ Category management ■ Brand extension ■ Brand equity measurement ■ Unique market research techniques ■ Planning skills ■ Database management	■ Advertising development ■ Customer service ■ Marketing process ■ Spending efficiency ■ Customer relationships ■ Customer targeting ■ Testing design
Selling	■ Supply chain management ■ Account management ■ Relationship development ■ Customer service ■ Building partnerships ■ Motivation and control ■ Planning	■ New account development ■ Merchandising ■ Presentation skills ■ Space management ■ Negotiation ■ Pricing and promotion ■ Trade marketing
Operations	■ Motivation and control ■ Process engineering ■ Industrial relations ■ Inventory control ■ Cost management ■ Productivity improvement ■ Planning ■ Health and safety ■ New facility development ■ Management training and development	■ Speed of response ■ Flexibility ■ Total quality management ■ Purchasing ■ Payment systems ■ Capacity utilization ■ Commercialization of new products or services ■ Method of supplier management ■ Property skills ■ Global operation

Figure 9.3 Examples of competencies that create a competitive advantage (*Source*: adapted from Davidson, 1997)

Figure 9.4 illustrates some questions that should be asked when attempting to match assets and competencies with potential market segments (Jobber, 1995).

Overall, the organization has to establish whether entering a particular segment is consistent with its long-term aims and objectives. If not then, no matter how tempting, entering the segment should be resisted. It will only divert company resources and management time away from the core goals of the enterprise.

Once the key areas of a company's capabilities have been identified they can be aligned with the attractive market segments already identified. An organization should enter segments that allow it to exploit current assets and competencies, or that will allow potential capabilities to develop into strengths. This is an area where adapting portfolio models more normally used to evaluate current products or business units can be useful. The Shell directional policy matrix, for

Marketing assets

Does the market segment allow a company to take advantage of its current marketing strengths? Successful situations are more likely to occur where a company's current brand identity, or method of distribution, is consistent with those required to enter the new target market.

Cost advantage

Entering a price sensitive segment would be consistent with the capabilities of an organization that has a low cost base.

Technological strengths

Where the organization has access to superior technology, is its use compatible with the market segment, and will it allow the company to gain any advantage?

Managerial capabilities and commitment

Does the company have the technical and managerial skills necessary to successfully enter a market segment?

Figure 9.4 Examples of assets and competencies matching with potential market segments.

instance, can be adapted to analyse market segment opportunities against corporate strengths. An adapted version of this model is shown in Figure 9.5.

Figure 9.5 Adapted Shell directional policy matrix applied to target market selection (*Source*: Shell, 1975)

Segment attractiveness

Figure 9.6 **Evaluating market segments for an imaginary organization/situation**

Weighted criteria are used as in the traditional usage of the model. In this case a selection of market attractiveness factors, from those discussed earlier, considered relevant in evaluating a particular sector are weighted according to their importance as judged by the organization's management. The same exercise is then undertaken of selecting a range of assets and competencies deemed relevant to this particular sector. These are again weighted. Choosing factors in relation to the specific area being considered ensures that the model is custom-made to the particular situation and organization under review.

Every potential market segment is then evaluated on a rating scale, normally of 1 to 10 (1 = poor, 10 = excellent), on each of the criteria. The overall position of the segment on each axis is established by multiplying the ratings by the weighting given to each factor (see Chapter 5 for full details). The result of such an exercise for an imaginary situation and organization is shown in Figure 9.6.

The most attractive segment is B as it lies in the box that is attractive on the horizontal axis, representing segment attractiveness, and has a strong fit with the company's assets and competencies, as represented on the vertical axis. This segment should be a priority for the company. Segment A is an attractive market but has only an average fit with the organization's assets and competencies. This may have potential and would be a higher priority for the organization than segment E. Segment E has medium attractiveness and medium fit with the organization's assets and competencies and should be selectively managed. The model suggests that targeting segments C and D is likely to be a poor investment.

This example illustrates how an adapted portfolio model can act as a screening device for identifying market segments that should be targeted.

The strategic nature of making target segment choices

However, as has already been stated, segmentation is a strategic process where qualitative and creative judgements have to be taken. Opportunities have to be evaluated on their strategic fit. Not only do the assets and competencies of the organization have to have synergy with a particular market segment, but wider issues have to be considered as well. Opportunities have also to be evaluated on the following somewhat subjective criteria:

- Ability to allow the creation of a sustainable market position.
- Compatibility with the corporate mission.
- Consistency with the organization's values and the culture. Segments that are a radical departure from current practice may challenge the prevailing values in the organization and the established status quo. The new segment may challenge the current power structure within the organization, which will create influential barriers to implementation.
- Ability to provide a focal point for action and future development in the organization.
- Ability to facilitate an innovative approach to market entry.
- Ability of the current organizational structure to service the target market. Does this opportunity lie between two areas of responsibility in the current organizational structure? This may lead to the opportunity never being seriously addressed.
- Compatibility with current internal information flows and reporting lines. Difficulties will arise where a segment does not sit easily with the current data collection or distribution systems. Segments in an innovative area may cause managers problems in terms of how to allocate targets and monitor progress. If this is linked to the problem already discussed under organizational structure, it may complicate issues such as areas of responsibility and reporting lines even further.

Illustrative Example 9.1: Centrica

Centrica's successful acquisition of the Automobile Association (AA) was an essential part of its strategy of building a household services business. Centrica's core business was initially gas distribution but the organization has also developed a Goldfish credit card with a unique loyalty scheme and home insurance services. The attraction of acquiring the AA was its membership of over 9 million. Car owners are still relatively affluent compared with other consumers and they need products such as motor, travel and holiday insurance. In fact the AA has around 2 million insurance customers and a credit card customer base of around 600,000. There is therefore the potential to cross-sell Centrica's products and services. Centrica judged that their assets and competencies have synergy with the AA's group of consumers. However, the AA's membership is spread across a wide range of consumers with different lifestyles and levels of affluence, making the successful achievement of Centrica's strategy more complex.

These factors of compatibility with the internal practices of an organization are likely to prove critical to the successful implementation of a new segmentation strategy. The newly entered segment has to have clear departmental ownership. Reporting lines and information flows have to be able to monitor its progress. In short, individuals within the organization have to embrace wholehearted the development of the new segment or failure will follow no matter how attractive the segment or how well the organization's overt assets and competencies might fit.

A successful selection process will have identified a market segment or segments that are in alignment with the company's assets and competencies and is also compatible with the wider organizational issues.

Positioning

Having selected a target market or markets the organization then has to decide on what basis it will compete in the chosen segment or segments. How best can it combine its assets and competencies to create a distinctive offering in the market? This has to be done in such a way that consumers can allocate a specific position to the company's product or service within the market, relative to other products. Consumers have to cope with a huge amount of product information. Consumers will position a product in their mind in relation to other products on the market based on their perception of the key attributes it contains. Consumers will see the key

Illustrative Example 9.2: The British Army

Early in 2000 the British Army launched a high-profile recruitment campaign, through a promotion called Operation Kenya. This promotion was fronted by the boxing world champion 'Prince' Naseem Hamed and a famous female UK television star Tamzin Outhwaite. Operation Kenya offered applicants the chance to win a week's training in Kenya with the King's Regiment. Joining the military is now more attractive than in the past as training is provided for 104 different careers within the Army and recruits are no longer required to join for 22 years of service as was once the case. Nevertheless, in order to maintain its forces at the current level of 109,000 the Army needs to enlist 15,000 new soldiers every year. The key age group the Army recruits from is 16–25 and the organization is therefore also promoting itself online. Individuals in this demographic group are heavy users of the internet. In 1999 between 40 per cent and 50 per cent of new recruits were attracted initially via the Army's internet site.

However, women make up just 7.7 per cent of the British Army and ethnic minorities account for an even smaller percentage of around 3 per cent. The Army has decided to target these segments more directly. Recent promotional activity has targeted females, highlighting the fact that 74 per cent of the careers in the Army are open to women. Ethnic minorities are being approached through adverts in the leading black newspaper *The Voice*.

attributes of Volvo as safety and durability. BMW's main attributes are based on performance, hence the 'The Ultimate Driving Machine' advertising slogan. When consumers consider the car market these two companies' products will be positioned relative to each other based on these perceptions. Companies can attempt to associate various qualities with their product as a way to help shape consumers' perceptions of their position in the market. A brand can be positioned using a range of associations (Kotler *et al.*, 1996):

- **Product attributes**. Heinz positions it products on the attributes of no artificial colouring, flavouring or preservatives
- **Product benefits**. Volvo positions itself using the product benefits of safety and durability.
- **Usage occasions**. The convenience store SPAR eight-till-late shops are positioned on the usage occasion. Customers use the shops when they need to shop out of normal hours or near to their homes. Kit Kat ('Have a break, have a Kit Kat') links the brand to tea and coffee breaks in the UK market.

- **Users**. Ecocover cleaning products are positioned as environmentally friendly products for the green customer.
- **Activities**. Lucozade is positioned as an isotonic drink for sporting activities.
- **Personality**. Harley Davidson motorbikes are positioned as a macho product with a free spirit.
- **Origin**. Audi clearly illustrates its German origins in the UK market by the use of the 'Vorsprung durch technik' slogan. The hope is that the product will be linked to the German reputation for quality engineering.
- **Competitors**. Pepsi-Cola is positioned as the choice of the next generation reflecting the fact that in blind tasting tests younger people preferred Pepsi over competitors' offerings.
- **Product class**. Kellogg's Nutrigrain bars are positioned as 'morning bars', a substitute for the traditional breakfast.
- **Symbol**. Esso petrol has used the symbol of the tiger to position itself in the market.

These are the various ingredients that can be used by an organization endeavouring to influence consumers' perceptions of the product offering. Companies have to decide which of these they can use and, more importantly, how they wish to position their product in the market *vis-à-vis* the competing options.

Four factors are of critical importance for successful positioning (Jobber, 1995):

- **Credence**. The attributes used to position the product have to be perceived to be credible by the target customers. It would be very difficult for a nuclear power generator to position itself as environmentally friendly.
- **Competitiveness**. The product should offer the consumer benefits which competitors are not supplying. Clairol launched a new shampoo, Herbal Essences, in the USA in 1995 which emphasized the brand's wholesome ingredients. By 1997 this was the fastest growing brand on the market and ranked number two behind Pantene.
- **Consistency**. A consistent message over time is invaluable in helping to establish a position against all the other products and services fighting for a share of the market. An organization that changes its positioning on a regular basis causes confusion in the consumer's mind. This will mean they have an unclear perception of exactly what are the key characteristics of the product.
- **Clarity**. The positioning statement an organization chooses has to create a clearly differentiated position for the product in the minds of the target market. A distinct message such as 'Bread wi' Nowt Taken Out' underlines the wholemeal old-world nature of Allison's bread.

Perceptual mapping

Mapping consumer perceptions can allow an organization to see where it is currently placed compared with competitors' offerings. A simple perceptual map is based upon two axes representing key attributes in a particular market. These attributes are identified though market research and are determined by consumers' perceptions of the important factors in a market. This could, for example, be price and quality, or style and performance, or a range of other issues. Products/companies, or more particularly brands, can then be placed according to their position on these attributes (see Figure 9.7).

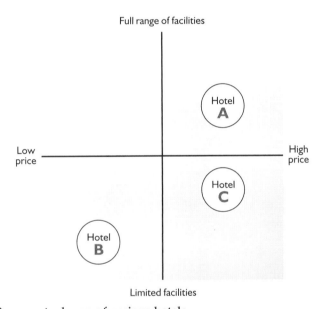

Figure 9.7 A perceptual map of various hotels

In the case of Figure 9.7, in the hotel market the key attributes are deemed to be the price and the facilities. Hotel A on this map is seen as expensive but with a full range of facilities. The Hotel B is perceived to be inexpensive but with limited facilities. Both of these are reasonably consistent offerings. Hotel C, however, is seen as expensive but with an intermediate level of facilities. This position does not offer any unique aspects. There may, of course, be more than two key attributes in a market. Figure 9.7 doesn't map out quality – Hotel C may be seen as having high service quality, for instance. To gain a fuller picture, obviously more than one positioning map can be developed. There are also more sophisticated three-dimensional mapping techniques available for marketers to use.

Through the use of perceptual maps marketers can establish the current situation in a particular market. There will then be a number of alternatives from which to choose.

Positioning alternatives

In a seminal work, Ries and Trout (1981) claim that when considering positioning there are three principal alternatives open to an organization:

- An organization can build on a current position to create a distinctive perception of the brand by consumers. Avis famously uses the 'We Try Harder' slogan to make a virtue out of being number two in the market.
- Having established the attributes that are most important to the consumer, the organization can see if there are any unoccupied positions that are desirable in consumers' minds and therefore viable opportunities. IDV Ltd used this approach when it launched Croft Original Sherry. The key product attributes in the sherry market from a consumer's perspective were the colour and the taste of the product. Consumers favoured a sweet taste, they also perceived that a light coloured sherry was more sophisticated than the traditional, darker coloured sherries (see Figure 9.8). There was at the time no sherry that had a light colour and a sweet taste and yet this combination was highly desirable to consumers. Croft Original

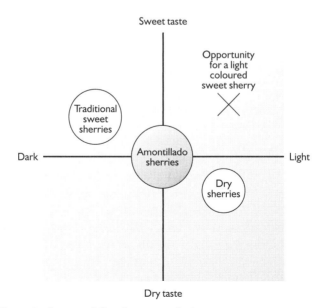

Figure 9.8 Perceptual map of the sherry market

entered the market with this unique positioning and now is the best selling sherry brand in the UK market.

- Due to changes in consumer behaviour, or where perhaps there has been a failure of the original positioning, a third alternative can be considered which is to reposition the brand. Campari has recently been relaunched in an effort to shake off its 1970s image as endorsed by Lorraine Chase. The new repositioning has a more macho feel, and even includes a notorious London underworld character 'Mad' Frankie Fraser in the advert. Both the soft drink Tango and the snack Pot Noodle have successfully been repositioned in recent years. However, repositioning can be difficult to achieve and there are several examples of brands that have been less successful at moving their position. Babycham abandoned the famous deer symbol and the trademark green bottle for a more masculine image in 1993. By May 1997 it had revived both the bottle and the Babycham deer and went back to its original, more female-orientated positioning.

There are alternative views on the correct approach to successful product/brand positioning. One view is that an organization should identify one unique selling proposition (USP) for a product and concentrate purely on that aspect. The whole focus of this approach is to be seen as the brand leader on that key attribute. For example, Gortex fabric is seen as the leading fabric for breathable, waterproof, lightweight clothing material. The most effective USPs are based on quality, service, price, value or advanced technology (Ries and Trout, 1981).

An alternative approach to stressing a USP, based on a functional aspect of the product, is to concentrate on an emotional selling proposition (ESP). The product can be distanced from functionally similar rivals by appealing to unique emotional associations. An example of this is Alpha Romeo's positioning on the heritage and image of the traditional Italian sports car.

Both these approaches stress one key aspect of the product. However, there is a view that more than one factor can be used to position a product. As has been mentioned earlier, Volvo is positioned on safety and the compatible factor of durability. Whichever approach is taken, there are a number of positioning mistakes that can be made by an organization:

- **Underpositioning**. In this situation consumers have only a very limited perception of the brand and are unaware of any distinguishing features.
- **Overpositioning**. Consumers have a perception that the brand is only active in a very focused area, when in fact the brand covers a much broader product range.

- **Confusion**. Consumers have an unclear view of how the brand relates to competitive offerings.

Positioning is concerned with establishing an organization's product in the mind of a customer, in a position relative to other products in the market. Inevitably, therefore, making decisions about branding strategy will be a crucial aspect of this process.

Illustrative Example 9.3: Buzz

In 1996 KLM acquired the budget airline AirUK and formed KLM UK. The aim was to create a middle market brand to sit between premium-price, business-orientated carriers and low-cost, no-frills airlines. The KLM UK brand, however, tended to fall between the two dominant segments in this market and appeared to be underpositioned. In particular, it failed to attract consumers in the budget segment of this market, a sector that has been growing by an average of around 25 per cent a year. As a result KLM decided to target the low-cost market directly by launching a separate brand called Buzz, positioned as a budget offering. This brand aims to compete directly with established airlines such as Ryanair and easyJet. Building on consumers' criticisms of budget carriers advertising low prices that only represent a small proportion of the seats actually on offer, Buzz hopes to create a unique positioning in this sector by presenting itself as a transparent and honest airline with clear and understandable pricing policies.

Creating brand equity

The overall aim of branding decisions is to create an identity for the product or service that is distinctive and also in line with the targeting and positioning decisions already taken. Organizations should strive to produce a brand equity that delivers value to the consumer. This will result in either the customer showing greater brand loyalty or being willing to pay a premium price for the product. Brand equity according to Aaker is 'a set of assets and liabilities linked to a brand's name and symbol that add to or subtract from the value provided by a product or service to a firm and/or that firm's customers' (Aaker, 1991).

Brands that contain high equity have strong name awareness, strong associations attached to the brand, a perception of quality and have high levels of brand loyalty (see Figure 9.9). To create a brand that exhibits these characteristics takes time and investment. For instance, of the top fifty UK grocery brands, four have their origins in the 1800s; sixteen date from the period 1900–50; twenty-one between 1951 and 1975, and only nine have been introduced to the market in the years since 1975 (Hooley *et al.*, 1998). However, once established, a successful brand will, in its own right, become a valuable asset to an organization.

Figure 9.9 The constituents of brand equity (*Source***: Aaker, 1995)**

Brand valuation

There has been a trend in recent years for companies to try to turn the general concept of brand equity into a specific financial valuation for these organizational assets and to account for them on their company balance sheets separately from goodwill. Accountants have largely been at the forefront of this approach and have developed a range of factors seen as indicators of a brand's value. All are linked to the ability of the brand to sustain higher returns than competitors. These factors include:

● **Market type**. Brands operating in high margin, high volume and stable markets will carry a higher valuation than brands in less profitable or stable sectors. The confectionery or beer markets have traditionally been seen as less liable to changes in technology or fashion. Deciding on the potential of a market type, however, is full of difficulties. Even the drinks industry now shows signs of more regular changes in consumers' behaviour. It should also be borne in mind that one of the aims of developing a strong brand is to allow a company to compete on other factors than price in order to make strong margins even in what could be seen as commodity markets.

The Andrex brand of toilet roll has consistently made strong margins in the UK market. More importantly, it has gained higher margins than any of its competitors over the last thirty years from what is essentially a commodity product.

- **Market share**. Brands that are market leaders are deemed to command a premium because competitors will find it difficult to overcome consumers' tendency to buy the dominant brand. In effect, holding the market leadership position is seen as a barrier to entry for other brands.

- **Global presence**. Brands that either are, or carry the potential to be, exploited internationally obviously carry more value than brands within a purely domestic market. Developments in e-commerce may lower barriers to establishing a global brand name and therefore set a potential challenge to the high values placed on current global brands. There is also, obviously, the potential for the current global brands to end up as the dominant players in the e-commerce market thereby reinforcing their position and value.

- **Durability**. Some brands manage to maintain a contemporary appeal and retain their relevance to customers over a long period of time. These brands have created strong customer loyalty and become an established player in the market. A study by Blackett found that brands such as Cadbury in the chocolate market, Gillette in razors, Kodak in film and Colgate in toothpaste, were all the brand leaders in their market areas over the period 1931 to 1991 (Murphy, 1992). Such long-term brand leaderships are therefore likely to generate high valuations.

- **Extendability**. Brands that have the ability to be extended into related markets or stretched in new markets offer greater value than brands with more limited options. The Bic brand, for example, has been successfully extended from disposable pens into a number of other disposable markets such as cigarette lighters and razors. Andrex in 1987 had 39 per cent of the toilet paper market; by 1994 this share had dropped to 28 per cent due to increased competition from discounters (Kapferer, 1997). However, the potential to extend the brand allowed the company to enter related markets for products such as kitchen paper, paper tissues etc.

- **Protection**. Brands that have some protection from being copied though patents or registered trademarks or designs, potentially offer greater value. However, this protection has in reality been limited. In particular, retailers have launched own label products with similar packaging to market leading brands.

The factors considered so far have generally been developments from an accountancy perspective. However, there is a range of other significant factors marketers perceive to be crucial in terms of judging the brand's potential value.

- **Superior products and services**. Brands that offer the consumer products and/or services that are superior to those of competitors

---

Illustrative Example 9.4: Amazon.co.uk

In December 1999 the research group MMXI Europe published a table of the top internet sites in the UK. MMXI rated Amazon.co.uk as the leading online retail site in the UK based on figures that showed the site was visited by 841,000 unique visitors in the year. Amazon UK's parent American site, Amazon.com, was in second place in the table with Jungle.com and Tescodirect.com in third and fourth place. Amazon had managed to attain this position by building its reputation on efficient service and delivery. Online retailing has developed rapidly – initially consumers worried about an online retailer's ability to fulfil and successfully deliver their orders. Increasingly, though, consumers' expectations are that online companies will deliver and meet the basic prerequisites of a satisfactory service. That element of a business's operation has therefore almost become commodity-driven. What separates the competition will increasingly be dependent on the consumers' perceptions of the brands on offer.

Amazon.com has stated that its goal is to offer the world's broadest selection of products online. The company believes there are no categories of merchandise that it could not eventually offer over the internet. In the USA the company is already offering goods such as software, toys and home improvement products and is exploring the possibility of selling cars online. In the UK it has begun to extend its range into DVDs and videos.

The online market is, however, becoming increasingly competitive. Amazon faces direct competition in the book and music markets from competitors such as BOL.com, eighth in the MMXI table. Increasingly, though, the company is facing indirect competition from others such as Freeserve and EGG, the latter establishing itself as an online retailer. Cars are already being sold online by several organizations including the Consumer Association through its Carbusters site.

Amazon also has to consider developments in new technology. Interactive television and wireless application protocol (WAP) mobile phone technology (see illustrative example 2.1) could become major competitive channels of distribution to the current internet technology.

Amazon has benefited greatly from being a first mover in the online retailing sector. The challenge for the company is to build on this advantage in the face of a rapidly expanding market that is attracting in both direct and indirect competitors.

---

create greater value. Brands that are perceived to deliver clear benefits to the consumer, such as quality, style, or cheapness, present the company with a clear asset in the market.

- **Country of origin**. The identity of the country of origin, as already mentioned earlier in the chapter (page 184), can either attach or deduct value from a brand. Association with Scotland is seen as attaching value to fresh food products in countries such as France. Association with Britain, however, has been deemed to have a negative image by consumers in certain market sectors such as telecommunications. This resulted in British Telecom for example, re-branding itself as BT as a way of distancing itself from its country of origin and appearing more international. Conversely, in the clothing market in the USA, association with Britain is seen as positive, much to the benefit of brands such as Barbour (jackets etc.) and Church's shoes.

- **Market domination**. The brand's ability to gain extensive coverage in the market, a dominant position in the distribution channels, and the ability to command good shelf positions are all assets of considerable value. Most of these attributes accompany brand leadership and merely add to the potential that market position gives a brand. There is some limited evidence, however, that affluent customers are now moving away from the major brands as a way of standing out from the crowd. In Japan there has even been the development of a retail clothing store, Seibu, successfully selling high quality clothing that carry no branded labels.

Strategic brand management

Successful brand development is reliant on far more than creating a strong image through the marketing communications mix. This is the area of which the consumer will be most aware, but the less visible elements are crucial ingredients in creating a strong brand (see Figure 9.10). Factors such as providing product quality, continuous product development and high levels of service are potential components of a successful brand yet are not as visible as elements of the communications mix. Significantly, marketing communication skills are generally co-ordinated by agencies outside the organization, while the other components of successful brand development have traditionally been reliant on the company's internal assets and competencies. However, a number of alternative approaches to the structure and ownership of crucial elements of brand development and delivery have emerged over the last thirty years. Organizations now are faced with a number of decisions on the best way to gain access to the assets and competencies needed to support a brand successfully. This had led to a number of

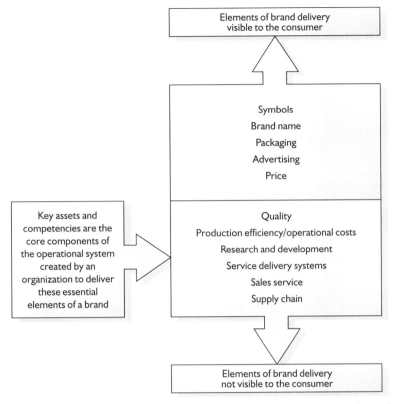

Figure 9.10 The visibility of core elements of a brand (*Source*: Adapted from Davidson, 1997)

alternative ways of structuring the business functions that support successful brands. Organizations have the option of co-ordinating these activities without necessarily owning all the assets and competencies needed. The capability to support a brand can be obtained through various forms of relationships and alliances (see Figure 9.11).

Organizations have tended to use one of four main options in structuring their operations to gain access to the assets and competencies they require:

- **Manufacturer's brand system**. Companies such as Kellogg only produce products under their own brand name. Kellogg owns the majority of the business operations except for the retail outlets selling the product. In some areas third party distribution systems may be utilized.
- **Retailer's own brand system**. Retailers such as The Gap or Marks & Spencer only supply goods carrying their retail brand name. Manufacturers under contract to the retailer carry out production. Often distribution is contracted out. Product development is sometimes undertaken by a third party, such as a design agency, but more

Type of brand marketing system	Finance	Brand development	Product development	Production	Distribution	Retailing
Manufacturer's own brand system					(shaded)	(shaded)
Retailer's own brand system			(shaded)	(shaded)	(shaded)	
Franchise brand system			(shaded)	(shaded)	(shaded)	
Manufacturer's private label brand system		(shaded)		(shaded)		(shaded)

(shaded) Shaded boxes represent area of the business fully or partly handled by a third party

Figure 9.11 Alternative options for the structure/ownership of key capabilities necessary to support successful brands (*Source*: Adapted from Davidson, 1997)

frequently it is a shared activity with the retailer taking an active role.

● **Franchise brand system**. Organizations such as Benetton and Burger King are franchise operations. Benetton contracts out parts of its manufacturing activities. However, key skills relating to core aspects of the brand's quality, such as pattern cutting and dyeing operations, are kept in house. Warehousing is also kept inside the company operations and is an area where considerable investment has been made to allow fast distribution around the globe. The retail outlets are mainly franchise operations. Although these retail outlets are one of the most visible aspects of the brand this is not a core area of competence owned by the organization. Key competencies lie in the areas of product design, brand development, management of key areas of production and distribution, supplier and retail franchise management.

● **Manufacturer's private label brand system**. Some companies concentrate on manufacturing products to be sold under a retailer's own label, such as Marks & Spencer. These companies have no control over branding or the retail outlets – instead, they create their competitive position through highly efficient manufacturing skills, customer service and new product development abilities. There are examples of organizations, such as Weetabix, producing both their own branded products and goods for retailers' own brands.

Optimizing the assets and competencies available to an organization is obviously a crucial step in creating appropriate operational systems to support a brand.

Brand name strategy

The operational structure an organization develops is not the only area of strategic decision making associated with brand management. An organization also has to decide its policy for naming brands across all its products and services. Branding decisions for any new products can then be taken within this framework. The focal point of decisions on branding strategy is about the emphasis the organization wishes to place on creating a distinctive offering in the market against the weight it wishes to place on the origin of the product or service (see Figure 9.12).

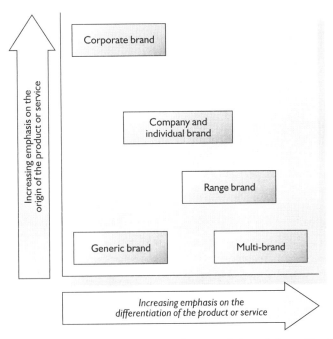

Figure 9.12 Alternative branding strategies (*Source*: Adapted from Kapferer, 1997)

Between the extremes offered by these two approaches lie several options available to an organization when considering an overall brand strategy:

● **Corporate brand**. Organizations following this approach use one corporate name across all products. Heinz would be a classic example of this unified approach. Individual products merely carry a descriptive name under the corporate umbrella Heinz brand, hence Heinz Baked Beans, Heinz Cream of Mushroom Soup, Heinz Tomato Ketchup. Linking the individual products together creates a strong overall image. It also gives the opportunity to create economies of scale in marketing communication and possibly distribution. The clear danger is that if there is a problem with an individual product the reputation of all the products may suffer. Virgin has used the corporate brand name across its entire product portfolio. Its high profile problems with the Virgin rail franchise in the UK may over time have a negative impact across its other operations. The fact that this does not yet appear to have happened is a testament to the strength of the core brand name.

- **Multi-brand**. Multi-branding or discrete branding is the complete opposite of the corporate branding approach. With multi-branding each product is given its own unique brand name. The aim is to build completely separate brand identities. This is appropriate if the organization is competing in a number of different segments and the consumers' perceptions of a product's position in one segment may adversely affect the consumers' perceptions of another product. A classic example of this approach would be Proctor & Gamble, who produce a range of washing powders such as Daz, Ariel and Bold aimed at discrete sectors of the market.

- **Company and individual brand (endorsed approach)**. Unilever used to practise a multi-brand approach with its washing powders but recently has been moving closer to the strategy of linking a company name to an individual brand name. Their products now have Lever Bros as a high profile endorsement on the individual brands such as Persil, Radion and Surf. This can be used in different ways. Endorsing a product with the corporate name gives a new product credibility while at the same time allowing the new brand some degree of freedom. A fixed endorsed approach entails the corporate brand name being given a consistent profile against each individual product's brand name in the range. For example, all Kellogg products give individual product brand names the promi-nent position on the pack, while the same secondary weighting is given to the company brand name. (This is different from Heinz where the prominence of the corporate brand is sacrosanct.) Cadbury takes a more flexible approach to the corporate endorsement – it is more or less prominent depending on how independent they choose to make the brand.

- **Range brand**. Some organizations use different brand names for different ranges of product, in effect creating a family of products. Ford has done this to an extent, using Ford for its mass-market car range and Jaguar for the upmarket executive car range. Volvo, Ford's latest acquisition, has its own distinct brand values that appeal to a particular market segment and therefore will become another brand family for the Ford group.

- **Private brand (distributor's own brand)**. An organization may decide to supply private brands, in particular retail brands. In this case the private brand is owned and controlled by the distributor who will make decisions regarding the product's position in the market. The distributor is likely to use either a strategy of corporate or a company and individual brand for its products.

● **Generic brand**. This strategy involves the product having no brand name. The product's packaging merely states the contents of the package, for instance flour or washing up liquid.

Each of the approaches to branding outlined above has advantages and disadvantages. These are summarized in Figure 9.13.

Branding strategy	Advantages	Disadvantages
Corporate brand	■ The strength of the corporate brand is conveyed to all products ■ Promotional costs are spread across all products	■ Any new product failure has the potential to damage the corporate brand ■ The positioning of the corporate brand constrains decisions on the quality and pricing for individual products
Multi-brand	■ Allows individual differentiation of brands ■ Allows products to occupy different positions in the same market, i.e. a premium and a discount brand from the same parent company ■ Current brands are insulated from any new product failures	■ Each brand requires a separate promotional budget ■ Market sectors have to contain enough potential to support more than one brand ■ Highly focused brands are hard to reposition once a market enters decline
Company and individual brand	■ Product can be supported by the reputation of an existing corporate brand while at the same time the individual characteristics of the specific offering can be emphasized	■ A new product failure has the potential to cause some damage to the company brand ■ The positioning of the company brand constrains decisions on quality and pricing of the individual product
Range brand	■ The strength of the brand is conveyed to all the products in the range ■ Promotional costs are spread across all the products in the range	■ Any new product failure has the potential to damage the range brand ■ The positioning of the brand constrains decisions on quality and pricing for individual products
Private brand	■ Demands little promotional spend by producer ■ Producer can concentrate on gaining cost efficiency through volume production	■ Marketing decisions controlled by distributors ■ Removes the producer from direct contact with the market
Generic brand	■ Limited promotional budget, reduced packaging costs	■ Competition becomes based mainly on price and service levels

Figure 9.13 Advantages and disadvantages of brand strategies (*Source*: Adapted from Brown and McDonald, 1994)

Combined brand strategies

Obviously large organizations may use a mixture of brand strategies to manage their large product portfolios.

3M employs a number of approaches to brand its broad range of products. The 3M brand name is used as an umbrella brand on all products aimed at the professional market, including cameras, overhead projectors and video tapes. On Post-it Notes the individual brand name is accompanied by the 3M company brand name. This approach is also adopted for the company's general consumer products, where 3M is used as an endorsing brand name in small print.

The umbrella brand name Scotch is used on most consumer products. This includes the company's video tapes aimed at the consumer market, where the presence of a 3M connection is hard to identify. Initially 3M consumer scouring pads were sold under the generic product name and the Scotch-brite brand. In response to competitor's actions, the scouring pad product was given the specific individual brand identity of Raccoon. There are also some variations on these major branding themes within 3M. For instance, aerosol glue aimed at the professional market is branded with a large 3M logo but also carries the Scotch brand name in smaller print.

Each of these branding decisions at 3M has been taken to make the greatest competitive impact in a particular market. 3M is not alone in having such a sophisticated brand portfolio – many large organizations have quite complex brand structures.

The approach an organization adopts to branding is a crucial decision relating to the overall strategy the company has decided to pursue. The branding policy should be developed in the light of:

- the nature of the product or service
- the pattern of consumer behaviour in the specific market
- the company's competitive position

When companies develop new products the branding decision will invariably be taken according to the general branding strategy of the organization. Multi-brand orientated companies will tend always to create a new brand for the new product. For other companies the decision will depend on the nature of the target market. If it is very different from the organization's current markets they may decide to introduce a new brand. Toyota did this when they entered the upmarket executive car market, introducing the Lexus brand. This is a rational approach where the target market is large enough and has the potential profitability to justify investing in creating a new brand. Companies may, however, choose to use a current brand name and opt for a brand extension or brand stretching policy.

Brand extension

There are occasions when an organization will try to extend the use of a brand name to new products in the same broad market. Brands that carry high brand equity are candidates for brand extension as they have the ability to increase the attractiveness of the new products. The Pretty Polly hosiery brand has been extended into the wider but related lingerie market (Tucker, 1998). The Pretty Polly brand is seen as fashionable, young, exiting and innovative – all qualities Sarah Lee, its holding company, feels can be extended to other markets.

Brand stretching

Brand stretching takes place when an organization stretches a brand into new unrelated markets. Virgin is an obvious example of this, moving from the record industry to airlines, railways, financial services and cola drinks. Marks & Spencer and Tesco have both moved from mainstream retailing into financial services. Both are examples of brand stretching. This policy is more likely to be successful where the original brand values are compatible with the aspirations of the new target group.

Brand revitalization

Over a period of time, it is likely that an organization will be required to undertake actions to improve the performance of a brand. This can occur for a number of reasons such as the advent of new technology, changing consumer behaviour or new competition. The options open to a company in these circumstances are either to increase sales volume or to raise the brand's profitability. Brand revitalization and brand repositioning are two approaches that can be employed to increase the sales volume of a brand.

Brand revitalization involves gaining sales volume by expanding the market for a brand. Four significant opportunities exist that can expand a market:

● **Enter new markets**. One approach is to expand into new geographical areas. Irn-Bru, the Scottish soft drinks, brand has recently expanded into the Russian market as a way of increasing sales.

Illustrative Example 9.5: JCB

JCB is an international brand originally associated with the company's core business, manufacturing mechanical diggers for use by civil engineers on construction sites. The diggers are painted a distinctive yellow and wear the JCB logo in large black lettering. They are instantly recognizable. Recently the company decided to extend the brand, through partnership agreements, beyond its industrial market sectors to new market areas. Research exposed the fact that particular age groups perceived the brand differently. The brand associations of yellow, durable and diggers were common to all age groups. Adults also associated the brand with quality, functionality and Britain. Children, however, linked it with characteristics such as big, muddy and fun. As a result of this research the company decided to target three new market areas: toys, fashion and hardware. Three brand ranges were created – JCB Junior, JCB Works and JCB Sitemaster.

JCB Junior is a range of durable toys meant to last. Children can buy toy hard hats, work benches and diggers. The toy range is a return to a more traditional approach in this market where children can recreate an adult world. They are promoted under the strapline 'Big things for little people'. JCB Works is a range of sturdy outdoor clothing comprising items such as fleeces, jumpers, combat trousers, footwear and sports equipment. These items are designed to reflect the JCB brand values of strength, functionality and integrity. The JCB Sitemaster range is made up of hand tools, power tools and other outdoor power products. Once again the products reflect the values of quality and durability.

Reactions to these brand extensions have been positive in the UK and JCB are developing the ranges on offer as well as expanding geographically by launching them across other European markets.

- **Exploit new market segments**. Once the initial market segment has been fully exploited a company can then expand by targeting new market segments. Johnson & Johnson's baby shampoo was stagnating until they moved the brand into a new market segment of adults who wash their hair frequently.
- **Increase the frequency of use**. This can be achieved by actions such as:
  - appealing to consumers to use products on new occasions. Kellogg have been attempting to increase sales of their Cornflakes brand by promoting the proposition that the product should be eaten as a supper-time snack as well as a breakfast cereal.
  - providing incentives to purchase, such as frequent-flyer programmes which promote the sale of airline tickets.

- **Increase quantity used**. This can be achieved by:
  - increasing the size of the 'normal-sized container' such as the popcorn or soft drink containers offered in cinemas. If consumers accept this size as normal then consumption will increase.
  - undertaking advertising campaigns promoting larger portions as normal, such as Weetablix suggesting eating three Weetabix at a time rather than two.
  - removing barriers to consumption. Thus companies can offer low calorie chocolate or soft drinks as a way of removing a major obstruction to consumer purchase.

Illustrative Example 9.6: Iceland.co.uk

In March 2000 Iceland, the UK supermarket chain, announced an £8 million rebranding exercise for all of its 660 retail outlets, which were to be rebranded as Iceland.co.uk. Iceland was the first UK food retailer to offer a nationwide home shopping service and the first to run a UK television campaign to promote supermarket home shopping. The aim of the rebranding exercise is to combine its online web-based service and its traditional retail outlets.

This is the first time a major UK retailer has changed its core brand to embrace the expanding e-commerce based market. The company believes its stores are a major marketing tool for promoting its web-based business. The decision reflects its belief that customers will increasingly buy commodity food items online while still undertaking other non-basic shopping through the traditional retail high street.

The new corporate identity will be displayed on all retail outlets, delivery vans, packaging and other marketing communications material. The brand will also be repositioned by highlighting the company's increasingly ethical reputation, by incorporating promotional messages on its vehicles about the company's stance on genetically modified foods and its charitable activities. The company was the first UK retailer to ban genetically modified ingredients in its foods. It is also phasing out artificial flavouring and colours in its products and will only use freezers that comply with environmental guidelines. In fact, it has begun selling its own brand, called Kyoto, of environmentally friendly freezers over the internet. It recently stopped stocking Norwegian prawns in response to Norway's continuing whaling activities.

The company is also considering linking up with other 'ethical brands' via the internet. The idea is to develop 'affinity portals' with partners that have similar ethical attitudes and may involve cross-promotion of brands or offering a range of brands through the Iceland.co.uk website.

Brand repositioning

Brand repositioning is undertaken in order to increase a brand's competitive position and therefore increase sales volume by seizing market share from rival products. When repositioning companies can change aspects of the product, change the brand's target market or both. This gives four repositioning options (see Figure 9.14.):

Figure 9.14 **Alternative options available for brand repositioning**

- **Image repositioning**. This takes place when both the product and the target market remain unchanged. The aim is to change the image of the product in its current target market. In the early 1990s Adidas were seen as reliable but dull. The company created an image of 'street credibility' in an attempt to reposition the brand to appeal to the consumer in the sports shoe market. Tango, the Britvic soft drink, has been transformed during the 1990s from a minor UK brand into a brand showing dynamic growth. This has been achieved by creating an anarchic image for the product through a major promotional relaunch that was aimed to appeal to consumers in the critical 16–24 age group.
- **Market repositioning**. Here the product remains unchanged but it is repositioned to appeal to a new market segment. Lucozade, a brand of carbonated glucose drink, was originally targeted as a product for individuals suffering from illness, particularly children. In recent

Illustrative Example 9.7: Adidas

In 2000 Adidas launched the first of a series of new advertisements featuring famous sporting personalities in daring but eccentric situations. The advertisement shows a large fish lying in the middle of a street slowly dying. Suddenly Jonah Loma appears, picks up the fish and runs down the road, through a car wash, crashes into a van, before finally throwing the fish into the sea at the local harbour. The viewer is then addressed by a diver who surfaces from the harbour waters to announce that 'Wearing Adidas makes you more caring about fish . . . and alligators . . . and cats . . . and elephants. And even people'. The aim is to promote the brand to a young market segment without being dull or worthy by referring to the technicality of the product. The use of humour is part of the strategy of repositioning the brand in the mind of a key consumer group.

years it has been repositioned as an isotonic drink aimed at young adults undertaking sporting activities.

- **Product repositioning**. In this situation the product is materially changed but is still aimed to appeal to the existing target market. In the early 1990s Castlemaine XXXX lager was altered, with its alcohol content being increased from 3.7 per cent to 3.9 per cent for pub sales and 4 per cent for cans sold in supermarkets. The packaging was also changed as the size of can was changed from 440 ml to 500 ml. These changes were instituted to address the changes in consumer tastes in the product's target market.

- **Total repositioning**. This option involves both a change of target market and accompanying product modifications. Skoda has managed under Volkswagen's ownership to reposition itself totally. The product quality and design has changed significantly and the brand now has credibility with new, more affluent consumers. This has also allowed the brand to expand its sales outside its Eastern European heartland.

Raising a brand's profitability

If a brand is in a static or declining market and a company judges that the brand has finite potential then it may be prudent to force the maximum profitability out of the product. This can be achieved by:

- **Raising prices**. Although this may lead to a drop in sales it is likely to improve margins dramatically. In a declining market competitors may be dropping out of the market, restricting consumer choice.

Thus consumers who still purchase the product may have little choice but to accept the higher price.

- **Cutting costs**. This action will obviously be a matter of management judgement as it will mean ceasing to invest in the brand and may hasten its decline.
- **Cutting the brand's product range**. Rationalizing the range of marginal product lines will save additional costs whilst having a limited impact on overall sales.

Brand extinction

Inevitably, over a period of time, brands die. They may last for decades, or in some cases centuries, but even well-established brands can falter. This can happen for a number of reasons:

- **Intense brand competition**. Weak brands face increasing competition from both overseas brands entering domestic markets and the growth of retailers' own label brands. This leads to poor profitability for brands with small market share and in the end withdrawal from the market.
- **Acquisition and mergers**. Companies that acquire brand names or undergo a merger often rationalize the portfolio of brand names owned by the new organization. Since acquisition, Nestlé has over time replaced the Rowntree brand name on its products.
- **Rationalization**. Organizations periodically review their brand portfolio and may decide that in relation to their promotional budgets they cannot sustain the range of brand names that they have propagated. The Rover Group has over the last forty years ceased to use such

---

Illustrative Example 9.8: Reckitt & Coleman

The UK company Reckitt & Coleman merged with the Dutch firm Benckiser in 1999 to create the world's largest household cleaning products enterprise Reckitt Benckiser. This new organization has a large portfolio of brands. Inevitably there will need to be a rationalization of the brand portfolio so that marketing expenditure can be focused on growing key brands rather than spreading spend too thinly. Whilst some key brands, such as Dettol, Disprin, Vanish and Harpic, will be reinforced with greater investment, other brands, such as Frank's Red Hot and French's Mustard, are likely to be either sold or discontinued.

famous brand names as Triumph, Austin, Morris, Riley and Wolseley. The Jaguar and MG brands have been lucky to escape this cull.
- **Globalization**. In order to create global brands, companies have also rationalized domestic brands in particular markets. Mars changed the name of Marathon chocolate bars in the UK to the Snickers brand name in order to create a consistent brand image internationally.
- **Weak brand management**. Brands also falter through mediocre marketing, uncompetitive production costs or poor quality. It is an ignominious end for what should be the key asset of any organization.

Summary

Targeting aims to align an organization's assets and competencies to attractive market segments. Once these market segments have been identified an organization has to decide how it will position its product in the market, relative to the competition. One key aspect of this positioning process is branding.

An organization's assets and competencies can be used to create new products and services, to unlock the potential in market segments that are not currently served, either by the company in question, or by companies in general. Product development and innovation are critical areas that have to be considered in any strategic plan and will be addressed in Chapter 10.

References

Aaker, D., *Managing Brand Equity*, Free Press, 1991

Aaker, D., *Strategic Market Management*, 4th edition, Wiley, 1995

Buckley, A., *The Essence of Services Marketing*, Prentice Hall, 1993

Brown, L. and McDonald, M., *Competitive Marketing Strategy for Europe*, Kogan Page, 1994

Davidson, H., *Even More Offensive Marketing*, Penguin, 1997

Hooley, G.H., Saunders, J.A. and Piercy, N.F., *Marketing Strategy and Competitive Positioning*, 2nd edition, Prentice Hall, 1998

Jobber, D., *Principles and Practice of Marketing*, McGraw-Hill, 1995

Kapferer, J., *Strategic Brand Management*, 2nd edition, Kogan Page, 1997

Kotler, P., Armstrong, G., Saunders J. and Wong, V., *Principles of Marketing: The European Edition*, Prentice Hall, 1996

Murphy, J.M., *Branding: A Key Marketing Tool*, 2nd edition, Macmillan, 1992

Ries, A. and Trout, J., *Positioning: The Battle for Your Mind*, McGraw-Hill, 1981

Shell Chemical Company, *The Directional Policy Matrix: A New Aid to Corporate Planning*, Shell, 1975

Tucker, J., 'Pretty Polly set for lingerie push', *Marketing*, 23 April 1998

Further reading

Davidson, H., *Even More Offensive Marketing*, Chapters 9 and 10, Penguin, 1997

Doyle, P., *Marketing Management and Strategy*, Chapter 6, Prentice Hall, 1994

Kapferer J., *Strategic Brand Management*, Chapters 6, 7 and 11, 2nd edition, Kogan Page, 1997

Chapter 10

Product development and innovation

About this chapter

Product development is a strategic necessity. In terms of product development, organizations can modify, imitate or innovate. A rigorous New Product Development (NPD) process is essential to avoid marketing failures. Additionally, managers must address the concept of innovation across the entire organization.

The strategic agenda

It is essential that all organizations develop products. Product development and innovation are the 'life blood' of any business. By definition, development and innovation are strategic activities that shape the future. The creation of an acceptable product offering involves many strategic decisions. For example, building on core competencies, matching resources to market opportunity and co-ordinating activities across functional boundaries are all accepted strategic activities which normally determine the success or failure of our products. Given that many organizations now face difficult commercial conditions – static/declining demand and intense competition – innovation and product development should top the agenda of today's (and tomorrow's) successful organizations. In essence, all organizations must evolve or they will perish. Product development and innovation allow organizations to evolve.

It is important to define 'product' in its broadest sense. What counts is the total product offering – this provides benefits to the customer. Hence, the process of product development involves not only innovation of the core product, but innovation in areas such as support services and production processes. Business cannot afford to view innovation in the narrow sense of technical/scientific development, but rather as a management process. Such a process focuses creative effort with the intention of developing products perceived as delivering superior benefits. Innovative projects require the right balance of creative, technical and managerial skills. Blending these factors together fosters an organizational culture that embraces innovation, product development and strategic success.

The nature of products and product development

As stated above, products must be considered in terms of the total product offering. The term 'product' covers goods, services, ideas and information. In reality, most products are combinations of these items. Service-based products tend to be intangible in nature. Above all, products must meet needs and deliver benefits to the user.

Kotler *et al.* (1999) defines a product as having three levels. Firstly, a **core product** defines the fundamental need being met. Fundamental needs are generic in nature (e.g. transport, data storage or self-esteem). Secondly, the **actual product** is the specific offering aimed at meeting a core need. This includes attributes such as styling, branding, performance features and packaging. Finally, the **augmented product**, which enhances the actual product by offering additional services and benefits, making the product a more attractive proposition to the consumer. Examples include factors such as after-sales support, maintenance and affordable finance.

It is important to consider product development at each of the above levels. Organizations must fully understand their core product(s) – what need does it meet? Then they must develop actual and augmented product offerings that are attractive to specific customers groups. As an illustration, consider Orange plc:

Core	**Actual**	**Augmented**
Communications	Mobile phone network	Voice mail
	Handset	Insurance
	Brand image	against loss

One school of thought suggests that in certain markets advances in quality management, manufacturing systems and information technology will tend to generate competitive products indistinguishable from each other. Therefore, the only way to differentiate products is at an augmented level – who offers the best service and support? Indeed, the augmentation may become such a vital part of the product offering that it is absorbed into the actual product. It becomes an integral, essential part of the product. For example, when buying a new car the warranty package is an integral part of the product offering.

Fundamentally, a product delivers a set of benefits to a customer, in order to meet a need. Organizations must strive to understand this process fully and be certain that their product offering best matches not only need, but customer expectation.

Illustrative Example 10.1: Persil tablet – the importance of new products

---

The weekly wash is not normally an activity associated with innovative products. This changed when Unilever launched Persil tablets. The concentrated 'soap powder' tablets eliminate the need to measure detergent doses correctly and provide customers with a more convenient method of washing garments. Persil is reported as gaining around 10 per cent market share (total market value approximately £1000 m) within three months of launch. Being first into the market with a tablet product enabled Persil to take customers from its rivals.

Product development strategy

There is much debate relating to product development strategies. For example, how is the term 'new product' defined? The reality is that few products are 'new' in the sense of being innovative, unique or novel. Most 'new' products are updates and revamps of existing goods and services. Jain (1997) views new product strategy in terms of three categories (see Figure 10.1):

- **Product improvement/modification**. Unless products are to be replaced by completely new entities they must be upgraded and enhanced as a matter of necessity. The process can have two possible aims: (i) maintaining the competitive position in an existing market, and/or (ii) adapting the product in order to appeal to other market segments. Major changes may result in the need to reposition a product offering within a given market. Conversely, organizations may only make minor changes aimed at ensuring the products remain up to date.

> **Product improvement and modification**
>
> **Product imitation**
>
> **Product innovation**

Figure 10.1 Product development strategy

- **Product imitation**. This strategy involves capitalizing on the initiatives of others and suits organizations that are risk averse and/or have limited funds to invest. Clearly, there are potential ethical and legal problems with this option and organizations must define the line between imitation and copying. The strategy is most effective when the 'new' version of the product brings some additional dimension of added value.
- **Product innovation**. This involves bringing new and novel ideas to the market place. Product innovation my be aimed at: (i) replacing existing products with new approaches and items which enhance customer satisfaction, or (ii) providing diversification in order to target opportunities in new markets. Clearly, organizations should expect a correlation between risk and diversification.

Booz *et al.* (1982) classified 'new' products using the categories shown in Figure 10.2. Again this demonstrates that truly original, innovative products represent only a small proportion of total development.

Type of Product Development	Nature
1. New to world	Often scientific or technical development, high risk/return activities which can revolutionize or create markets
2. New product lines or line additions	Such products can be: (i) new to the provider as opposed to the market place, or (ii) additions to the product ranges already on offer
3. Product revision	Replacements and upgrades of existing products. This category is likely to cover the largest single number of new product developments. Additionally, this may cover changes aimed at generating **cost reductions** – no perceived change in performance but more economic product/provision of the product
4. Reposition	Aiming to diversify away from existing markets by uncovering new applications, uses or market segments for current products

Figure 10.2 Types of 'new' product

New product development process

Regardless of whether we are developing a 'new to world' product, a new product line or simply aiming to reduce cost, we need a new product development (NPD) process. All organizations require some mechanism, or process, which enables ideas to be evaluated and, when appropriate, translated into commercial products. Such a process provides a vital ingredient in the fight for commercial success. Indeed, Davidson (1997) cites lack of rigorous process as a factor commonly contributing to the failure of new products.

NPD processes take many shapes and forms. It is vital that any process is driven by an overall NPD strategy, otherwise development activities will lack co-ordination and focus. This concept is expanded upon later in the chapter.

Stages commonly found in NPD processes include:

1 **Idea generation**
   New product ideas have to come from somewhere. This may be via a formalized technical research and development process or from systems that scan the business environment, enabling the organization to identify trends, customer requests and competitors' intentions. Market research certainly has a role to play in this process. Equally, management needs to encourage staff to suggest product development ideas and have systems to enable and reward such activity.

2 **Idea evaluation**
   Next, ideas must be screened in order to establish what is feasible and where opportunities exist. Ideally, ideas are screened against strategic objectives by demonstrating how they are likely to contribute to such objectives. It is important to establish criteria against which all ideas are evaluated. This provides a consistent approach to decision making and the safeguard of rigorous testing. Evaluation is likely to include marketing and operational/production criteria.

3 **Concept development**
   Having passed through a screening process, ideas are developed into product concepts. This stage involves initial technical and marketing evaluations. Having established the technical/operational feasibility and resource requirements, marketing (often using secondary data – general industry trends, key competitor profiles, etc.) evaluates the potential for the product. A marketing strategy needs to be outlined: target segment(s), product positioning and marketing goals, such as market share.

4 **Business evaluation**
   The aim is to evaluate commercial potential and investment requirements. Sales volume, revenue and cost projections will establish the

viability of the project. Clearly, this is more difficult when dealing with diversification or highly innovative products. Often organizations have predetermined returns on investment, which projects must demonstrate they will meet.

5 **Product development**

This stage turns the concept into an actual product. The product development stage tends to be dominated by technical and operational development. There is a need to examine both the development of the product (styling, features, performance, branding, etc.) and the means of its production/delivery (manufacturing, administration, after-sales support, etc.). This stage may see the building of a prototype and the use of market research to establish the final product offering. To gauge market-place reaction, products may be test marketed with groups of actual consumers.

6 **Product launch**

Using the knowledge and targets generated in the previous processes, a final plan is developed. This includes all the other elements of the marketing mix. For example, a final price is set, a promotion campaign is designed and the build up of stock begins within the distribution channels. It is vital that the product has the correct marketing, operational and logistical support to make it a success. Competitor and customer reaction should be monitored and the product offering 'fine-tuned' if required. Where resources are limited, or where high degrees of uncertainty exist, the product may be introduced using a 'roll-out' strategy. This entails a phased launch, gradually building market coverage.

Given the importance of new product development, managers must endeavour to make the process as rigorous and objective as possible. Only in this way can organizations maximize the likelihood of success and minimize the chances of progressing with poor ideas. However, there is a dilemma: while a robust development process has its advantages, there is increasing commercial pressure to do things quickly. This may result in corners being cut and ultimately mistakes being made in the new product development process. So, the reality of business life means management has to develop the right products in an increasingly shorter time frame. How can we enable this? Adhering to the following principles should optimize the entire process:

1 **Multi-functional teams**

There is much evidence to suggest that projects go more smoothly when a multi-functional team is in control. By taking people from different functional backgrounds (e.g. production, marketing, design and finance) a balanced viewpoint is obtained. For example, problems relating to the manufacture/provision of the product are addressed early in the project. Additionally, the multi-functional approach promotes 'ownership' of the project and staff can be more committed and motivated.

2 Completeness and evaluation

NPD can be viewed as a six-stage process (see above). The simple process of completing all these steps can increase the likelihood of product success. Undertaking each stage in a systematic manner and building an ongoing evaluation into the process may not guarantee success, but it will reduce the chances of failure. So-called 'evaluation gates' at the end of each stage can review the potential product and whether the NPD process has been properly conducted.

3 Customer involvement

Often market research is used to evaluate possible ideas and to review products after launch. It may be advisable to integrate the 'voice of the customer' into the entire project. This is possible by having an ongoing process of market research that takes place during each development stage or by having customer representation on the multi-functional team.

4 Parallel processing

Traditionally, NPD has been viewed as a sequential process – activities follow each other in sequence. It may be possible to conduct some activities concurrently, in other words undertaking a process of parallel development. Encouraging functional areas, departments and individuals to work more closely has a number of advantages. Firstly, this overlapping, parallel approach reduces overall development time. Secondly, as activities are being undertaken at the same time, they can share information and a more interactive approach can be taken. This can improve the overall quality of the process. To illustrate, a technical and marketing feasibility assessment could be conducted as one process, generating a more vigorous product/market specification.

5 Strategic direction

NPD requires a strategic focus and clear links must be established between overall corporate strategy and the NPD process. As previously stated, strategic objectives can be used as a template against which new product ideas are evaluated.

Additionally, the process of strategic analysis and audit should provide valuable information (external and internal) relating to the development of product offerings. The aim is to integrate into one coherent framework: (i) technical development – improving the technical capability of the product; (ii) process development – improving the provision/production of products and services, and (iii) marketing strategy. Figure 10.3 illustrates this.

Figure 10.3 Strategic direction of NPD

6 Knowledge management

This concept is closely related to strategic direction. Increasingly, organizations are developing knowledge management strategies. Mobilizing and managing the knowledge base of the organization is rapidly becoming a management priority. The collective experience and accumulated learning within the organization can be vital to successful NPD. The organization needs to facilitate the development of, and access to, information. Enabling technologies and methods include benchmarking, brain-storming, computer networks, 'group-ware' – software products enabling work and knowledge to be shared (e.g. Lotus Notes) – and data warehousing. O'Connor and Galvin (1997) define data warehousing as constructing a high-level database of all operating and customer data, and making such a database available to support decision making.

Why do products fail?

It is reasonable to suggest that an understanding of the pitfalls of product development can help us avoid them. When addressing this question, managers need to consider the nature and background to NPD, as some types of development activity are inherently more risky than others. Additionally, the organization's attitude to risk and investment has a bearing on the situation.

Common reasons for failure can be summarized as follows:

- **Under-investment**, where the project is short of funds and lacks the investment required to establish/sustain it in the market place.

- The product fails to deliver any **customer benefit**. This can happen with technical or scientific advance. While the technology may be innovative, it must be perceived as innovative by the market place, otherwise it is unlikely to be adopted. Additionally, the product must perform to the required performance parameters. Remember, quality is defined as 'fit for purpose'. There needs to be a clear definition of market segment and how the product offering is positioned.

- **Forecasting error** is a common source of failure. It was once said, '. . . forecasting is difficult, especially if you're forecasting the future'. This is certainly true! Often, forecasting errors relate to over-optimistic forecasts of demand and/or underestimates of costs. Managers need to examine the assumptions supporting forecasts as well as the forecasting techniques used. Also, timescales for planned development have to be realistic.

- **Internal politics**, trade-offs and compromise can result in problems. The project may lack the support and commitment of staff and vested interests may conspire against its success. Equally, trade-offs, and other such factors, may result in the project drifting from its original target, as internal conflict distracts management. Internal conflict has been the graveyard of many good product ideas.

- **Industry response** is vital. For example, success may be completely dependent on retailers stocking products or on the response of competitors – what happens if they drastically cut price? Such factors are less controllable, but good quality market research and competitor intelligence can lessen the negative effects.

While some factors are unpredictable, and projects are a 'hostage to fortune', most issues are simply a matter of management and marketing. Applying a sound, structured approach to NPD and having effective project management should move the odds in your favour. Products need a product champion – a leader/manager who gets things done. In turn, this leader needs the support of the organization.

Managing innovation

The term 'innovation' means different things to different people, with common definitions relating to scientific advance and the development of high-technology products. However, the reality is that innovation is a far broader activity. Essentially, innovation is about changing established products, processes and practices. Innovation must blend creativity, clear thinking and the ability to get things done into one process. Ultimately, the market place will judge innovation. New ideas need support, commitment and resources if they are to be effectively implemented.

Illustrative Example 10.2: The Carphone Warehouse – innovation drives sales

The mobile phone has developed rapidly, and will continue to do so. New models are packed with features (internet access, voice activation, graphics capability, etc.). Such innovation is important in generating sales. As Charles Dunstone, Chief Executive of the Carphone Warehouse, states, 'For some people mobile phones are like trainers – they've got to have the latest model'. Indeed, the company now sees the majority of sales being generated by customers changing to newer, more advanced phones as opposed to first-time buyers. Essentially, technical innovation is driving replacement demand.

Organizations cannot remain focused on the past. The static organization that believes 'the old ways are the best' will flounder. Innovation means change. Such changes are not normally single events, but are complex combinations of actions and functional activity. Note that innovation and invention are not one and the same, as innovation is concerned with the commercial application of ideas.

Senior management should address the issue of innovation and create a culture and infrastructure to support the process. After all, organizations that continue to learn and effectively translate this learning into product offerings are the ones who will prosper.

Innovation creates the environment for successful product development. Product improvement and modification, product imitation and product innovation (where the product is truly new or novel – see Figure 10.1) all stem from the overall process of innovation.

Having established the importance of innovation, how do organizations facilitate the process? Figure 10.4 summarizes common enablers. **Teamwork** is vital, as successful innovation requires a combination of skills and functional activity (e.g. marketing, research and design). Innovation tends to flourish where frequent contact and good working relationships exist among groups. The **exchange of information** and ideas should be encouraged, as this not only facilitates innovation but also enhances teamwork. Information flow and effective communication contribute greatly to creativity. However, it is important to recognize that more information is not necessarily better – information overload should be avoided. There is a need to be focused on the external environment. **External inputs** relating to market trends, customer perception, technological development and competitor activities are vital inputs into the overall process. The organization must be receptive to new ideas/change and have the capacity to evaluate such concepts. Clearly, **senior management** has a role to play in the process. They need to develop appropriate strategies and act as facilitators to the process. This normally involves taking calculated risks and allocating required resources (see the following section). Consequently, senior managers need to be committed to long-term growth as opposed to short-term profit. If it is to work properly, innovation requires the correct systems and support. Frequently, this relates to organizational culture. Creating the right organizational climate is important, as the wish is to challenge existing practice and generate creativity. **Systems**, such as communications networks, computer-aided design and project management structures, need to be in place.

Figure 10.4 Generating innovation

The organization must foster and exploit innovation. Group and individual motivation are important. **Reward** and recognition for innovation helps generate ideas and fosters a collaborative atmosphere. Additionally, the role of the individual must not be neglected in the discussion of innovation. While the organization can facilitate and foster innovation, individuals have to take ownership. People need to have the courage, skill and motivation to make things better. Only this type of commitment will see the process to completion.

Risk and the innovation dilemma

Inevitably, conflict between innovation and operational efficiency will occur. All organizations need to develop new ideas and translate such ideas into new products if they are to remain competitive. Equally, organizations require stable and efficient day-to-day operations in order to accomplish basic tasks effectively. Indeed, many views of manage-

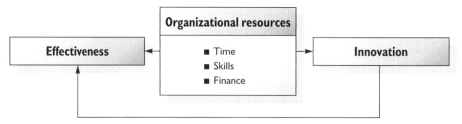

Figure 10.5 The innovation dilemma

ment, and management techniques, tend to focus on eliminating waste, reducing cost and optimizing the use of assets. Figure 10.5 illustrates the principle.

So, should management focus resources on generating innovation or ensuring optimum efficiency? This is a dilemma, to which there is no easy answer. The answer may be a hybrid solution, attempting to balance innovation with operational effectiveness. A key maxim is that innovation should be fostered, but never allowed to disrupt activities. Clearly, the nature of the industry and/or product life cycle is important. So-called 'sunrise' industries which are research and design led (telecommunications, biotechnology, etc.) will have a different innovation profile from more mature industries, or service sector industries. Such industries tend to be affected more by process and customer service based innovations.

Innovation and operational effectiveness cannot be seen as mutually exclusive. They are interlinked, with one supporting the other. Given these factors, innovation should lead to operational effectiveness – however this is defined. Remember, innovation is invention plus commercial exploitation, and there is little point in pursuing innovations that do not lead to operational effectiveness. The question is not should we innovate, but rather how we support and resource the process, given other often more immediate demands.

Assuming organizations have the right factors in place (as outlined in the previous section) it can be argued that innovation will eventually pay for itself several times over. However, in order to stimulate the process, forward-looking organizations allocate funds to such activities. A number of methods are commonly used for this purpose.

● Gap analysis is used to establish the difference between desired and projected future revenue requirements. Management then examines how much of the 'gap' can be closed by innovation. This provides an 'innovation target'. Resources can then be allocated to the new

product development areas and innovations most likely to close this
gap.

- An alternative is to allocate a percentage of sales revenue to an
'innovation fund' and request internal bids for this money. These bids
are then evaluated and screened, with funding being given to the
strongest.
- Additionally, we can seek collaborative ventures, partnerships and
external funding (e.g. government grants, venture capital).

Organizations, and individuals, need to balance the risk associated in
innovation with the potential return. Higher risk projects invariably
need to demonstrate greater potential returns. Pearson developed the
concept of an uncertainty map (Henry and Walker, 1991) which helps in
the understanding of the concept of risk and uncertainty in innovative
projects. Pearson identifies two key variables. Firstly, uncertainty about
the endpoint – what is the project likely to result in? Secondly,
uncertainty about process or approach – how will the endpoint be
achieved? The model is adapted (see Figure 10.6) to reflect the
importance marketers attach to market reaction and product development issues. High degrees of uncertainty relating to market reaction
tend to exist when organizations are dealing with: (i) innovative new

Figure 10.6 Marketing uncertainty map

technologies, with the potential to create markets, or (ii) diversifying away from core customers or markets in order to find new applications or markets for existing products. In terms of product development it is important to consider development issues and the infrastructure required to deliver the product (distribution, after-sales support, etc.).

The model gives four possible situations with varying degrees of uncertainty and helps management convert ideas and concepts into workable solutions:

- **Quadrant 1 – Exploratory research**. Here there is much uncertainty. Innovation needs to be nurtured over time and immediate commercial gain cannot be expected. Typically, this involves state-of-the-art technical research and development of new technologies. Risk relates to two factors: (i) the work may be resource intense and divert resources away from more commercial activities, and (ii) no actual exploitable benefits may be generated. While activities in this area may require to be shielded from commercial pressure, this cannot be done indefinitely. Such activities require to be evaluated and either developed further or dropped. This requires a clear focus in terms of likely commercial outcomes and overall strategic goals. Given the right management structures risks can be kept to acceptable levels.
- **Quadrant 2 – Developmental activity**. This situation sees clear marketing goals and a well-defined market reaction, but uncertainty as to how such outcomes can be achieved. Many NPD projects fall into this category. For example, marketing has defined a specific need, but there is a debate as to the means of satisfying such a need. Given the high degree of uncertainty over how to achieve outcomes plus a requirement to commit (often substantial) resources, risk factors can be high.
- **Quadrant 3 – Market development**. The method and technologies are proven and well understood and uncertainty of outcome relates to applying such methods to new opportunities. The process of market development aims to find new applications and target new markets or market segments. As businesses move away from core markets, uncertainty will increase. Innovation revolves around the creative use of market information, creative segmentation and positioning.
- **Quadrant 4 – Market penetration**. The uncertainty pertaining to outcomes and method is low, and there appears to be an immediate opportunity. The organization needs to align its assets and competencies in order to capitalize on this. The problem is often one of speed of response. Here, innovation relates to flexibility, recognizing opportunity and adaptation of product offering.

Summary

Product development and innovation are strategic activities. Given the increasing competitiveness of the business world, organizations and their product offerings must evolve to survive. It is vital that management understand the true nature of their core, actual and augmented products. It is often the augmentation – enhancing the actual product via additional services – that generates commercial success.

Product development falls into three categories: product improvement/modification, product imitation and product innovation. It is product innovation that brings new and novel ideas to the market place. Regardless of the degree of innovation, a new product development (NPD) process is required. Essentially, this is a six-stage process covering:

1 idea generation,
2 idea evaluation,
3 concept development,
4 business evaluation,
5 product development, and
6 product launch.

The NPD process can be enhanced by using factors such as multifunctional teams and customer involvement to instil a market focus and ensure operational problems are resolved in advance of launch. Additionally, it is important that all product development has a strategic direction, with the process integrated into overall business strategy. To develop products successfully we must understand the pitfalls of NPD. Such pitfalls relate to factors such as underinvestment, failing to deliver customer benefit, forecasting errors, internal conflict and competitor response.

Innovation is effectively a management process aiming to bring together creative thought, technical/process development and commercial exploitation. Organizations need the right climate to promote innovation. They need to encourage teamwork and the ongoing exchange of information, coupled to support and reward systems. In this way, it is possible to innovate across their entire field of business operations. Managers need to consider the risks and returns associated with such activity.

References

Booz, Allen and Hamilton, *New Product Management for the 1980s*, Booz, Allen and Hamilton Inc., 1982

Davidson, H., *Even More Offensive Marketing*, Penguin, 1997

Jain, S., *Marketing Planning & Strategy*, 5th edition, South-Western, 1997

Kotler, P., Armstrong, G., Saunders, J. and Wong, V., *Principles of Marketing*, 2nd European edition, Prentice Hall, 1999

O'Connor, J. and Galvin, E., *Marketing and Information Technology*, Pitman, 1997

Pearson, A., cited in Henry, J. and Walker, D. (eds), *Managing Innovation*, Open University/Sage Publications, 1991

Further reading

Davidson, H., *Even More Offensive Marketing*, Chapter 11, Penguin, 1997

Chapter 11

Alliances and relationships

About this chapter

Increasingly, businesses have recognized the importance of alliances and joint ventures to future success. In marketing, vertical marketing systems (VMS) demonstrate the benefits co-operation can bring. Additionally, organizations need to build relationships with a range of 'markets'. Therefore, a broader definition of marketing is required.

Introduction

The saying 'no man is an island' could easily be adapted to 'no business is an island'! No organization can exist in isolation. All organizations depend on establishing and developing relationships. In short, they must develop relationships with other organizations (suppliers, distributors, etc.) and, even more critically, with customers. Indeed, this latter relationship provides the fundamental basis of all marketing activity.

Alliances, joint ventures and other co-operative strategies are now widely recognized as effective strategic solutions to the challenges of the commercial world. Many commentators predict that the future of many organizations depends on their ability to successfully enter, and manage, collaborative ventures. The coming decade will be one of strategic collaboration.

Marketers readily acknowledge the importance of building relationships with customers. We have seen the emphasis move from

transaction marketing (focusing on single sales) to relationship marketing (focusing on customer retention and building meaningful customer
relationships).

When considering inter-organizational relationships, or relationships
with customers, increasingly there are moves away from conflict and
towards collaborative-based strategies and philosophies. In this chapter, we examine the role of alliances within marketing strategy and
principles of relationship marketing.

**Illustrative Example 11.1: McKean Foods – haggis maker needs
US alliance**

The internet has opened up global opportunities to Glasgow-based food
manufacturer McKean Foods. Their website attracts interest from all over the
world, with a 40 per cent increase in sales of haggis via online operations.
Popular products include the 500 g 'Warrior' haggis and the larger 'Chieftain'
haggis – a big favourite on Burns' Night. Around 80 per cent of website hits
originate from North America. Such interest is pleasing, but also frustrating as
US Department of Agriculture restrictions mean the company is unable to
export its product to the United States. Despite the UK having some of the
world's most stringent hygiene regulations and the company achieving the
highest level of European food safety accreditation, they are unable to service
this growing demand due to US import regulations. McKean is looking at the
possibility of a partnership with a US-based manufacturer, thus enabling the
company to meet demand in North America.

Alliances

At a strategic level, managers aim to 'add value' by ensuring the
organization has the optimum level of assets and competencies.
Increasingly, strategic thinking recognizes that it is neither wise, nor
feasible, to attempt exclusively to provide or own this optimum level of
assets and competencies. Rather than do everything themselves, it may
be more feasible to enter into partnership arrangements with other
organizations. For example, two manufacturers could set up a joint
distribution system and both benefit from economies of scale. Telecommunications and computer manufacturers could combine their
technical expertise to produce a range of integrated products. While the
concept of alliances is now more common, it is hardly new. The history
of business is littered with good, and bad, examples of collaborative
ventures.

What motivates an alliance? There is no single answer to this question. Any number of factors can initiate such action. Common factors include:

- **Globalization**. Businesses are increasingly able, or indeed compelled, to compete on a world scale. Alliances and joint ventures are a means of responding to this challenge. Shortening product life cycles, the globalization of technology, and political change means the world is becoming a smaller place with more opportunity/necessity for collaboration. For example, parts and components can be sourced worldwide, or organizations can now more readily seek partners to distribute their products in previously inaccessible markets. Joint initiatives give access to expertise and contacts in local markets and greatly help the process of market entry. It should be noted that while world markets are increasingly open, some less developed economies (e.g. China) may insist on joint venture agreements as a condition of market entry, thus ensuring inward investment.
- **Assets and competencies**. As previously stated, there is a recognition that organizations cannot be truly effective at all activities. The move towards downsizing has seen organizations concentrate on core activities and contract out non-essential activity. Additionally, the cost (plus shortages of skills) associated with product development may facilitate joint activity. This allows market opportunities and new technologies to be developed at a relatively lower cost. Complementary activities and/or management skills can lead to inter-organizational synergy – the combined effect of two or more organizations working together is greater than their individual effect. To illustrate synergy, consider the following example. In-House Cuisine provides a restaurant delivery service – customers order via In-House Cuisine from a directory of top restaurants and In-House's uniformed waiters collect the meal and deliver it to the customer. The scheme has now been extended to hotels, with the Scottish Tourist Board allowing hotels with limited restaurant services to retain their three-star status by using In-House Cuisine as a form of room service.
- **Risk**. Collaboration is often born from the need to reduce risk. The sheer financial commitment may be so great that a consortium approach is required to spread the financial risk across a number of participants. A 'go-it-alone' strategy may incur other risks. Co-operative ventures can promote industry standards and common practice. For example, JVC's alliance with Sharp and Toshiba helped establish VHS as the industry standard for video recorders. Thus, 'go-it-alone' firms risk being isolated from accepted industry practice and technical standards. Additionally, joint activity can reduce the time

taken to develop products, thereby reducing the risk associated with launching them.

● **Learning and innovation**. Collaborative ventures provide great opportunities to learn and innovate. Technology and skills transfer are often essential in generating meaningful commercial benefit. Indeed, Morrison and Mezentseff (1997) attribute sustainable competitive advantage (generated via collaborative ventures) directly to learning and knowledge transfer. Consider the alliance between Rover and Honda. When active, this collaboration enhanced Rover's expertise in total quality management. The expertise and skills gained during the venture proved more durable than the alliance.

When examining the concept of alliances, it is important to consider the various forms such ventures may take. The scope of alliances ranges from highly formalized agreements involving ownership, to informal co-operation based on little more than a handshake. Johnson and Scholes (1999) summarize alliances in terms of four main categories.

Firstly, **acquisition and mergers** involve taking formalized ownership. This includes co-operative or hostile takeovers. Commonly, this is driven by: (i) possible efficiency gains which lead to lower operating costing in areas of activity – procurement, transaction processing and operational scale, and (ii) synergy effects, where combined activity leads to greater 'added value' than the two organizations could hope to generate separately. Acquisition strategies normally look to benefit from eliminating duplicated activities. For example, the merger of the Leeds and Halifax Building Society (subsequently converted into a bank) has seen the rationalization of the branch network.

Secondly, **consortia and joint venture** activities involve independent organizations entering into specific project agreements or setting up jointly owned ventures. Consortia are groups of companies in partnership, normally to develop large-scale projects. For example, the 'Eurofighter' project brings together a Europe-wide consortium of defence, electronic and aerospace companies developing the next generation of military aircraft.

Thirdly, **contract and licensing** agreements are legal, contractual agreements whereby the right to a product/activity is assigned to an independent operator. Common forms include subcontracting and franchising arrangements. Such agreement can allow organizations to focus on core activities, while contracting out work to specialist operators. For instance, the prison service has experimented with contracted-out transport and custodial services to Group–4 – a private security firm.

Finally, **networks** are informal agreements of co-operation built on working relationships and mutual benefit, as opposed to contractual agreement or ownership. Networks can also take the form of opportunistic alliances that, while informal, focus on specific opportunities. For example, a group of independent local retailers may join together and launch a customer loyalty card, as a response to increased competition from national retail chains.

For any alliance to stand the test of time, there needs to be strategic and cultural fit. **Strategic fit** essentially means that the core assets/ competencies of the partners are configured in such a way as to complement each other and offer more effective pathways to strategic goals than generic internal development. As previously stated, strategic fit relates to efficiency, synergy and, on occasions, legal necessity. Strategic fit needs to be clearly defined and must offer sustainable competitive advantage. **Cultural fit** is vital if organizations are going to work together. For any partnership to be successful, there is a need for the partners to have similar aspirations, goals and attitudes. For example, joint ventures between a fast-moving entrepreneurial company and a highly risk-averse conservative organization could be difficult to achieve. The question of cultural fit is pivotal in the selection of a partner and type of alliance.

A marketing perspective on alliances can be illustrated by examining the development of **vertical marketing systems** (VMS). A VMS approach offers an alternative to the traditional view of distribution channels. Traditional distribution channels involve a chain of independent companies, each pursuing individual goals. Each channel member aims to optimize its position, normally at the expense of other channel members. The resultant tension and conflict between the buying/ selling organizations within the channel tends to lead to distrust, erosion of margins, higher costs and other lingering problems. A VMS approach aims to integrate channel members into one cohesive unit, with common objectives and distribution being actively managed across all channel members. Such an approach has the advantages of: (i) reducing overall cost by avoiding repetition and reducing administration, and (ii) enhancing quality and effectiveness by means of joint problem solving and shared expertise. Figure 11.1 illustrates both activities.

VMS ventures tend to operate in one of the following ways. They can be **corporate** – all parties in the VMS having common ownership. Alternatively, it is possible to have an **administrative** VMS – independent organizations agreeing to conform to common standards and compatible interlinked systems, normally determined by the dominant partner. For example, Ford car dealerships, although independent, conform to service, stock-holding and marketing criteria set by the Ford Motor Company. Finally, there are **contractual** VMS agreements which have legally binding obligations. For example, the SPAR retail chain is

Figure 11.1 Traditional and VMS marketing channels

a group of independent retailers who sign up to a centralized buying agreement.

To examine a practical VMS example, consider Marks & Spencer. M&S has remained at the forefront of British retailing for longer than most commentators can remember. Although the mighty M&S has recently experienced troubled times, its enduring appeal and acknowledged strengths flow from its relationships with suppliers. Over decades, it has developed innovative and mutually beneficial supplier partnerships. Close working relationships enable the company to effectively manage the entire supply chain. Indeed, supply chain management will prove increasingly vital as M&S faces future challenges.

Relationship marketing

The concept of relationship marketing takes marketing back to basic principles. It recognizes the fundamental importance of sustaining customer relationships in order to generate customer loyalty and repeat business. Additionally, relationship marketing acknowledges a broader view of marketing, and defines a number of 'markets' which must be addressed in order to optimize customer relationships. Christopher *et al.* (1994) identify a six market model relating to the organization's relationships (see Figure 11.2).

Undoubtedly, customer markets should be the primary focus of any organization. Previously, marketing has tended to focus on finding new customers and winning new business. Modern marketing practice

Figure 11.2 The six market model (*Source***: Christopher *et al.*, (1994)**

(relationship marketing) now recognizes the importance of retaining customers and generating repeat business. Relationship approaches aim to develop customer alliances, whereby the customer not only sees the organization as their preferred provider, but actively recommends others to use their products and services. This 'elevated status' is more achievable when a broader view of marketing is taken. Such a view recognizes the role of 'markets', other than the direct customer, in developing customer relationships.

Supplier markets are important, as strong supplier links and joint innovation enable the overall supply chain to be optimized. This leads to reduced cost and potentially enhances the overall quality of the customer experience. **Employee markets** recognize the importance of recruiting and retaining the right staff. Ultimately, it is staff who, directly or indirectly, deliver the desired levels of customer satisfaction. Closely related to the employee market is the concept of **internal markets**. The idea of internal markets and internal marketing is examined in Chapter 12. The concept uses marketing principles (segmentation, targeting and the 'mix') internally. By treating employees, departments or functions as customers, we can deliver internal services and support more effectively, thus motivating staff, improving effectiveness and, ultimately, enhancing the external customer experience. External groups can have a significant influence on the organization and its customer base. Marketing strategies may need to consider such **influence markets**. For example, management may need to build relationships with financial analysts, the media, local communities and campaign groups. Finally, **referral markets** lead to new business. Organizations that deliver high degrees of customer services are well placed to receive customer referrals. Additionally, referrals may come via other parties (e.g. trade groups, distributors) and relationship marketers must strive to establish a wide referral network.

The process of relationship marketing is summarized by Kotler *et al.* (1999) in terms of creating and further developing 'value laden' relationships with stakeholders.

Developing relationships

There is a strong body of evidence supporting the economic case for relationship marketing. For example, Reichheld and Sasser (1990) illustrate that relatively minor improvements in customer defections can generate significant improvements in profit. As relationships are built on mutual benefit, what benefits does relationship marketing bring to customers? The approach typically benefits customers in that: (i) it requires marketers to have a much closer understanding of customer needs and therefore provide more appropriate solutions to customer problems; (ii) it may result in schemes rewarding customer loyalty, and (iii) it fuses together all aspects of the business, making the entity more customer-focused and responsive to customer need.

Having clearly established the benefits of a relationship approach, organizations must consider how they can move from transaction-based marketing (focusing on single sales) to sustainable relationship-based strategies. Common principles of relationship marketing are:

- **Use appropriately.** Like any technique, relationship marketing works better in certain situations. Not all transactions are relational in nature. For example, impulse buys or one-off purchases generally don't require, or offer, scope to develop relationships. Indeed, attempts to install a relationship approach in such circumstances may simply agitate potential customers. Relationship strategies work well in high-involvement purchases categorized by: (i) complex decision making; (ii) a degree of risk associated with purchase; (iii) a requirement for ongoing support, and/or (iv) regular purchase. To be worthwhile, the additional revenue generated needs to exceed the cost of any relationship programme. Organizations may well prioritize customers in terms of relationship potential, with higher priority being given to certain segments or type of customer.

Illustrative Example 11.2: Costa Coffee – strategic relationships

Coffee has now become a hot market! Driven by changing lifestyle patterns and the popularity of US TV shows featuring coffee houses (e.g. Friends, Frasier) the coffee market is emerging as one of the fastest growing retail sectors.

The UK market leader Costa, owned by Whitbread, has embarked on a programme of rapid expansion. Strategic relationships with other parts of the Whitbread group are vital to building the chain. David Thomas, Managing Director of Whitbread Restaurants and Leisure states, 'In addition to stand-alone coffee retail outlets, we are developing opportunities for the brand in our existing retail and leisure businesses' (e.g. Marriott Hotels). Additionally, outlets are opening in airports and railway stations. By building working relationships with other outlets, Costa in well placed to extend its brand and develop long-term relationships with the consumer.

- **Establish relationship drivers**. If a relationship strategy is feasible, what are the key components driving success? Market research techniques facilitate an understanding of what is important to building/maintaining relationships. By identifying how customer expectations are set and evaluated, organizations are more able to generate positive interactions. For example, if it is found that key customer service attributes are accurate order processing and delivery time as per agreed schedule, it is possible to allocate resources to ensure such expectations are met (or even exceeded).

- **Build customer value**. Businesses need to adopt a value-building approach to relationships. There are three basic approaches to generating customer value. Firstly, there are **financial benefits**, where the relationship has some economic benefit to the customer. For example, Tesco was the first major supermarket chain to introduce a customer loyalty scheme. 'Tesco Clubcard' points can be exchanged for goods or discounts. The firm now plans to enhance the scheme by creating three classes of loyalty points – gold, silver and bronze – with higher spending customers receiving bigger awards. Secondly, there are **social benefits**. Here, relationships are based on social contact, belonging, support and personal inter-action. For example, friendly relationships with clients may provide the basis of a hairdressing business. Brand loyalty may also be based on this concept. In the fashion market, people adopt brands as a symbol of lifestyle and group identity. Thirdly, **structural benefits** stem from close operational association. For instance, manufacturers and retailers could implement automated stock control/replenishment to facilitate a 'just-in-time' approach to inventory management.

- **Retain customers**. It is a normal fact of business life that long-established customers tend to be more profitable than new or occasional customers. They tend to be larger, more frequent consumers and major sources of referral business. Therefore, organizations need not only to measure retention, but to guarantee that all employees are aware of its importance. The ideas outlined above all have a role to play in retaining customers, but organizations must actively seek to strengthen ongoing business relationships. Common methods include corporate hospitality, sending referral business to customers and briefing clients on new developments. A key step in many retention programmes is to establish a relationship management structure within the organization. This involves: (i) identifying which customers (or customer groups) merit special attention, and (ii) assigning account/relationship managers to develop and implement a relationship plan. Such a plan requires specific objectives and strategies aimed at enhancing the organization's business position with that target group.

Amazon – the internet bookshop – offers a practical illustration of relationship marketing. Obviously, as a virtual bookshop Amazon has no direct, face-to-face contact with its customers. However, its website allows customers to write book reviews, read what others thought of a given text, and track the progress of individual orders. The process engenders a feeling of belonging – a social benefit.

Summary

Increasingly, businesses need to recognize the importance of alliances and joint ventures. A collaborative approach has much to commend it, and is being driven by factors such as globalization, risk reduction and the need to share learning and generate innovation.

Alliances can range from acquisition and merger, through to networks based on informal co-operation. To be successful, organizations need to seek partnerships where strategic fit exists. Strategic fit relates to factors like economy of scale, synergy benefits resulting from complementary assets/competencies and, on occasion, legal necessity. Cultural fit is also important as it sustains relationships.

Relationship marketing is a vital component of business success. To be truly effective, organizations must recognize that they serve a range of 'markets'. They need to consider a broader definition of marketing, one that embraces 'markets' such as employees, suppliers, internal function, referral sources and influences. However, relationship marketing is not applicable in all cases. When applicable, organizations must strive to identify the key relationship drivers, build customer value and do everything reasonable to retain customers.

References

Christopher, M., Payne, A. and Ballantyne, D., *Relationship Marketing*, Butterworth-Heinnemann, 1994

Johnson, G. and Scholes, K., *Exploring Corporate Strategy*, 5th edition, Prentice Hall, 1999

Kotler, P., Armstrong, A., Saunders, J. and Wong, V., *Principles of Marketing*, 2nd edition, Prentice Hall, 1999

Morrison, M. and Mezentseff, L., 'Learning alliances: a new dimension in strategic alliances', *Management Decision*, 35(5/6), 1997

Reichheld, F. and Sasser, W., 'Zero defections: quality comes to services', *Harvard Business Review*, Sept./Oct. pp. 105–111, 1990

Further reading

Hooley, G.H., Saunders, J. and Piercy, N., *Marketing Strategy and Competitive Positioning*, 2nd edition, Chapter 8, Prentice Hall, 1998

Chapter 12

The strategic marketing plan

About this chapter

Planning is an integrative, co-ordinating activity that gives focus to the organization's activities. Strategic and tactical decisions are made at corporate and functional levels. Addressing the analytical, behavioural and organizational aspects of planning can help overcome the many barriers to success. While the format and presentation of marketing plans may vary, a common purpose exists – to identify, select and implement appropriate marketing activities.

Corporate and marketing plans

Marketing managers plan in order to complete tasks on time and without exceeding pre-set resource limits. It is likely that objectives, targets and budgets will be set as part of the overall corporate planning and budgeting process. The task is to translate these factors into a workable marketing plan.

When developing a plan, the process involves choosing certain courses of action and ruling out other possible options. Planning should be systematic, structured and involve three key components: (i) objectives – what has to be achieved; (ii) strategy (or actions) – defining how the objectives are to be achieved, and (iii) resource implications – the resources required to implement the strategy.

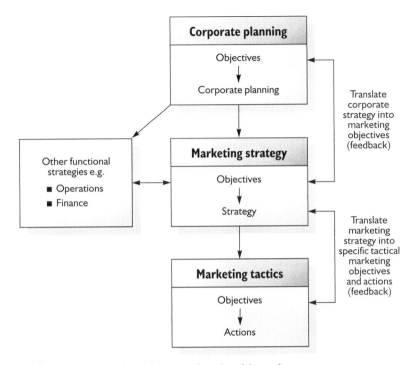

Figure 12.1 Corporate and marketing planning hierarchy

Clearly, it is important to understand the interface between marketing and corporate strategy. This is best illustrated by considering the hierarchical structure of an organization. Senior management formulates objectives and strategy for the entire organization (or a strategic business unit – SBU). Managers in various functional areas, such as marketing, contribute to the process by developing specific functional strategies and ultimately tactics to achieve these corporate objectives. Effectively, the process involves a hierarchy of plans, with strategy at one level becoming the objective(s) at the next. Additionally, this process provides feedback on the success/failure of any strategy. Figure 12.1 illustrates the concept.

Corporate planning

The corporate plan will define objectives for the entire business and should co-ordinate the various functional strategies (marketing, operations, human resource management, finance, etc.) to deliver the overall corporate objectives. It is important that functional strategies are interrelated (see Figure 12.1). For example, if the marketing strategy

Figure 12.2 The strategic process

focused on developing high levels of customer service in order to retain key customer groups, both the operations and human resource management functions would have a role to play in delivering this. Corporate strategy can be summarized as being:

- **Integrative**. The process **co-ordinates functional activity** towards a common goal and takes a 'whole organization' view of the corporation. By defining corporate targets, normally in financial terms, collective targets are set for the functional groups.
- **Providing focus**. Strategy defines the scope of the business – the general nature of activities and markets served. This **strategic direction** allows functional areas to develop appropriate strategies and tactics.
- **Important**. By its very nature, corporate strategy is the process of making major business decisions. It defines business direction over the **long term** and is critical in setting the overall resource profile available to the organization.
- **Matching**. There is a need to match the organization's activities and resource base to the current and future business environment.

A useful summation of corporate strategy management is provided in Figure 12.2. This model takes a top-down view of the overall strategy process. It identifies the five components vital in achieving corporate success:

1 **Vision.** Senior management and other stakeholders must establish an overall vision of what the corporation should be. This defines the basic need they fulfil and establishes the generic direction of the business.
2 **Corporate objectives and strategy**. Collective goals and strategy define the 'benchmarks' for success, and ways of achieving success. This level co-ordinates corporate activity and initiates activities to achieve desired results.
3 **SBU/functional objectives and strategy**. Corporate strategy translates into objectives and plans for individual elements of the business. This may take the form of SBUs (Strategic Business Units – divisions within a company) or functional activities. For example, a hotel chain could divide its business into three SBUs – accommodation, food and beverage, and conferences and leisure.
4 **Resources**. For a given strategy, the need exists to match resources to strategic intent. This process normally involves annual budgeting.
5 **Structure**. Management must develop the appropriate organizational and staffing structures to facilitate success.

Successful businesses ensure these factors are aligned in order to turn strategic intent into business reality.

Marketing plans – strategy or tactics?

There are two types of marketing plan – strategic and tactical. This distinction generates much confusion and debate: is it a strategy or a tactic? This question may be academic when facing the reality of the business world, as the distinction between the two will vary from organization to organization and manager to manager. However, much of the confusion can be removed if characteristics common to strategic plans and tactical plans can be identified.

● **Strategic marketing**. This takes a longer-term time frame and broadly defines the organization's marketing activities. The process seeks to develop effective responses to a changing business environment by analysing markets, segmentation and evaluating competitors' offerings. Strategy focuses on defining market segments and positioning products in order to establish a competitive stance. Marketing strategy tends to embrace all of the mix, or significant components of the mix (distribution strategy, communications strategy, etc.). Problems in this area tend to be unstructured and require external, often speculative, data.

	Strategic marketing	Tactical marketing
Time frame	Long term	Short term
Focus	Broad	Narrow
Key task(s)	Defining market and competitive position	Day-to-day marketing activity
Information and problem solving	Unstructured, external, speculative	Structured, internal, repetitive
Example	New product development	Price discounting

Figure 12.3 Strategic and tactical marketing

● **Tactical marketing**. This takes a shorter-term time frame and concerns day-to-day marketing activities. It translates strategy into specific actions and represents the ongoing operational dimension of marketing strategy. Tactical marketing tends to deal with individual components of the marketing mix elements (sales promotion, advertising, etc.). Problems are often repetitive and well structured with data being internally generated.

Figure 12.3 examines the differences between strategic and tactical marketing.

Why does planning matter?

The organisation needs a strategic marketing plan in order to adapt to a changing business environment. Given the basic business premise of 'success through effectively meeting customer needs' it is clear that organizations must continually adapt and develop to remain successful. Strategic marketing facilitates this process and provides robust solutions in an increasingly competitive world. Essentially, the plan should provide a systematic framework with which to analyse the market place and supply a well-defined way to pursue strategic goals.

However, the truly successful plan goes further than the simple process of planning. It is a vehicle to communicate, motivate and involve staff in fundamental business activities. Too often planning is viewed as a restrictive process based on programming events and generating paperwork. Remember, plans need employee commitment and 'ownership' to achieve results.

The key reasons for planning are summarized as follows:

- **Adapting to change**. Planning provides an opportunity to examine how changes in the business environment have affected or will affect the organization. It enables management to focus on strategic issues as opposed to day-to-day operational problems.
- **Resource allocation**. Planning allows us to deploy resources to effectively meet opportunities and threats. No plan can succeed without appropriate resources. When a strategic perspective is taken, organizations are better placed to marshal the resources required to meet strategic 'windows of opportunity'. Doyle (1994) defines strategic windows of opportunity as changes that have a major impact in the market place. Strategic windows include factors such as: (i) new technology; (ii) new market segments; (iii) new channels of distribution; (iv) market redefinition – where the nature of demand changes; (v) legislative changes and, (vi) environmental shocks – sudden unexpected economic or political change. Essentially, the process involves aligning marketing activities with opportunities in order to generate competitive advantage.
- **Consistency**. By providing a common base to work from (e.g. techniques and assumptions) the overall decision-making process can be enhanced. Additionally, common methods and formats should improve internal communication.
- **Integration**. As a strategic process, planning should facilitate the integration and co-ordination of the marketing mix. By providing a strategic focus it should be possible to generate synergy from the individual elements of the marketing mix.
- **Communication and motivation**. The plan should clearly communicate strategic intent to employees and other stakeholders. Clear objectives and an understanding of the individual, or group contribution to the process serve to generate 'ownership' and motivation.
- **Control**. All control activities are based on some predetermined plan. The planning process should set meaningful targets, thus defining the criteria by which success is measured.

Barriers to successful planning

Few would argue with the concept of planning. In any activity, a plan provides a fundamental basis for success. Marketing plans should offer exactly what is required – optimizing the use of marketing techniques and resources in order to make the most of marketing opportunities. However, even the most charitable of marketing managers would view this statement as naive and unlikely to be fully achieved. If managers view planning as 'fine in theory' but failing in practice to deliver its full potential, where does it go wrong?

Clearly, barriers must exist to successful planning. Often, these barriers are more to do with the human aspects of the business management. They involve people, politics, skills and culture, to a greater degree than formal systems, methodology, and data.

Common barriers to successful planning are:

- **Culture**. The prevailing culture may not be amenable to marketing plans. If the fundamental principles of marketing are not accepted by the organization, any move towards being market-led and customer-orientated could be dismissed as 'not the way we do it'. Often we see considerable resistance to change and gradual regression back to old work practices.
- **Power and politics**. All organizations are subject to internal politics. The development of strategic planning becomes a battlefield where vested interests fight each other's proposals and squabble over status and resources. This process absorbs much management time and can result in ill-advised compromise and unnecessary delay.
- **Analysis not action**. Much time and energy can be wasted by the process of analysing data and developing rationales for action, as opposed to simply acting. While a rigorous process is commendable, it should not displace action. This 'paralysis-by-analysis' barrier tends to substitute information gathering and processing for decision making. Perhaps surprisingly, many planning systems do not promote action and are more concerned with reviewing progress and controlling activity, rather than tackling strategic issues.
- **Resource issues**. In any planning situation, the potential exists to negotiate over resources. Indeed, a major aspect of the process is to match resources to strategic aims. Managers must take a realistic view of the resource position and endeavour to ensure resources are not over-committed or needlessly withheld.
- **Skills**. In some instances, managers do not have the skills (project management, forecasting, etc.) required to make the best use of the planning process. Here, planning takes on a ritual nature – a meaningless but 'must-do' annual task. Often, planning is reduced to incremental increases/decreases in annual budget and fails to examine opportunities for business development.

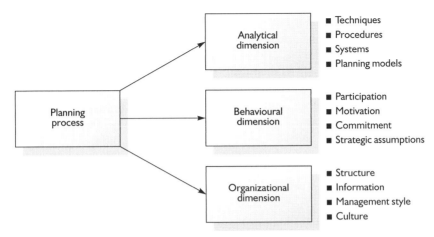

Planning process → Analytical dimension
- Techniques
- Procedures
- Systems
- Planning models

Planning process → Behavioural dimension
- Participation
- Motivation
- Commitment
- Strategic assumptions

Planning process → Organizational dimension
- Structure
- Information
- Management style
- Culture

Figure 12.4 A multidimensional model of marketing planning (*Source*: Piercy, 1997)

Many of these barriers relate to the implementation of plans rather than the planning process itself. Chapter 13 deals with the issue of implementation in detail. However, sound management practice would advocate the inclusion of implementation as part of the planning process. Indeed, Piercy (1997) suggests a multidimensional model of planning. This considers the analytical dimension, the behavioural dimension and the organizational dimension of any plan. Figure 12.4 summarizes the model.

- **Analytical dimension**. Analytical tools, techniques and models are important, as they provide a framework to tackle issues and identify/solve problems. While formalized planning systems have the advantage of offering a common (corporate-wide) systematic approach, to be truly effective they must address behavioural and organizational issues.
- **Behavioural dimension**. Here we focus on the people aspects of the planning process. Plans only become successful because of the support, participation, motivation and commitment of people. There is a need to understand and fully communicate the strategic assumptions underpinning the strategy. Plans must address behavioural factors in order to gain the support so vital to smooth implementation.
- **Organizational dimension**. Strategic planning takes place within the context of a given organization. Therefore, it will be influenced by organizational factors, such as culture and style of management. Remember, organizational structures determine the flow of informa-

tion, as well as defining responsibilities and reporting lines. Major strategic initiatives may require radical organizational changes.

By taking this 'multidimensional' approach to planning and actively considering behavioural and organizational issues within the planning process, it is possible to enhance the overall likelihood of success.

The structure of a strategic marketing plan

What does a strategic marketing plan look like? While the answer to this question will vary from organization to organization (in terms of structure and presentation), marketing plans perform a common function and have common components. Indeed, McDonald (1999) views marketing planning as a systematic way of identifying, selecting, scheduling and costing activities in order to achieve objectives. Such definitions focus on the purpose, as opposed to the structure, of planning.

Regardless of precedent and planning formats, strategic plans tend to have common elements. Marketing managers would expect a strategic plan to cover: (i) industry analysis; (ii) internal analysis; (iii) opportunity identification; (iv) objective setting; (v) formulation of strategy; (vi) proposed marketing programmes and actions, and (vii) implementation and control – including financial forecasts.

Figure 12.5 presents an annotated example of a strategic marketing plan. Note that this figure does not attempt to portray the definitive marketing plan. It merely illustrates the component parts common to such plans.

Strategic marketing plans take on many different guises. The content, structure and complexity of a plan will vary. While planning formats and conventions are largely a matter of historic precedent within the organization, the key imperative is to generate action. Plans should address critical issues in a way that is relevant to the organization. For example, promoting decisive marketing initiatives within a limited timescale.

Approaches to marketing planning

The development of a marketing plan is a significant and time-consuming activity. All planning is essentially objective-driven – objectives are translated into actions. A number of schools of thought

Figure 12.5 Illustrative example of a strategic marketing plan

exist as to how the task is best approached. The standard approaches to planning are:

● **Top-down**. Senior managers develop objectives and strategy. Managers at an operational level are then required to implement these strategies. This approach is said to encourage professionalism and promote a corporate strategic view of marketing activity.

- **Bottom-up**. Here, authority and responsibility for formulation and implementation of strategy is devolved. Senior marketing managers approve, and then monitor, agreed objectives. It can be claimed that this approach encourages ownership and commitment.

Hybrid systems are also common, where objectives are 'top-down' and responsibility for the formulation/implementation of strategy is devolved.

Summary

Strategic planning offers a systematic and structured approach to choosing and implementing certain courses of action. Corporate plans define overall business objectives, while providing focus and co-ordinating functional activities. Such plans need to align the stake-holders' vision to the objectives, strategy, resources and structure of the strategic business units.

There is a need to differentiate between marketing strategy and marketing tactics. Essentially, strategic marketing focuses on defining segments, establishing competitive positions and co-ordinating all the elements of the mix. Tactics translate strategies into action and deal with day-to-day marketing transactions.

Planning allows organizations to adapt to a changing business environment and provides a framework for resource allocation. Additionally, sound planning promotes a consistency of approach and facilitates integration of activity, communication, motivation and control of activities. In order to achieve these benefits, we must overcome the numerous barriers to successful planning. These include culture, internal politics or lack of the requisite skills to make planning a successful activity. Truly successful plans make use of analytical techniques but also address the behavioural and organizational dimensions of the process.

The structure and content of a strategic marketing plan will vary. However, plans tend to have common elements – industry analysis, internal analysis, opportunity identification, formulation of strategy, marketing programmes/actions and implementation/control.

Formulating marketing plans can take a top-down, bottom-up or hybrid approach.

References

Doyle, P., *Marketing Management & Strategy*, 2nd edition, Prentice Hall, 1994

McDonald, M., *Marketing Plans*, 4th edition, Butterworth-Heinemann, 1999
Piercy, N., *Market-led Strategic Change*, 2nd edition, Butterworth-Heinemann, 1997

Further reading

Aaker, D., *Strategic Market Management*, 4th edition, Chapter 17, Wiley, 1995
Piercy, N., *Market-led Strategic Change*, 2nd edition, Chapter 12, Butterworth-Heinemann, 1997

Strategic implementation

- Strategic implementation
- Control

Part 3 examines issues relating to implementation and control. Any strategic activity must address two basic issues – selecting a competitive strategy and putting it into practice. Implementation and control address the second issue. Managers should never underestimate the importance, or indeed complexity, of 'putting it into practice'.

Chapter 13 assesses the general issues pertaining to implementation and how to build effective implementation approaches within the context of marketing projects. Chapter 14 is concerned with the application of financial measures, performance appraisal and benchmarking as control mechanisms. The concept of control loops applied to marketing is also examined.

Chapter 13

Strategic implementation

About this chapter

Implementation is critical to the success or failure of any venture. Basic generic management principles (e.g. leadership, team building and delegation) contribute to the process. Marketing managers must evaluate the ease, or otherwise, of implementation and deploy project management techniques to achieve desired goals. Additionally, 'internal marketing' can ease the process of implementation.

Implementation – stressing the importance

A key maxim in business is: never acquire a business you don't understand how to run. Equally, it would be true to say: never adopt a strategy you don't understand how to implement.

It can be said that, in terms of strategy, planning is the easy part. With a basic grounding in marketing, most managers could sit down with a blank sheet of paper and develop an outline marketing plan. This plan may contain all the correct 'buzz-words'. Ideas relating to market penetration, segmentation, globalization and competitive advantage would fill the page and a clear concise way forward formulated. However, it is not that simple. While many managers could produce such an outline, how many could implement it? Without implementation, the plan remains some ideas on a piece of paper.

In the context of marketing the goal will be to achieve and/or maintain a marketing orientation – success by a process of understanding and meeting customer need. It is doubtful if a marketing strategy can be implemented where this orientation does not exist. Achieving such a view is dependent on the quality of management and their understanding of marketing as a business philosophy.

It is reasonable to suggest that implementation is often a key determinant in the success or failure of any strategic activity. Therefore, it should be an integral part of any marketing strategy. This view is supported by examining the history of corporate strategy. Recent times have seen a move away from corporate planning to the concept of strategic management. The main difference is that strategic management addresses the issue of implementation.

Success vs failure

Two dimensions determine the success of a strategy: the strategy itself and an organization's ability to implement it. A useful starting point in considering success or failure is outlined in Figure 13.1. Bonoma (1984) examines the appropriateness of the strategy and the effectiveness of execution skills, thus establishing four general positions:

- **Success**. The ideal situation: an appropriate strategy and a strong ability to execute such a strategy. This should present little or no problem.

Figure 13.1 Strategy and execution (*Source*: Adapted From Bonoma, 1984

- **Chance**. Here the strategy is poor, perhaps lacking detailed analysis or not building on existing strengths. However, it may be saved by effective execution. This may be such that we can adopt and adapt from a weak opening basis and, with luck, do what is required. Clearly, the degree of 'inappropriateness' is highly significant. Is the strategy able to be saved? Notwithstanding this question, this position always brings a high degree of risk.
- **Problem**. We are doing the right things badly. The strength of strategic planning is dissipated by poor execution. Often the true value of the strategy is not fully recognized and it is dismissed as being inappropriate.
- **Failure**. A no-win situation. With failure on all levels there is a danger of struggling on with implementation and simply 'throwing good money after bad'. Organizations should try to learn from such situations. Do not make the same mistake twice.

Clearly, there is an issue of subjectivity within defining good/bad and appropriate/inappropriate and it is all too easy to be wise after the event. It is simple to classify a strategy as inappropriate after it is deemed to have failed. The key quest is to ensure strategies fall into the 'success' category. Formulating an appropriate strategy has been dealt with in the preceding chapters of this book and we will now focus on the execution of strategy – in other words, implementation.

Effective implementation can be viewed in terms of:

1 Understanding the fundamental principles of implementation.
2 Assessing the ease, or otherwise, of implementing individual projects.
3 Applying project management techniques.

Fundamental principles

Having stressed the importance of implementation we turn to the issue of what factors are required for success. These are summarized in Figure 13.2.

Any successful strategy must be supported by each of these components. These cover the human aspects of business and a more objective process approach to management. Note that these factors can have either a positive or negative effect on a given project. Each is considered in turn.

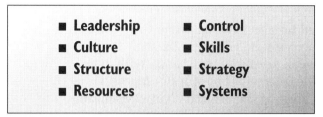

- ■ Leadership   ■ Control
- ■ Culture   ■ Skills
- ■ Structure   ■ Strategy
- ■ Resources   ■ Systems

Figure 13.2 Key elements in implementation

Illustrative Case 13.1: Kall Kwik – implementing a national marketing strategy

Kall Kwik operates a UK-wide chain of outlets offering design, print and copy services to business. The organization faces the challenge of implementing clients' marketing strategies across a distributed, geographically dispersed, network. Kall Kwik Centre owners provide local service, while adhering to centrally set quality, pricing and production time standards. The network of local Kall Kwik Centres allows multi-site client organizations (e.g. retailers) to implement marketing campaigns without incurring the high distribution costs normally associated with centralized print purchasing.

Leadership

The role of the leader is to get the best out of people and deal with the unexpected. They should be viewed as facilitators. This is achieved by creating an environment where actions can take place. Leaders require effective people skills such as negotiation and delegation. Often leaders acquire their leadership position by means of technical expertise. This can be dangerous, since their primary function is to facilitate rather than undertake the work themselves. The leader needs transferable management skills in addition to technical and marketing competence. Adair (1984) summarizes leadership as:

1 **Task needs** – aiming to complete the project.
2 **Group needs** – developing team spirit and morale.
3 **Individual needs** – harmonizing the above with the needs of the individual.

Depending on circumstances, the leader will emphasize task, group or individual needs (see Figure 13.3).

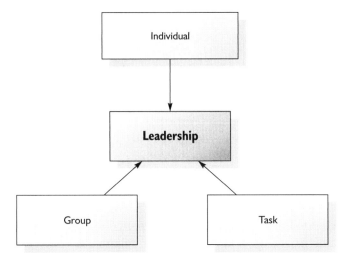

Figure 13.3 Leadership

Leaders need to adopt an appropriate style of management. If a crisis looms then a more direct autocratic style may be called for. However, under different circumstances a participative style may be best suited. Hence leaders can move from task, individual or group orientation depending on the circumstances.

Culture

Much management theory relates to corporate culture. Culture can be defined as a combination of shared values and beliefs. These are commonly reinforced with corporate symbols and symbolic behaviour. For example, a company may wish to pursue a culture of openness and accessibility. The symbol of this may be to encourage all staff to dress informally on a Friday, to promote a more relaxed atmosphere.

Great care must be taken when implementing strategy. If the strategy goes against the dominant culture it is likely to fail unless a major effort is made to develop and maintain support. This could be achieved via staff training, appraisal and restructuring. The strategist needs to be sensitive to the shared values that exist within the organization. Normally it is best to work with, as opposed to against, such values.

Structure

The structure of any organization, or project, has two primary functions. Firstly, it defines lines of authority denoting levels of responsibility. Current management thinking promotes a move towards flatter structures with more devolved authority. Secondly, structure is a basis for communication. Structures can filter out information, making senior management remote from the customer. In the area of implementation consideration should be given to how communication occurs.

In relation to developing marketing strategy, it can be advisable to have multifunctional teams. A group with a diverse range of backgrounds can promote ownership of projects, identify operational problems in advance and enhance overall quality.

Resources

Any project needs to be properly resourced. Leaders have the role of obtaining and making optimum use of resources. The resourcing of projects is often more to do with internal politics than actual need. In many organizations there needs to be a more objective process of resource allocation. Resources will ultimately relate to finance and staff.

Resourcing is normally budget driven. However, there is now a recognition of the importance of being time focused. For example, a three-month time delay is likely to be more serious than a minor budgetary overspend. The concept of 'time-to-market' is dealt with in a later section.

Remember, implementation never takes place in a vacuum – things change and it is important to be flexible and build in an acceptable degree of contingency (additional resource to be called on) within any implementation strategy.

Control

Control is simply a way of making sure what is supposed to happen actually happens. The term itself – control – often appears to have negative connotations and is seen as limiting and coercive in nature. This should not be the case. Astute management can develop effective control systems.

The basic approach is a simple feedback loop. You measure progress, compare against some pre-set standard and if required take action. Given the importance of control the concept is expanded upon in the next chapter.

Skills

The appropriate skills mix is required in order to achieve any aim or goal. Within the context of implementing marketing strategy, 'softer'

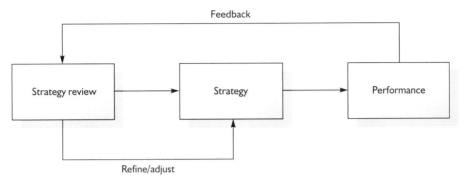

Figure 13.4 Reviewing strategy

human resource management (HRM) skills can be lacking. It should be remembered that project management is a skill in its own right. To summarize, successful implementation requires skills such as:

- Technical/marketing skills, e.g. design, market research, industry analysis.
- HRM skills, e.g. delegation, performance appraisal, training.
- Project management skills, e.g. budgeting, resourcing, forecasting.

Strategy

To state the obvious, there must be a strategy to implement. However, the fact that a strategy exists may not be apparent to everyone. Additionally, the strategy may not be seen as appropriate by all staff. The project leader must ensure people are aware of the strategy, the reason for it and their role in making it work.

Potential strategy should be screened to ensure that it is appropriate to current circumstances. For example, what is the basis of competitive advantage? What organizational changes need to take place?

The development of strategy is an ongoing activity. During and after the implementation phase, management should review and adapt policy as required. While the overall objectives remain intact, there may be changes in how we set about achieving such targets. Figure 13.4 illustrates this point.

Systems

Several systems are important in the implementation process and fall into two general groups: reporting and forecasting. It is necessary to have systems which aid management decision making. Note that these are aids to decision making and not replacements for decision making.

Figure 13.5 The Seven S's

Such systems will cover areas such as finance and budgeting, project evaluation/refinement and market research. The key factor is often the interpretation of information rather than the system itself.

The Seven S's

The 'Seven-S' model developed by McKinsey & Co. provides a useful summation of these ideas. The model can be adapted as seen in Figure 13.5 and split into: (i) human resource management (HRM) – dealing with the people-based aspects of implementation, and (ii) process – the policy, procedures, reporting and systems aspects of implementation.

Assessing ease of implementation

It is now possible to test and evaluate the likely ease of implementation. Firstly, strategic fit – how easily will the strategy fit into current activities? Unsurprisingly, the easier the fit the less likely implementation problems are to occur. However, it must be recognized that an easy fit does not guarantee success. The strategy must be right for the business environment.

Primarily, the concern is with the level of change associated with the implementation. The greater the change, the greater the management challenge and the greater the perceived benefit of the change needs to be. Hence there is a need to consider the potential pay-off and the amount of change required to achieve this. Figure 13.6 illustrates the relationship between change and importance:

- **Overhaul.** Here implementation will have a significant impact and face significant challenges. Given that a high degree of change is likely, one must expect increasing levels of resistance and risk as the strategy has only a limited fit with current activity. There needs to be compelling strategic reasons and significant support for this strat-

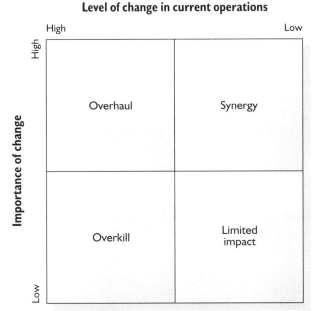

Level of change in current operations

Figure 13.6 Strategic fit

egy's implementation. Such activities are likely to involve factors such as restructuring, downsizing, mergers and overhauling business culture.

- **Synergy.** The word can be defined as 'working together'. The combined effect of high importance and relatively limited change offers a potentially 'easy ride'. Problems should be limited and risk of failure is reduced. However, great problems occur when a strategy is deemed to fall into this category, only to find that it is not the case and far more change is required. The organization needs to be doubly sure it has the required synergy before embarking on this route.

- **Limited impact.** Low levels of change affecting relatively unimportant areas of activity. Often a series of such activities can yield incremental change. This could represent a stage-by-stage approach to change, where relatively minor changes are introduced over a period of time. This option of incremental activity can be used where resources are limited or a phased consolidated approach is deemed more appropriate.

- **Overkill.** This has high risk and limited impact importance. Questions have to be asked. Why are we doing this and what is the pay-off? Care is needed in order not to alienate staff and disrupt activity. Such projects often occur as a result of political manoeuvring and compromise.

Successful management requires an appreciation of the nature of change and its subsequent impact on the organization and individuals. The process starts with an awareness of the need to change, then progresses to a transition phase and finally reaches some pre-determined state. Normally, the transition stage is the most critical as it is fraught with risk and uncertainty.

Management must assess the level of change associated with a project and deploy strategies relating to the management of change. For example:

- **Justification.** Have supportive evidence in the form of facts and quantitative/statistical data. Hard data often prove powerful allies.
- **Commitment.** Try to involve others via group problem solving, participation and communication. Such factors tend to generate commitment to change.
- **Learning.** Change is often difficult to achieve and mistakes will be made. Learning from mistakes is important. Remember, experience is the name we like to give our mistakes.
- **Incrementalize.** It may be better to have an overall strategy that can be broken down into a series of smaller ongoing changes, as per the 'limited impact' strategy.
- **Operations.** Ensure that change is reflected in operational activities through the appropriate systems, structures, policies and monitoring. In this way, change becomes a permanent feature and the organization avoids slipping back into old practice.

People, power and politics

When addressing the issue of implementation there are no panaceas. However, not all staff will be equally supportive of a given marketing strategy. Hence it is wise to consider the likely levels of support and resistance that may exist relative to a given project. Piercy (1997, p. 591) sets out general categories into which staff can fall (see Figure 13.7).

Those with influence, often the appropriate decision-making unit (DMU), need careful consideration. Common tactics include:

- Converting or isolating opposition.
- Upgrading the status of influential supporters.
- Recruiting the active involvement of non-involved supporters.
- Negotiation and trade-off with vested interest.

Influences over issues

Figure 13.7 Key players' matrix

In short, the success of any programme requires sufficient influence and support. This becomes more complex when the project generates high levels of change.

The issue of supporters and their influence tends to relate to the dreaded, but vital concept of internal office politics. Within the organization, political behaviour can be either desirable or undesirable. Often this depends on your perspective. Good strategies can flounder on the rocks of political self-interest and behaviour.

Kakabadse (1983) identifies seven common approaches to playing the political game:

1 Establish who the interested parties are – the stakeholders.
2 Consider their comfort zones. What do they value, fear or tolerate?
3 Work within these comfort zones.
4 Use networks – those interested or influential.
5 Identify 'gatekeepers' and adhere to the norms of the network.
6 Make deals for mutual benefit.
7 Withhold and withdraw. Consider withholding information and know when to withdraw from areas of conflict and dispute.

Arguably, political behaviour is an essential part of strategy implementation. This view requires management to identify key players and consider their potential reaction to strategic initiatives. Remember, the art of politics is about influencing people when you cannot rely on direct authority. By considering the political dimension related to the project it is possible to gauge resistance and support, develop justification and counter-argument in advance of critical decisions.

Additionally, you may be able to develop influence via various power bases. For example, controlling resources, having access to people and controlling the flow of information. These can all assist in playing the political game.

Internal marketing

No discussion relating to the ease, or otherwise, of implementation would be complete without considering the potential use of internal marketing. Internal marketing focuses on the relationship between the organization and its employees. Berry and Parasuraman (1991) define the process in terms of viewing employees (or groups of employees) as internal customers.

Definitions of this type encompass the work traditionally within the remit of the personnel/human resource management function (recruitment, training, motivation, etc.). Few would argue with the importance of staff in relation to implementation. Therefore, can marketing techniques be used to motivate employees and ease the path of project implementation?

By applying the marketing concept internally, it may be possible to enhance the likely success of a project. Factors such as internal segmentation and application of the 'mix' may well have a role to play. Consider the following:

- **Segmentation.** The process of dividing groups into sub-groups with similar characteristics. This is perfectly feasible within any organization. For example, senior managers may have different training needs from other staff. By grouping like types together more effective training and communication is possible.
- **Product.** This may well be the focus of strategy and accompanying process of change. Equally, the individual's job or function could be viewed as an 'internal product'. The internal product, service or task is a component in delivering the overall strategy.
- **Promotion.** Clear communication has a vital role to play in establishing success. The project manager could design a 'promotional campaign' stressing the benefits of a new strategy. In all cases, communication is an issue that must be considered when planning implementation.

Organization		
Segment 1	Segment 2	Segment 3
Influential supporter Internal mix I	**Influential opposition** Internal mix II	**Non-involved supporter** Internal mix III

Figure 13.8 Internal marketing

- **Place.** How to get the 'product' to the internal customer. Channels of distribution for information, services and training can be developed and optimized. These could include team briefings, seminars and day-to-day business interactions.
- **Price.** This is a complex issue. While it is relatively easy to cost factors like training, communications vehicles and other associated tangible costs, it is worth remembering that a price is also paid by the group and/or individual. This 'psychological' price is difficult to measure, but important. It takes the form of uncertainty, loss of status, stress and loss (hopefully short-term) of operational efficiency.

In its simplest form internal marketing offers a framework (the 4 P's) which can lay the foundations of successful policy implementation. It offers the marketing concept as a way to achieve specific strategic goals. Figure 13.8 illustrates how the concept could be applied to an organization. Here we segment by level of support. However, other criteria (e.g. department or management level) could be applied.

Applying project management techniques

The ability to manage a project is a skill in its own right. Such skills are 'transferable' and can be applied to any situation. Therefore, they adhere to general principles which can be learned by the marketing strategist.

Essentially, project management involves achieving unity of purpose and setting achievable goals within given resource and timescale parameters. Efforts tend to focus on integrating activity, building teamwork and monitoring progress. Marketing projects are rarely simple and often have to be achieved while overcoming unforeseen problems and barriers. Effective project management deals with such problems as and when they arise.

Figure 13.9 summarizes common tasks in project management. Each task is reviewed in turn.

- **Objective setting**   ■ **Team building**
- **Planning**   ■ **Crisis management**
- **Delegation**

Figure 13.9 Project management

Objective setting

An overall strategic objective will be broken down into a series of sub-objectives. It is important that these are clear, concise, understood and accepted by team members. A useful acronym is to develop SMART objectives. These add focus and relate to the task(s) required.

S   **Specific**. They should be clear and task orientated.
M   **Measurable**. Objectives must be measured in order to establish progress.
A   **Action**. They should be task related and promote activity.
R   **Resourced**. A realistic resource base has to be allocated to enable progress.
T   **Time**. There is a need to make the objective time focused. How long will it take?

Planning

Having established what is to be achieved, planning breaks an activity into a series of structured manageable tasks, co-ordinates these tasks and monitors progress.

Tasks can happen in series or in parallel. So-called 'parallel processing' – running several tasks simultaneously – has several advantages. It can reduce the overall timescale for the project and reduce the risk of a delay in one task delaying the entire project. Figure 13.10 illustrates this point.

Increasingly there is an awareness of being time focused. Business is now adopting a time-to-market (T-t-M) philosophy. This T-t-M approach advocates the importance of reducing the overall time taken to implement a project. Consider the potential benefits of reducing implementation time. Firstly, a commercial return is produced sooner. Secondly, by being early into the market the opportunity exists to gain a price premium and/or market share. The T-t-M focus is achieved by parallel processing and, conversely, spending more time developing a robust planning specification.

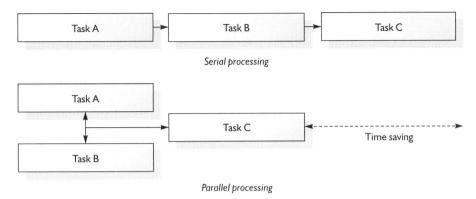

Figure 13.10 Serial vs parallel processing

Delegation

Effective managers realize they cannot do everything themselves – they know that management is the art of delegation. The art is often to balance the degree of delegation with the appropriate span of control. The manager needs to understand the strengths, weaknesses and group dynamics of the team members.

Illustrative Example 13.2: Ericsson – time to market

The mobile phone industry provides an illustration of how critical time-to-market cycles can be. Although the market is booming, it is characterized by intense competition and rapid technological development. Ericsson – the manufacturer of mobile phone handsets – has recently seen its market share drop within this growing market. These difficulties are largely attributed to the delay in launching a key product (the T28). The company is quoted as stating that the T28 was nearly a year late and that they had to cancel the T36 because it had only a short market life. Such delays caused Ericsson to miss out on demand for low-cost handsets aimed at the expanding pre-pay mobile phone market.

Many managers have a problem with letting go and need to remember that delegation extends the capacity to manage and frees the leader from the mundane. Additionally, if staff are encouraged to take decisions, overall decision making can be improved. The people 'on the spot' are more likely to have a fuller grasp of the situation and be able to make effective decisions.

Key principles of delegation include:

- Focus on the objective. Be crystal clear about what has to be achieved but flexible in how it is to be achieved.
- Delegate authority not just responsibility. Empower people to make decisions and manage resources.
- Test people on smaller and less important tasks and gradually give the more able employee greater scope.
- Explain how tasks are monitored and define circumstances in which they should refer back to senior management.
- Refrain from undue interference but be watchful.

Team building

Clearly there is a need to use the skills and capacity of the team to the optimum level. It is important to have a core goal as this gives the team a focal point. Each team member must understand their contribution to this collective goal. As Wickens (1997) states, teamwork does not depend on people working together but upon working to obtain the same objective.

A winning team has the right combination of skills. These should blend and complement each other. The environment should be positive and supportive but not complacent or overly relaxed.

Basic team-building principles which can be applied to a marketing project are:

- Encourage a positive supportive environment. It is acceptable to make mistakes but ensure the team learns from them.
- Show and encourage respect for each other. Encourage constructive criticism as opposed to personal attack.
- Link individual reward to group performance.
- Disagreement and discussion should not be suppressed and ideas should be listened to. However, this should not detract from effective decision making.

Crisis management

There will be times when things go dramatically wrong and a crisis point is reached. The basic premise of crisis management is to take urgent action in response to unexpected events. By definition, the process is reactive in nature and invariably is a turning point. However, it does not negate prior planning. Management can develop a series of scenarios and have appropriate responses available as a contingency. This scenario planning allows a crisis management approach to be developed in advance.

Additionally, we may be given prior warning of a pending problem. Often there is a gradual worsening of events until the point of crisis is attained. If these signals are picked up early enough decisive action can be taken before the problem becomes a crisis.

A key idea is to maintain confidence and for management to be clearly in control. Basic techniques include:

- Assess the situation coolly and establish the facts before taking any rash action.
- Draw up a plan of action and establish a management structure.
- Set up a communications system to receive and disseminate information.
- Separate the trivial from the important and prioritize tasks.
- Be decisive and take responsibility.

Summary

Do not downplay the importance of implementation. Organizations need not only to consider the development of strategy, but also to address issues that turn strategy into reality.

The key to successful implementation is the application of basic management principles – leadership, systems and resourcing are all important. Such factors must be taken within the context of the organizational culture and business environment that exists.

Prior to implementation, it is wise to consider how easy the tasks are likely to be. This relates to the importance of the task and the level of associated change. The attitude and influence of interested parties will also have a significant impact on the ease, or otherwise, of implementation.

Internal marketing techniques and the deployment of standard project management principles, such as objective setting, planning and delegation, facilitate a workable framework for the implementation of strategy.

References

Adair, J., *Action Centred Leadership*, McGraw-Hill, 1984

Berry, L. and Parasuraman, A., *Marketing Services: Competing Through Quality*, Free Press, 1991

Bonoma, T., 'Making your marketing strategy work', *Harvard Business Review*, Vol. 62, No. 2, March–April, pp. 68–76, 1984

Kakabadse, A., *The Politics of Management*, Gower, 1983

Piercy, N., *Market-led Strategic Change*, 2nd edition, Butterworth-Heinemann, 1997
Wickens, P., *The Road to Nissan*, Macmillan, 1997

Further reading

Piercy, N., *Market-led Strategic Change*, 2nd edition, Chapters 14 and 15, Butterworth-Heinemann, 1997

Chapter 14

Control

About this chapter

Control mechanisms aim to translate strategic plans into specific actions. The purpose is to ensure that behaviour, systems and operations conform to corporate objectives/policy. Marketing managers need to be aware of a range of control variables: financial measures, budgets, performance appraisal and benchmarking.

Introduction

The term 'control' has received a bad press. The phrase smacks of coercive action, limiting freedom and keeping costs to an absolute minimum. The reality is somewhat different and managers should consider the control process as simply a mechanism to protect strategic plans during implementation. Murphy's law states that, if anything can go wrong, it will go wrong. Hence a control system detecting and pre-empting the inevitable problems that accompany implementation is a valuable asset.

Control can be defined as attempting to guarantee that behaviour and systems conform to, and support, predetermined corporate objectives and policies. Such 'hard edged' views illustrate the importance of linking behaviour to overall strategic direction. This is a fundamental reason for having control systems.

Control – the basic principles

The basis of control is the ability to measure. In essence it compares what should have happened with what actually happened or is likely to happen. Given the importance of measurement, a tendency exists to measure what is easy to quantify rather than what is important. Project managers must guard against this and focus on the key areas. Good control systems often detect and rectify problems before they become significant and managers should remember that prevention is better than cure. Try to be proactive rather than reactive.

The process is broken down into a series of simple steps. Firstly, a target is set. Ideally, this is integrated into overall strategic planning. Secondly, a method of measurement has to be determined and implemented. Finally, measured results are compared with the pre-determined target(s) and corrective action, if required, is undertaken.

There are two sides to the control equation – inputs and outputs. If only output is considered then the system is one of inspection as opposed to control. Correctly addressing both sides of the equation allows management to optimize the process and take a strategic view. Typical inputs include:

- **Finance**: investment, working capital and cash.
- **Operations**: capacity, usage, efficiency and application of machines, systems and other assets.
- **People**: numbers, quality and skills of staff.

Output is measured in terms of overall system performance. Performance is derived from a combination of efficiency and effectiveness:

- **Efficiency**. How well utilized are the inputs? Do we make maximum use of finance, minimize cost and operate at optimum levels of capacity?
- **Effectiveness**. Are we doing the right things? This relates to actual performance and will include sales revenue, profit, market share and measures of customer satisfaction.

Remember, it is better to pursue effectiveness. For example, a company may be a very efficient producer (low cost, high volume, etc.) but relatively ineffective at finding buyers for its goods.

Control systems can operate as simple feedback loops. Figure 14.1 illustrates the concept. However, more sophisticated systems of **feedforward control** are possible. Such systems try to pre-empt problems by anticipating the effect of input(s) on overall performance. However, such systems are more complex and consequently more difficult to set up.

Figure 14.2 illustrates the application of a basic control loop to the marketing management process. Here marketing objectives, such as increasing market share, are translated into performance targets. These

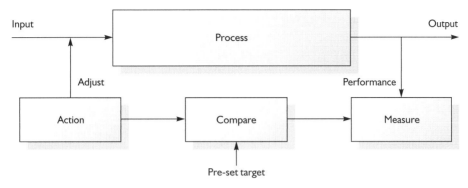

Figure 14.1 Feedback control

targets define a specific measurable basis against which managers will be judged. The objective of increasing market share would be quantified. For example, we may aim at a 7 per cent increase over twelve months. Responsibility for achieving the target is assigned and actual performance is evaluated against planned performance. The adjustment of the process is achieved by management action and/or altering the objectives or standards within the system. In this way, the system becomes flexible and can react to changes in performance and the business environment.

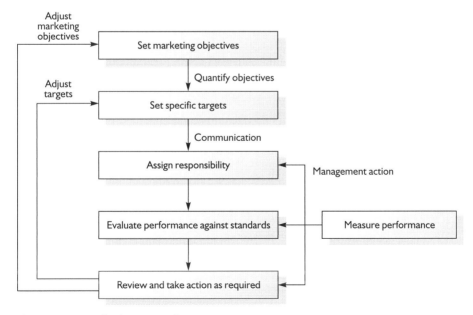

Figure 14.2 Marketing control systems

What makes an effective control system?

Control systems require careful design. Generic principles exist which are common to all effective control mechanisms. As with management processes, it is important to retain a degree of flexibility and common sense. The project manager can deploy the following principles to ensure effective control:

- **Involvement.** This is achieved by encouraging participation in the process. Management can achieve desired results via consultation. For example, staff could contribute towards setting targets. Their own staff development needs could be considered along with the required tasks. Correctly applied, the process enhances morale, promotes ownership and develops the skills base of employees.
- **Target setting.** There are two important factors. Firstly, the target criteria should be objective and measurable. How this is assessed needs to be communicated and agreed in advance. Secondly, it needs to be achievable but challenging.
- **Focus.** Recognize the difference between the symptoms and the source of a problem. While it may be expedient to treat the symptoms, tackling the source of the problem should eliminate it once and for all.
- **Effectiveness.** The tendency exists to measure efficiency as opposed to effectiveness. Efficiency is the usage and productivity of assets. Effectiveness is about doing the right things. Ideally, we want measures of efficiency applied to areas of effectiveness. In reality we tend to apply efficiency measures to areas easiest to measure. Be careful to measure what is important, not what is easy to quantify. Additionally, measurement should be accurate, valid and consistent.
- **Management by exception.** Management attention is directed to areas of need. Identifying what constitutes an exception to the norm is a useful exercise in its own right. The process involves setting tolerances and benchmarks for normal operation. Management action only becomes a priority when pre-set limits are breached. Figure 14.3 shows a simple tolerance control chart. This is based on planned sales revenue plus or minus a tolerance of 5 per cent. If the levels are broken, or in a proactive system appear as if they may be breached, management will begin to take an interest in the process.
- **Action.** Good control systems promote action. Such systems do not just detect problems, they solve problems. Basically, actions adjust the inputs to the process. For example, extra resources could be made available to deal with a backlog or a process or procedure could be redesigned to make it more effective.

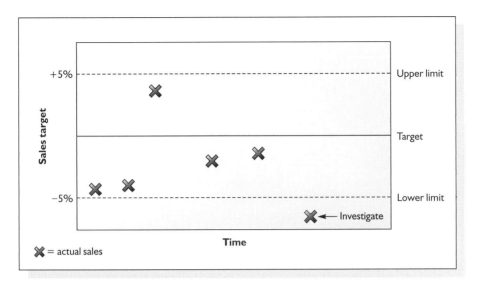

Figure 14.3 Tolerance control chart

Problems of control

A good control system is not easy to develop. The project manager requires an awareness of the general problems associated with control systems. No system is perfect and no control system offers one hundred per cent accuracy. Often, the concern is keeping operations and plans within acceptable limits.

Three problems are commonly associated with control systems. Firstly, such systems can be **costly**. Here the benefits of control and subsequent improvements are outweighed by the cost of the control mechanism. This often relates to large bureaucratic systems – layer upon layer of administration is built one upon the other. This is self-serving rather than customer-focused, often absorbing resources that would be more effectively deployed in core activities. Secondly, control systems **stifle effort and creativity**. Such systems promote uniformity and conformance to pre-set targets. They become barriers to innovation. Thirdly, control promotes a view of **inspection as opposed to development**. Systems often deal with the symptom rather than the root of the problem. Here, we tend to be constantly 'fire fighting' and looking for the quick fix as opposed to developing a better overall method of operation. The effect is to filter and/or suppress information from those with the power to radically overhaul a poor system.

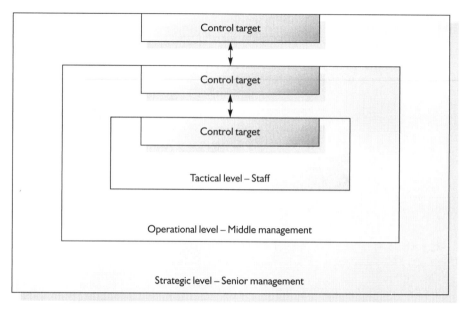

Figure 14.4 Cascade control

Management control

Having reviewed the basic concept of control, we can now focus on the key aspect of management control. Management control takes place at a number of different levels within the organization (see Figure 14.4). Control criteria apply to strategic, operational and tactical levels. The control variables at one level become targets for the next level down. Effectively, this means that a 'cascade' system of control is in operation. Senior/strategic levels use fewer, more critical, control variables. These are predominantly financial in nature and focus on divisional or strategic business unit (SBU) targets. The operational level relates to project or departmental activities and encompasses financial and non-financial information. The tactical level relates to group or individual performance and the focus is on productivity.

Good performance means that employees (at all levels) have a clear view of what the priorities are, what they should be doing currently, how their area of responsibility contributes to overall performance and what levels of achievement are acceptable.

Management control will focus on finance, performance appraisal and benchmarking. The relative importance of each may vary with the level of management. Financial measures will give both short and long-term control data and are fundamental to decision making. Perform-

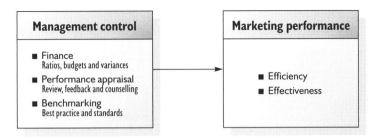

Figure 14.5 Management control related to marketing

ance appraisal examines the personnel and human resource aspects of management. Finally, benchmarking is a means of comparison and identification of best practice. As Figure 14.5 illustrates, management control is applied to marketing in order to establish marketing performance. Remember, performance is a function of efficiency and effectiveness.

Financial control

Financial control techniques are vital to successful strategy. Such techniques apply to both the planning and operational phases of projects. We will focus on three main financial control activities: ratios, budgeting and variance analysis.

A basic understanding of financial terminology is required. Ultimately all business activities are measured in financial terms and managers require a grasp of accounting terms. Key terms include:

- **Assets.** Items that have value to the business. Assets are subdivided into two categories. (i) *Fixed assets* – retained by the business, in the long term, for continual use. Typical examples include buildings, machinery, vehicles and long-term investments. (ii) *Current assets* – items that are readily convertible into cash, or cash itself. Such assets are to be used in the short term. Typical examples include stock, cash and debtors (those owing the organization money).
- **Liabilities.** Financial obligations owed to others. (i) *Current liabilities* are those debts which must be paid in the near future. Therefore cash will be required to meet current liabilities. (ii) *Capital* invested by the owner can be classified as a liability as it is technically owed to the owners.

Ratio analysis	
Use	Application
■ Trend analysis ■ Comparison ■ Highlight key areas	■ Profitability ■ Liquidity ■ Debt ■ Activity

Figure 14.6 Use and application of ratios

Ratios

A simple and effective control technique is to express performance in terms of ratios. Ratios should not be used in isolation but should be considered in relation to trends and comparisons with planned or standard ratios. Remember, they are no more than indicators and rarely identify the source of a problem. However, managers can identify key ratios for their areas of responsibility. These ratios provide a quick and effective way to establish performance and highlight areas warranting more detailed analysis. Figure 14.6 outlines the uses of ratios.

Ratios represent a snapshot of the firm's financial/productivity position and fall into four general categories (see Figure 14.6): profitability, liquidity, debt and activity. When calculating ratios it is important to be consistent with the terms used. For example, how is profit defined – before or after tax?

Profitability ratios

Here, effectiveness is measured by evaluating the organization's ability to produce profit. Profit margin is expressed in terms of a ratio of profit to sales. The profit margin is a key trading concern. Clearly, the profit margin can be enhanced by raising selling price and/or reducing costs.

Return on capital employed (ROCE) is expressed as net profit as a percentage of capital. It examines to what extent an investment is paying off. It can be applied to an entire business or to specific projects requiring capital investment. ROCE is used to indicate the extent to which an investment is justified or to compare investment opportunities.

Examples

$$\text{Gross profit margin} = \frac{\text{Profit}}{\text{Sales revenue}}$$

$$\text{Profit} = \text{Revenue} - \text{cost}$$

$$\text{Net profit margin} = \frac{\text{Profit after tax}}{\text{Sales revenue}}$$

$$\text{Return on capital employed} = \frac{\text{Net profit}}{\text{Capital employed}}$$

Liquidity ratios

Ratios evaluate the ability to remain solvent and meet current liabilities. The firm needs to be able to convert assets into cash in order to meet payment demands. If the current ratio is more than 1, sufficient assets exist to meet current liabilities. The quick (or acid-test) ratio gives a stricter appraisal of solvency as it assumes stock is not automatically convertible into cash. Ideally, this ratio should be 1 to 1. However, many businesses operate with lower acceptable ratios. If the ratio is too high it may suggest that the organization does not make optimum use of its financial assets (e.g. holding too much cash).

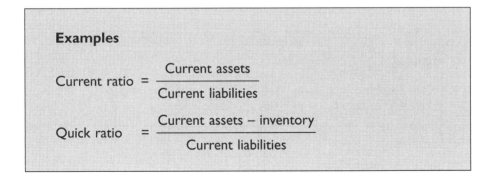

Examples

$$\text{Current ratio} = \frac{\text{Current assets}}{\text{Current liabilities}}$$

$$\text{Quick ratio} = \frac{\text{Current assets} - \text{inventory}}{\text{Current liabilities}}$$

Debt ratios

These ratios help determine the company's ability to handle debt and meet scheduled repayments. They examine the extent to which borrowed funds finance business operations. If creditors begin to outweigh debtors this may signify overtrading – an inability to collect money owed.

Examples

$$\text{Debt to assets ratio} = \frac{\text{Total liabilities}}{\text{Total assets}}$$

$$\text{Debt to credit ratio} = \frac{\text{Debtors}}{\text{Creditors}}$$

Activity ratios

These ratios determine how effective the organization is at generating activity, such as sales from assets. These activities often relate to business cycles or processes, such as the time taken to turn over stock or collect debts. For example, the greater the stock turnover the better for the organization. An additional example, common in retailing, is sales per unit of floor space. This gives a measure of retail effectiveness.

Essentially, such ratios measure the relationship between inputs to outputs.

Examples

$$\text{Inventory turnover} = \frac{\text{Sales}}{\text{Inventory}}$$

$$\text{Sales per square foot} = \frac{\text{Sales}}{\text{Floor space}}$$

$$\text{Productivity} = \frac{\text{Units produced}}{\text{Number of employees}}$$

Budgeting

The processes of strategic development and budgeting are intrinsically linked. To be blunt: no budget equals no strategy! The budgeting process translates marketing strategy into financial terms which, whether we like it or not, are the way all plans are expressed, evaluated and controlled.

Budgeting is the single most common control mechanism. It serves not only to quantify plans but also to co-ordinate activities, highlight areas of critical importance and assign responsibility.

Many industry practitioners would agree with Piercy (1997). He talks about the 'hassle factor' – difficulty, time, negotiation, paperwork, etc. – associated with budgeting. This serves to highlight two points, Firstly, budgeting is about resource allocation. Secondly, budgeting is a political process (negotiation, bargaining, etc.) necessary to obtain required resources.

Before managers can prepare a budget there are certain fundamental requirements which must be met. These relate to:

- **Budget guidelines.** The organization's policy and procedure relating to budget formulation must be understood. These set out assumptions, methods and presentational requirements.
- **Cost behaviour.** Management must understand what drives costs within their area of responsibility. Additionally, it is important to be clear on how costs are allocated. For example, what is the basis of overhead cost allocation?
- **Timescale.** A specific time period needs to be set. This could be for a fixed budgetary period, such as a financial year, or alternatively a 'rolling budget' could be prepared. Here, the budget is split into manageable time periods, and outline forecasts are updated at regular intervals. New periods are added as the budget progresses.
- **Objectives.** Specifically, what are we aiming to achieve and how is it being assessed? Corporate or departmental goals should be translated into resource and subsequent budgetary requirements.

Approaches to budgeting

Many approaches exist to formulating a budget. Most organizations have developed a historic way of approaching the task. Recent times have seen a move towards greater objectivity and the need to justify assumptions and requirements. Common methods of budgeting are:

- **Historic.** Traditionally the main determinant of a future budget is previous expenditure. Organizations simply base the budget on previous financial data. Adjustments are made for factors like inflation and level of activity. The model is basically incremental in nature – last year, plus or minus some factor, with managers concentrating on justifying or challenging changes.

- **Zero-based.** Budgets are systematically re-evaluated and senior management establishes priority within the context of overall financial constraints. The process involves examining activities and deriving the cost and resulting benefit from these activities. Alternative methods of achieving objectives are simultaneously considered and there is often a trade-off between activities. The method relates to analysing objectives and tasks and is highly 'political' in nature.

- **Activity-related.** Here budgets are based on often crude measures of activity. Simple calculation rules such as percentage of sales, or average industry spend, are used as precursors to determining available funds.

Variance analysis

Finally, in this section on financial control, variance analysis is reviewed. Basically, this examines the variation between actual and planned results and is a concept applicable to a range of activities. It is commonly used along with budgetary control. The actual results are compared with budgeted forecasts and then the variance is examined in order to determine the reason for the difference. Variance analysis allows the organization to identify the main areas of concern and break problems down into component parts. For example, in marketing, variance analysis is often applied to sales price and sales volume. Standard formulae are useful in calculating the effect of these variables on overall revenue:

- Variance in sales revenue = Actual revenue – planned revenue
- Variance due to price   = Actual volume × (planned price – actual price)
- Variance due to volume   = Planned price × (actual volume – planned volume)

Consider the following example. We plan to sell 4200 units at £25 per unit. However, due to market conditions, we actually sell 3850 units at £16 per unit. Hence the variance in sales revenue is:

Variance in sales revenue $(3850 \times 16) - (4200 \times 25) = -43\,400$

Variance analysis can be used to determine whether the loss of sales revenue is predominantly due to the lower than expected volume or failure to maintain planned price:

$$\text{Variance due to price} = 3850 \times (16 - 25) = -34\,650 \quad 80\%$$

$$\underline{\text{Variance due to volume} = 25 \times (3850 - 4200) = -8750 \quad 20\%}$$

$$-43\,400 \quad 100\%$$

Therefore, we can see that 80 per cent of the failure to achieve planned revenue is due to the lower unit price. Management could then investigate why we failed to achieve the planned unit price.

Variance analysis is not limited to price and volume calculations. A wide range of factors can be analysed in this fashion (e.g. profit, cost and market size).

Performance appraisal

Performance appraisal concerns achieving better results from groups and individuals. A performance appraisal framework is based on planned objectives, levels of achievement and competence. The focus is on the control and development of staff, and is critical to project implementation. Effective performance appraisal requires managers to have good people skills and appraisal should be constructive in nature. It is about doing a better job. Three key skills are involved: reviewing performance, giving feedback and counselling.

- **Reviewing performance.** The performance of individuals, or groups, should be reviewed continuously as part of normal management activity. Additionally, there may be a formal review which summarizes activity. Try to use objective criteria as a basis of review. Such criteria should be communicated and agreed in advance. Work and personal development plans should be considered in tandem with set criteria.
- **Giving feedback.** Feedback relating to performance is based on actual results, or observed behaviour. It is important not to focus just on the negative but to try to give credit where it is due. When giving feedback, be specific and describe rather than judge results. By reference to specific actions and behaviours, managers can more readily focus on key aspects of improvement.
- **Counselling.** Performance appraisal should be positive in nature. In order to build on strengths and overcome weaknesses, management may well have to counsel staff. This is particularly relevant to areas

of underperformance. Counselling needs to consider performance, not personality, and to invite a degree of self-appraisal. Aim to identify and agree problems and then choose required actions.

Benchmarking

In order to be 'the best you can be', it pays for organizations to compare themselves with leading performers. Benchmarking provides a method of enabling such comparisons to take place.

Benchmarking is defined as:

> A systematic and ongoing process of measuring and comparing an organization's business processes and achievements against acknowledged process leaders and/or key competitors, to facilitate improved performance.

However, benchmarking is more than just copying. The process is about continuous improvement and becoming a learning organization. The credo is one of adaptation rather than adoption. Ideas, practices and methods have to be screened and adapted to specific business situations Benchmarking falls into three general areas:

- **Competitive analysis** – reviewing competitors' activities, strategy and operations so that the organization can improve its performance.
- **Best practice** – determining the best way of undertaking an activity. This could involve examining activities in unrelated areas of business or industry. For example, a computer manufacturer could benchmark a mail-order retail company in order to improve its stock control system. Equally, best internal practice could be identified and spread to other units or departments within the organization.
- **Performance standards** – targets to be met or surpassed. For example, if the average industry conversion of enquiries into sales was 1 in 20 and the organization achieves 1 in 25, what does this say about its sales process?

The process of benchmarking

Benchmarking comprises a four-stage approach. This is illustrated using the 'Deming cycle' (Watson, 1993): plan, do, check and act (see Figure 14.7). The planning stage involves identifying what to study and who or what should act as the benchmark. Common areas to

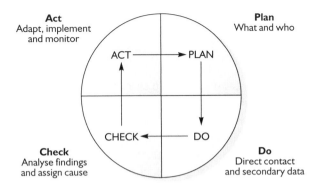

Figure 14.7 **The Deming cycle applied to benchmarking** (*Source*: Watson, 1993)

benchmark are customer service levels, logistic and distribution methods, product quality and 'time-to-market' cycles. Organizations will benchmark against competitors, acknowledged leaders or success-ful internal activities. Next, conduct research. This may involve co-operation and direct contact with the benchmark. Alternatively, secondary data may be used to establish standards and actions. The data are then analysed. This involves establishing the extent of performance gaps and identifying assignable causes for such gaps. Finally, the lessons learned are adapted, as appropriate, and applied in order to generate improvement in performance.

Controlling marketing performance

In contrast to mechanical systems, marketing activities are inherently more volatile. This is due to a constantly changing business environ-ment driven by the needs and wants of the market. Measuring marketing performance is a process of determining appropriate criteria by which to judge activity. Kotler (1997) identifies four main areas associated with the control of marketing activity (see Figure 14.8):

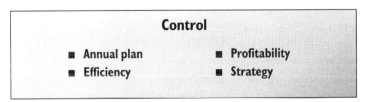

Figure 14.8 **Control of marketing activities**

Illustrative Example 14.1: British Airways – measuring marketing success

Organizations spend a great deal of time and money marketing their products, therefore they require objective measures relating to the effectiveness of such expenditure. British Airways is reported to evaluate marketing success via measurement of awareness, feedback on customer satisfaction and market share data. Additionally, a more focused approach is applied to specific promotions. These measure factors such as repeat business and level of sales.

- **Annual planning.** This has the purpose of evaluating the extent to which marketing efforts, over the year, have been successful. Evaluation will focus on analysing sales, market share, expenses and customer perception. Commonly, sales performance is a major element of this analysis. All other factors provide explanation of any variance in sales performance.
- **Profitability.** All marketing managers are concerned with controlling their profit levels. By examining the profitability of products, or activities, it is possible to make decisions relating to the expansion, reduction or elimination of product offerings. Additionally, it is common to break distribution channels and segments down in terms of profitability. Remember, it is important to have a systematic basis for allocating cost and defining profit.
- **Efficiency control.** Efficiency is concerned with gaining optimum value from the marketing assets. Managers are looking to obtain value for money in relation to marketing activity. The promotional aspects of marketing (sales, advertising, direct marketing, etc.) are commonly subject to such controls. Figure 14.9 displays examples.
- **Strategic control.** There is a need to ensure that marketing activities are being directed towards strategic goals and that marketing is an integral part of the overall process of delivering value. A strategic review will aim to assess that marketing strategy, and subsequent implementation, is appropriate to the market place. A review of this nature will take the form of a marketing audit – a comprehensive examination of all marketing activity to assess effectiveness and improve marketing performance.

   These areas of marketing control are general in nature and specific measures of marketing performance are required. Performance measures and standards will vary by organization and market conditions. A representative sample of the type of data required to

<table>
<tr><td>

Product
- Market share
- Sales
- Sales by segment
- Number of new products
- Warranty claims
- Return on capital employed
- Repeat purchase

</td><td>

Price
- Profit margin
- Discount levels
- Price by segment
- Price comparisons

</td></tr>
<tr><td>

Place
- Channel costs
- Channel volume
- Channel growth
- Delivery time
- Stock levels

</td><td>

Promotion
- Cost per contact
- Media coverage
- Sales per call
- Awareness levels
- Enquiries generated

</td></tr>
</table>

Figure 14.9 Control of marketing activity

control marketing activities successfully is shown in Figure 14.9. The aim is to break the general areas (annual plan, profitability, efficiency and strategy) into measurable component parts to which responsibility can be assigned.

Remember, in the context of marketing a balanced view is required. No one variable should dominate the control process. For example, marketing strategists have been guilty of following a credo of 'market share at any cost'. While such a variable is important, it is not a panacea and consideration needs to be given to other factors such as profitability. Additionally, marketing control should measure only dimensions over which the organization has control. Rewards, sanctions and management actions only make sense where influence can be exerted. Control systems should be sensitive to local market conditions and levels of competition. For instance, developing markets and mature markets may require different control mechanisms.

Summary

The essence of control is the ability to measure and take action. Control systems are concerned with efficiency and effectiveness and often operate as simple feedback loops. In marketing terms, control ensures that what is supposed to happen actually happens and is a mechanism to protect strategic plans when they become operational.

Effective control systems have focus, involve people and promote action. Management control extends to cover finance, performance appraisal and establishing and maintaining performance benchmarks. Marketing managers are concerned with the following control mechanisms: annual plans, profitability, efficiency of marketing and strategic control.

References

Kotler, P., *Marketing Management*, 9th edition, Prentice Hall, 1997

Piercy, N., *Market-led Strategic Change*, 2nd edition, Butterworth-Heinemann, 1997

Watson, G., *Strategic Benchmarking*, Wiley, 1993

Further reading

Piercy, N. *Market-led Strategic Change*, 2nd edition, Chapter 12, Butterworth-Heinemann, 1997

Chapter 15

Mini cases

Introduction

About this chapter

Mini cases are useful tools to employ in order to build an individual's skills of analysis and evaluation. They are also useful mechanisms for assessing whether examination candidates have acquired those key skills.

Skills

The whole aim of this book has been to increase your knowledge of marketing planning process and strategic marketing, in order to become more adept practitioners. The mini cases that follow enable you to practise the skills of analysis and decision making by allowing you to assess the strategic issues involved in a specific scenario. The scenarios outlined in the mini cases that follow are based on the situations faced by organizations in the real world. By using the models, concepts and processes covered in the previous chapters you should be able to identify and assess the strategic issues faced by the organizations summarized in the cases. You should then go on to formulate and evaluate the strategic options available to each organization in the context of the scenario with which it is faced. This is a skill you need to enhance in order to develop your ability to see your organization, competitors and industry sector in a wider strategic context. This ability, to tease out the key strategic themes that lie under the complex layers of operational details, is the essence of true strategic vision. Like any other skill the more an individual practices the more skilful they become. Once you have analysed and discussed these cases continue practising by applying the same procedure to articles about companies and business sectors from the daily press and business programmes on television. A great deal of satisfaction can be gained by anticipating the developments that are likely to occur next in an industry.

Assessment

Mini cases also allow examiners to assess whether you have acquired an in-depth knowledge of the subject. Your analysis allows you to demonstrate an ability to apply theoretical models and concepts in such a way that new insights can be gained about the situation of a particular organization in a specific context. Given the aim of the assessment, the questions on the CIM examination paper for Marketing Planning unit will be based on marketing planning processes, strategic decisions and operational decisions of the marketing plan.

The Marketing Planning paper requires you to analyse and evaluate the situation outlined in the case. You will fail if you merely describe or reiterate the mini case. You need to show some clear insight into the key issues facing the company in the case. Finally, any options you propose that the company should follow have to be based on the reality of the situation. In particular, they have to take into account the assets and competencies available to the organization in pursuing its strategic objectives.

Treatment of the mini case in an examination situation

On the Chartered Institute of Marketing's new Marketing Planning paper, there are usually three compulsory questions, which are set on the mini case in Part A of the examination paper. This section of the paper is worth 50 per cent of the total marks. The weighting of each question in Part A will vary from session to session, however, there may be two sections worth 20 per cent each and one worth 10 per cent. This means that you should spend around 90 minutes of your time on the mini case questions. This will include any time taken reading the case. Remember to note the number of marks available for each question and work out the amount of time and effort required for each question.

It is critical that candidates answer the questions set. Examiners do not expect pre-set structure to answers. Only give an outline marketing plan if the question expressly asks for one. SWOT and PEST analysis should only be given if they are directly relevant. The examiner is looking for your strategic insights into the scenario outlines, not a restructuring of the material presented in the mini case. Using one of the numerous models, such as the Boston Consultancy Matrix, Porter's Five Forces of industry structure or his Competitive Advantage Matrix, is a valuable way of structuring your answer. The model will provide a structure that is likely to give clarity to your answer and highlight the insights you have drawn from your analysis.

The new Marketing Planning examination papers will generally require you to analyse the data in the case study and you will often be expected to assess the main challenges in the marketing environment which are likely to impact on the case organization. You may be required to consider or evaluate the strategic growth options available for a company. You could also be asked to consider the role of branding within the organization or the service quality where appropriate. In some cases you will be required to propose a marketing plan, but given the time constraints this is unlikely. However, the examination questions may concentrate on specific parts of the planning process such as the marketing audit, strategic option choices, and marketing mix decisions to achieve the strategy proposed, therefore it will be important to answer the question set rather than to write out a marketing plan (unless specifically required).

The mini cases

Five mini cases follow, each highlight the situation faced by a specific organization.

The five cases are:

15.1 easyJet
15.2 Gillette
15.3 Howden Joinery
15.4 ACDA's Organic Retailing
15.5 Tesco Mobile

15.1 easyJet

EasyJet is a low fare airline that operates a number of routes within the European market. Haji-Ioannou, the owner of easyJet, founded the airline based on the belief that reduced prices would lead to more people flying. EasyJet's prices are low, for instance a return flight from Luton to Amsterdam would cost between £70 to £130. Flights, with a airline offering a full customer service package, could cost around £315 upwards.

The organization's main base is at Luton airport from where flights to European destinations such as Amsterdam, Geneva, Nice, Barcelona, Palma and Athens are available. The airline also flies UK domestic routes from Luton to Edinburgh, Glasgow, Belfast and Liverpool. Liverpool allows the company to gain access into the lucrative North of England market and is becoming a growing centre of activity for easyJet. Flights can now be taken from Liverpool to Nice, Amsterdam and Belfast.

Luton airport is around 30 minutes by road from north London and only 15 minutes from the London's main orbital motorway, the M25. The airport is ten minutes away from Luton railway station from where a 27-minute rail connection to London is available. A shuttle bus to the station is available every 10 minutes. A return rail journey for easyJet passengers is available at around £8 (Sterling). Liverpool airport also has good motorway connections.

Connecting flights are not part of easyJet's product offering. The airline merely carries passengers to and from single destinations. This allows the airline to eliminate costly ticketing processes as well as intermediaries, such as travel agents. The company also operates a paperless office policy and non-ticket flights. Simply by ringing the company's telephone number or using the company's Internet site customers can book a seat directly on their credit card. In autumn 1998, 40 per cent of bookings for a major promotion in the Times newspaper were via the Internet. Although a confirmation of the booking will be sent if requested, customers merely have to produce identification at the airport and quote the booking reference number to be given a boarding pass for their flight.

EasyJet flights are 'free seating'. Passengers are not allocated a specific seat when they check-in, instead they are given a boarding card that carries a priority number. The first person to check-in gets boarding card No 1 the next passenger boarding card No 2 and so on. Customers are then asked to board according to the order in which they checked-in occupying whichever seat they wish. The result is that passengers board the plane faster and tend to sit down faster than when they have to search for an allocated seat, as is the case in the more traditional airline operations. The faster passengers board an aircraft the quicker the plane can take off and the less time it spends on the tarmac. This results in reduced airport fees.

The fact that easyJet is not hindered by connections to other flights allows it to operate out of cheaper secondary airports such as Luton and Liverpool, rather than larger airports such as Heathrow or Manchester. EasyJet also exploits the lack of competition for time slots at Luton and Liverpool to keep the length of time its aircraft are on the tarmac to a minimum. Easyjet's aircraft are therefore airborne longer, creating more hours of revenue earning per aircraft, than companies operating out of larger and busier airports.

Premium priced airlines offer business class seats, which take up more room on an aircraft, and will normally operate with 109 seats on a Boeing 737–300. These airlines also require additional cabin crew in order to provide the level of service business class passengers demand. EasyJet operates without offering business class seats, which allows it to create 148 passenger places on a Boeing 737–300. Catering consists of a trolley from which cabin staff will sell drinks and a limited range of snacks, to passengers. The only 'freebie' on the flight is a copy of the airlines in-flight magazine called 'easy rider', which is printed on recycled paper. Cabin staff wear orange polo shirts and black jeans and have a more relaxed attitude and are more casual than traditional airlines. They appear as equally safety conscious as staff on other airlines.

EasyJet's telephone number is promoted widely. The company's telephone number, in bright orange, dominates the sides of the aircraft, where it has almost become part of the easyJet corporate image. The organization's approach to advertising has been described as "a guerrilla promotional approach", distinguished by attacks on the airline establishment and a series of PR stunts. Press and magazine advertising is widespread. Sales promotional activity has included joint promotions in national UK newspapers such as the Times and the Independent. The airline has also been the focus of a documentary series on UK television. The owner, Haji-Ioannou, has been featured in many business articles in the press, particularly for his high profile campaign against British Airways' launch of its own low cost airline operation called 'GO'.

EasyJet has also started targeting companies that wish to keep travel budgets under control. EasyJet emphasizes that they do not offer a loyalty scheme where business customers can build up loyalty points and gain free flights. The suggestion is that although executives may like this perk the executive's company could be saving hundreds of pounds per trip by sending their staff on easyJet flights.

The organization's latest plan is to develop a family of companies with a common theme, beginning with the launch of a chain of cybercafes. Although the branding for this venture has yet to be decided the working title is 'EasyCafe'. The company still has to take decisions, such as whether EasyJet's trademark bright orange colour is made a prominent feature of the cafes. Tony Anderson, who will oversee this new development, is quoted as saying that with these cafes ' we are targeting Joe Public, not the middle classes.'

(This mini case study has been prepared from secondary sources.)

Discussion questions

1 Identify the core capabilities of easyJet that can be used to grow the family of companies that Haji-Ioannou envisages. Try to use the value chain as part of this analysis.
2 EasyJet have decided to develop a group of companies beginning with the cybercafe concept. Determine the issues that need to be considered when making decisions on the organization's branding strategy, for the group as a whole and for the 'easycafe' concept in particular.

15.2 Gillette

Gillette has launched a new wet shave razor system, called Mach 3, onto the global market. This product cost £460 million and took seven years to develop. The company aimed to spend around £215 million launching this product globally of which approximately 10 per cent was to be spent in the UK. The main feature of this shaving system is that it has three blades. The key benefit is that it cuts 40 per cent more hair than Gillette's previous shaving system Sensor Excel and gives an extra–smooth shave. It also exerts less friction making shaving more comfortable. The Mach 3 is forecast to generate 17per cent category growth over two years, equivalent to selling 1.2 billion blades globally.

Wet shave customers can buy a shaving system or a disposable razor. With shaving systems the customer buys a razor handle which is refillable with blades that they can buy separately. The three main competitors in the wet shave market in the UK have the following market shares:

	Number of users of wet shave razors (Millions)
Gillette	9.0
Wilkinson Sword	2.8
Bic	2.6

Note: Bic concentrate on disposable razors.

The UK market is split between 54 per cent on systems and 46 per cent on disposables. 74 per cent of blade and razor purchases (shaving systems and disposables) are made by men for themselves. The male grooming market has grown over the last two years by £50 million. The shaving systems market alone is worth £113 million. This is broken down as follows:

Gillette	£105m	65%
Wilkinson sword	£ 32m	20%
Biro Bic	£ 11m	7%
Other brands, retailers own label	£ 13m	8%

When Gillette launched Sensor (a new razor system) in 1989 it went on to generate £3.65 billion in world-wide brand sales and sold nearly 400 million razor handles and eight billion blades. At the same time, because Sensor was an innovative product Gillette was able to charge a high price for the product. The fact that there was little interchangability of the blades with other systems meant that the customer was restricted to purchasing Gillette blades. Previous launches of new systems have typically been priced 15 per cent higher than the most expensive product available. The Mach 3 will be around 35 per cent more expensive. Replacement blades will cost £1.12 each. The aim with the Mach 3 is to capture new users into the Gillette franchise. To encourage millions of current Gillette users to trade up to the new system and to move current users of disposables into the refillable shaving systems sector.

Advertising for the Mach 3 will be identical globally. Television advertisements will use the same film from Asia to Europe, with only minor modifications to the script. The aim of the campaign will be to steal customers from its competitors (Wilkinson Sword in particular as its only major competitor in the systems market) and to aggressively grow the sector. Prior to the launch of the Mach 3 Gillette ran a television advertising campaign with the aim of persuading customers to move from disposable razors to the Gillette system.

(*This mini case study has been prepared from secondary sources.*)

Discussion questions

1 Referring to models of strategic formulation explain why Gillette continue to spend large amounts of money on new product development.
2 Identify and evaluate the strategic options that are available to Wilkinson Sword in this market.

15.3 Howden Joinery

Based in the UK, MFI is a vertically integrated business manufacturing and retailing kitchen and bedroom furniture and fittings. In 1999 the company's retail outlets were mainly large 'out of town' retail sites. MFI at this time had falling sales, rising losses, high debts and a low share price. In fact in December 1998 the share price had reached a new low of 28.5 pence a share. Since then the company has implemented a number of initiatives to increase sales and ensure its factories are operating at efficient levels.

Firstly, by the end of 2001, MFI aimed to have opened 20 smaller high street stores of about 370m². The aim was to have 50 of this type of retail outlet by 2003. In a further development, in twelve stores MFI were also testing the idea of selling bathrooms. Collaborative agreements were also being explored. In one of these the company negotiated an agreement with an electrical goods retailer named Currys to sell kitchen fittings and furniture alongside electrical appliances. Initially this took place in 50 Currys stores with the aim of the idea being developed in a further 50 stores by summer 2002.

MFI also aimed to expand internationally. It planned to expand its already profitable business in France, where it felt it could double sales and triple profits in a three to four year period. The company also had a joint venture in Taiwan which operated four stores.

Despite these developments, the fastest growing venture within the MFI group has been a business called the Howden joinery. This company is a chain of depots that supply kitchens to small builders. The idea of the business is to meet small builders needs by supplying kitchens that are easy to install whilst at the same time meeting the expectations of the builders' customers in terms of quality and design. The kitchens are supplied through local depots that hold stock and also contain a small showroom space. The depots are located on industrial estates which offer low rents, this also means they are often close to other suppliers which small builders use, such as plumbers' merchants and timber outlets. These depots can supply a builder with all the component parts needed to create a new kitchen. They can also supply other joinery items such as windows and doors. Rather than supplying the component parts that need assembling, all kitchen cupboards are fully assembled by Howden and ready for installation by the builder. This not only saves the builder time but also ensures that the final units are of a high quality.

Howden promote themselves by contacting local builders with mail shots and by staff ringing them up directly. The relationship between local staff and local customers is seen as a crucial aspect of the business. Howden staff help the builders to draw computer designs of proposed kitchens as well as providing builders with brochures which they can show to their customers. Howden's customers are offered trade discounts and easy credit terms. The normal MFI store reaches maturity after around eighteen months, however a Howden depot is still attracting new business four years after opening.

In the year 2000 there were around 100 Howden depots. By 2002 there were around 200 with the aim of there being 350 outlets by 2004 or 2005. In 2000 Howden's operating profits were £8.9m against the total group's profits of £44.9m. In 2001 Howden's profits had grown to £15.3m against what ING Barings Charterhouse Securities predicted would be profits of around £63m for the MFI group as a whole. MFI is now considering international expansion of the Howden business.

(*This mini case has been prepared from secondary sources.*)

Discussion questions

1 Identify and explain the sources of Howden's competitive advantage and make a judgement as to whether their current position is sustainable.
2 Evaluate the potential of franchising the Howden joinery business into overseas markets, both in the European and South East Asian markets. Consider the criteria that Howden should use in order to evaluate the potential of any new overseas market.

15.4 ACDA's Organic Food Retailing

Background

The past decade has witnessed a rapid growth in the consumption of organic produce within the UK and Europe. What began as a rather specialist fad amongst middle and upper-middle class families has become an increasingly important sector in the food business, with all of the major supermarket groups in the UK now offering organic ranges of produce. Indeed, stores nowadays offer organic versions of products ranging from fruit and vegetables to ready made meals and even nappies.

According to a recent survey by the UK Consumer's Association, around 29 per cent of UK consumers now replace some of their staple foods with organic versions. Of those purchasing organic produce, two-thirds cited 'health reasons' as the main influence on their switch to organic products. A further recent consumer survey indicated that the consumer's decision to buy organic has been influenced by a concern over the use of pesticides in farming, and a belief that organic products taste better and contain more nutrients than non-organic products.

The growth of interest in consuming organic foods has also been influenced by concerns in recent years over the safety of food; in particular, the recent BSE crisis over the safety of British beef and the controversy over GM foods. However, some food industry commentators have begun to question whether the claimed benefits of organic foods are fully justified and, in particular, have criticized the significantly higher price charged for organic produce compared to non-organic foods.

Food producers have been accused of encouraging consumers to believe that 'organic' automatically equals 'healthy'. Recent press coverage has included scientific data that raises concerns about the safety of organic farming, suggesting the potential for e-coli poisoning from the use of organic manure.

However, despite such concerns being raised within the media, there seems to have been little sign of any significant decline in demand for organic produce. Perhaps a more significant consumer concern has been about the possibility of retailers and producers exploiting the current demand for organic products and charging excessively high prices for organic versions of products. Some consumer groups have expressed concern that many retailers are jumping on the organic 'bandwagon' and using the label 'organic' as an excuse to charge premium prices.

In response to such accusations of price exploitation, organic food producers and retailers have argued that demand for organic produce still far outstrips current supply and the costs to farmers of converting to organic inevitably means that organic produce will be more expensive than non-organic.

The Soil Association (SA) acts as the lead body codifying and policing the majority of organic products in the UK. The SA has worked to promote organic farming since 1946 and its symbol is widely recognized as the consumer's guarantee of organic quality. The SA has established a 'multiple retailers working group' to educate supermarkets on organic standards and also organizes farm visits and produces educational materials to raise understanding of organic production techniques. The SA also works to lobby government for more financial assistance for farmers to encourage them to convert to organic production. At present the supermarkets are forced to source around 70 per cent of their organic produce from abroad as the UK farming industry is unable to meet current level of consumer demand.

Organic food retailing

Most of the major food retailers in the UK now offer a significant range of organic produce but organic products still account for only around 10 per cent of all foods sold in most supermarkets.

One of UK retailer has always prided itself on its pioneering stance, being one of the first supermarkets to stock organic produce back in 1983. Earlier this year, this retailer was voted Organic Supermarket of the Year for the second year running in a poll by one of the UK newspaper readers. This retailer was praised for the selection and quality of organic produce available, manner of display, quality of supporting information and for its knowledgeable and helpful staff. This company currently stocks around 650 organic products and plans to expand this to over 1000 during the current year. However, as this retailer has only 121 stores in the UK, based mainly in South of England, Midlands, East Anglia and Wales, it does not compete directly with the other major supermarket groups on a national scale.

The other major supermarket groups in the UK have also responded to the growth of consumer interest in organic produce and have introduced organic products alongside traditional products within their stores. At another main supermarket retailer in this sector, organic produce currently represents between 5–10 per cent of sales and the company plans to expand its sales steadily over the next two years. One of the top five retailers in the UK currently stocks around 200 organic foodstuffs and plans to grow this sector of its sales significantly. Other major supermarket groups in the UK have equally well-developed organic food policies that are planned to expand significantly over the next few years.

The major barrier to further growth in demand for organic produce is undoubtedly price. A recent survey by a health magazine found that 45 per cent of people choosing not to eat organic food stated that 'cost' was the main reason. The release of this study prompted a further round of highly critical newspaper articles accusing supermarket groups of exploiting the consumer interest in organic food and pricing it beyond the pocket of the average family.

Following the publication of the study, two supermarket groups in particular have announced plans for significant cuts in organic produce prices in an effort to attract further custom. A further retailer has announced its intention to sell organic products at more favourable prices and ACDA has launched its own-brand organic range that it claims will undercut the competition by 5–10 per cent.

ACDA – Retailing Chain

ACDA is a major retailer and, under its new US ownership, has already announced an aggressive price-based attack on the UK grocery market. Its management has claimed that its stance on organic produce pricing is simply an extension of its low price positioning strategy, offering 'permanently low prices'. ACDA's management has acknowledged that supply difficulties, together with the higher production costs of organic produce, will mean that organic products will cost more than their non-organic alternatives. However, they believe that by reducing the price of their organic range, it will be possible to broaden the appeal of organic food to middle and lower income households in the UK.

ACDA's management have recognized however that they need to be careful not to raise consumer expectations too much about the level of price cuts that can be expected in organic produce range as supply constraints and higher production costs will mean that prices will have to exceed those charged for non-organic products.

The company has already employed a marketing consultancy to devise a new brand name for the organic range which will be sold under the name ACDA 'Down to Earth'. A design consultancy has also produced a series of new store display units for the fruit and vegetables and display cards containing nutritional information that will accompany other organic products within ACDA stores.

Their own customer research has revealed that there is still considerable uncertainty amongst consumers about precisely what the term 'organic' means and how organic produce differs from conventionally produced products. This study also found that a significant number of consumers remain sceptical about the benefits of organic produce and believe that the additional cost of organic produce is not justified. As might be expected, the greatest resistance to organic produce was found amongst the lower socio-economic income groups (C2, D &E), although around 40 per cent of higher income groups (A, B, C1) also expressed some reservations about whether the organic produce was worth the extra cost involved. One significant criticism identified by the majority of respondents was the lack of knowledgeable staff within stores capable of answering questions about organic products.

This study has led ACDA's management to the conclusion that there is still a significant consumer education task to complete with regard to organic produce. They have also recognized the need to improve the training of store staff to equip them with the necessary knowledge to answer consumer questions about organic products.

(This case was written by Danny Moss and Ruth Ashford, The Manchester Metropolitan University. It was prepared from secondary sources and is fictitious but based on a major retailer).

Discussion questions

1 Assess the main challenges in the marketing environment which are likely to impact on ACDA's organic brand in the next two years, and explain the role of marketing information in conducting an external audit.
2 With reference to appropriate theory, identify and evaluate how ACDA could expand their retailing business within the next two years.
3 Specifically considering the role of ACDA's organic food brand, recommend the extended marketing mix decisions for your chosen growth strategies.

15.5 Tesco: Entering The Mobile Phone Market

The already crowded mobile phone market now faces yet another entrant as Tesco, the supermarket chain, announced the launch of a joint venture with mobile phone group O2. This will see a Tesco branded mobile phone service entering the market place. Tesco already retails other companies' pre-paid mobiles, and has been keen to launch its own brand service.

The UK telecoms market is already fiercely contested. Around 80 per cent of people own a mobile, making the market one of the most saturated in the world.

Both O2 and Tesco will jointly own Tesco Mobile, and the service will make use of O2's existing technology/network. Each company has committed to investing £8m into the joint project over the first two years of operation, after which it is expected to become profitable. The venture aims to attract 2 million consumers within 5 years. The partnership agreement is open-ended in nature with a 5-year 'lock-in' period during which neither partner may sell their shareholding. Senior managers will be drawn from both Tesco and O2.

O2's Chief Executive states ... "as the UK's biggest supermarket, with 14 million customers, Tesco is the cream of the crop when it comes to a vehicle for hitting the family market, complementing our other ventures perfectly" and "the terms of the joint venture create a sound and sustainable business model for both parties. O2 will make a return both through Tesco Mobile's earnings and more efficient use of our network capacity". Tesco's Chief Executive describes O2 as a good partner for Tesco, and states ... "customers tell us they want simplicity and value for money from a name they can trust and that is what Tesco Mobile will offer. The service will be convenient. You'll be able to buy handsets in store or over the Internet, and the charges will be clear and simple."

Tesco will view the project as a further development of their non-food sales, after a successful venture into financial services in association with the Royal Bank of Scotland. Additionally, Tesco has plans to launch a fixed-line phone service with Cable & Wireless. The deal would provide O2 with a means to reach new customer segments (e.g. housewives, older users) without any adverse effect on its existing more lucrative core customers.

The Tesco venture comes shortly after rival chain J Sainsbury announced that it had signed an exclusive deal with the Carphone Warehouse to launch a fixed and mobile telecoms service.

Discussion Questions

1 Summarize the key issues outlined in the case.
2 Consider Tesco's strategy, core purpose and values (see Appendix1). How does the new venture fit into such strategy/principles?
3 Discuss branding issues illustrated in the case.

Appendix 1: The Tesco Strategy

Source WWW.Tesco.com (2003) – Reproduced with permission of Tesco PLC

The Tesco Strategy

The Tesco strategy is for long-term growth, and focuses on four elements:

Core UK business

The UK business remains our core market. Our focused strategy of providing exceptional value and choice for customers ensures that we continue to grow market share.

Non-food business

We now have a 5% market share of a market worth £75bn in the UK, where our goal is to be as strong in non-food as in food. Our non-food offer encompasses electrical, home entertainment, clothing, homeshop, cookshop and, in our largest stores, white goods and furniture.

Retailing services

As customers' shopping habits change, we change and respond by providing new products and services. Our e-commerce business has grown rapidly. We are the worlds largest grocery e-tailer and operate our system in the international markets. Both tesco.com and Tesco Personal Finance demonstrate our ability to extend the Tesco brand. We recently announced that we would launch a fixed line phone service in 2003.

International

Tesco has successfully opened up new growth markets in Central Europe and Asia. The proportion of total Group space outside of the UK was 45% at the end of 2003/2003. We now operate in Hungary, Poland, the Czech Republic, the Slovak Republic, Thailand, South Korea, Taiwan and the Republic of Ireland. In May 2002 we opened our first store in Malaysia.

The Tesco core purpose and values underpin the Tesco strategy

Our Core Purpose is all about customers.

"Creating value for customers, to earn their lifetime loyalty."

This statement is at the centre of all we do.

Our two values drive the way we do business.

No one tries harder for customers:

- Understand customers better than anyone
- Be energetic, be innovative and be first for customers
- Use our strengths to deliver unbeatable values to our customers
- Look after our people so they can look after our customers

Treat people how we like to be treated:

- All retailers, there's one team . . .The Tesco Team
- Trust and respect each other
- Strive to do our very best
- Give support to each other and praise more than criticise
- Ask more than tell and share knowledge so that it can be used
- Enjoy work, celebrate success and learn from experience

Index